SUNDAY NIGHTS WITH WALT

Everything I Know I Learned from
"The Wonderful World of Disney"

RICHARD ROTHROCK

Theme Park Press
The Happiest Books on Earth
www.ThemeParkPress.com

Editor: Bob McLain

Layout: Artisanal Text

ISBN 978-1-68390-087-0

Printed in the United States of America

Theme Park Press | www.ThemeParkPress.com

Address queries to bob@themeparkpress.com

For
My Mother
Dorothy Higgins Rothrock
(1933–2002)
Who invented Sunday nights with Walt

Contents

Introduction

Growing up in the 1960s and 1970s, Sunday nights at my house were different from the other nights of the week. It was the only night when my mother made pizza. It was the only night of the week when we could drink soda. It was the only night of the week when we could have candy for dessert. It was the only night of the week when we were allowed to eat dinner in front of the television. And the only shows we ever watched were *Mutual of Omaha's Wild Kingdom* and *The Wonderful World of Disney*. (Mom sent us to bed as soon as *Bonanza* started.)

For almost the entirety of my childhood, *The Wonderful World of Disney* was always there, even as I grew from a boy to a young man of eighteen, and even as my family moved from the small towns and farms of rural Indiana to the coal and steel towns of West Virginia to the towering spires of the Motor City in Michigan. The only true anchors in that time were "pizza night," as it came to be called in our family, and Disney.

Like all of us growing up at that time, *The Wonderful World of Disney* was an eye opener to our world. Peering through that spinning kaleidoscope that always served as background for the episode title, we caught our first glimpses of what it meant to be a kid, what it meant to travel, what it meant—to borrow a phrase from the lyrics of the opening credits—to be in "this world where we each play a part." We learned about history. We learned about fantasy. We learned the magic of science, the glories of art, and the marvels of the earth, sea, and sky. We experienced the power of drama and the cleansing laughter of comedy.

We learned about faraway places and how they were populated by people like you and like me who had the same hopes and fears and joys and tears. And, more than anything, it taught us the miracle of imagination and how it can be harnessed and used to unite us all.

It taught me about life. It taught me how to be (and how not to be) an adult. It taught me the value of nature. I learned the ropes of friendship, romance, and how to make my way in the world. I learned to believe in the future. Most of all, it taught me how to dream.

So for the rest of this book I am inviting you over to my parents' house to share Sunday nights with Walt. In our kitchen, my mother has her homemade pizza (your choice of cheese, pepperoni, or sausage) set out buffet style on the top of the stove. My father has popped popcorn using his Mirro chrome popcorn popper (the only thing I remember my father ever cooking and the only night I can remember having popcorn outside of going to the movies). And our beverage selection, usually Coca-Cola, Pepsi-Cola, or 7Up, is set up on the kitchen table. Sometimes there would be Fresca or Tab or Dr. Pepper, depending on what flavor of the month my sisters and I were into.

The weekend is almost over. Tomorrow morning, we will each be back to school or back to work. But for right now, we have tonight to travel and to dream.

Fill up your Tupperware dinner plate and glass and come downstairs with me to the family room. Grab a TV tray and take a seat (green sleeper sofa, blue butterfly chair, white bean bag chair, or brown recliner) as we all gather around my father's 1964 RCA Victor color television set, which to my eyes still gave off the best color picture ever. Second helpings, refills, and dessert can be had during the commercials.

Now, quiet down! The NBC peacock is on to signal the start of the prime-time TV line up. The show is about to start...and for the next sixty minutes the world truly will be a carousel of color.

CHAPTER ONE

"And Now Your Host, Walt Disney"

I cannot remember the first time I watched *The Wonderful World of Disney;* it was just something my family always did. There was never even a question of which show we were going to watch. In order to better help you understand the uniqueness of the *World of Disney* in our lives, it is important for people born after 1980 to understand how television was back in the 1960s.

1960s TV 101

First, there were only three channels. That's right, three channels: ABC, CBS, and NBC. PBS did not go on the air until 1969. Larger cities like New York, Los Angeles, or Chicago might have a so-called independent station with no network affiliation like New York's WWOR or Chicago's WGN or Atlanta's TBS. Their schedules were mostly filled by reruns of cancelled network shows during the day and old movies at night. So, at best, in the big cities you had 5 or 6 channels to choose from. If you lived outside a major metropolitan area, you were limited to the Big Three.

Second, children's programs were limited to just a few times per week. The networks ran Saturday morning cartoons between the hours of 8am and noon. *Captain Kangaroo* ran weekday mornings on CBS. After school, local stations might fill the time between network soap operas and the news by showing Japanese cartoons like *Speed Racer, Marine Boy,* and *Kimba, The White Lion.* But that was it. The only other children's programming for the entire week was *The Wonderful World of Disney.*

The mainstay programming that children take for granted today had not begun. We had not yet visited *Sesame Street.* We could not take the trolley to *Mister Rogers' Neighborhood.* There was just "Uncle Walt" and his show on Sunday nights.

The Universe of Disney

Even as children, we understood that Walt Disney was a multimedia presence, the gold standard for children's programming. And our parents understood it as well. Besides *The Wonderful World of Disney*, he produced the hit shows *Zorro* and *The Mickey Mouse Club* (the original daytime TV show aimed squarely at children). Every year,Walt's studio released around a half-dozen live-action movies into theaters. Their subject matter ranged from zany comedies (*The Shaggy Dog, The Ugly Dachshund*) to nostalgic looks back at turn-of-the-century America (*Toby Tyler, Summer Magic, Pollyanna*) to out-and-out fantasies (*Darby O'Gill and the Little People, The Absent-Minded Professor*). Roughly every five years, Walt's animation department released a new full-length animated feature like *Sleeping Beauty* or *101 Dalmatians* or *The Sword In the Stone*. And his classic feature-length animated films, such as *Snow White and the Seven Dwarfs, Pinocchio, Dumbo,* and *Bambi*, were rereleased back into theaters on a rotating seven-year schedule.

When we weren't watching one of Walt's television shows or going to the theater to watch one of his movies, we were reading one of his comic books and following the adventures of Mickey Mouse, Donald Duck, Goofy, and Chip 'n' Dale. We listened to his records (Disney being the first studio to release soundtrack albums for their movies). We read novelizations of his movies. It's hard for post-1980 generations to comprehend a time when there were no VHS, DVDs, Netflix, or YouTube that allow us to watch practically any movie or TV show anytime we want. Back then, the only way to see a movie was to go to the theater or wait for it to be shown on television. If you wanted to see it, you arranged your schedule so you were sitting in front of the TV when it aired. When it was gone, it was gone. Buying and reading the novelizations of movies was our only way to relive them in our minds.

And that doesn't take into account all the toys, wristwatches, clothes, Davy Crockett coonskin caps, and stuffed animals we could buy and use in our everyday lives. Being kids, we didn't really understand the basic concepts of marketing synergy. All we knew was that it was easy to get Disney stuff and it was stuff we wanted to get.

Walt was also the man who held the keys to the Valhalla of all kid-dom—the original Magic Kingdom, the Happiest Place on Earth, Disneyland. The first theme park where every year he seemed to be creating yet another fantastic ride that reset the boundaries of what was possible, from Flight to the Moon, the Matterhorn Bobsleds, the Submarine Voyage, and the Disneyland monorail, to It's a Small World, Great Moments with Mr. Lincoln, Pirates of the Caribbean, the Haunted Mansion, and Space Mountain.

There was no one else like Walt Disney for us children living in the late 1950s or early 1960s. And all the elements above came together Sunday nights on Walt's television show.

Sunday Night TV: Disney vs. Sullivan

During the 1960s, even though the marketing term had yet to be coined, Sunday night television was the "must-see TV" of the week and the night belonged to two men: Walt Disney and Ed Sullivan. Their shows ran opposite each other. In America, you were either a Sullivan family or a Disney family.

Ed Sullivan hosted *The Ed Sullivan Show* on CBS from 1948 until 1971. It was television's premiere variety show and all kinds of comedy and musical acts got their first national exposure by appearing on his show. If you were a stand-up comedian or a singer or a rock band or novelty animal act, you knew you had arrived when you got the call to appear on *Ed Sullivan*. The show aired for 60 minutes from 8:00 to 9:00pm EST. I cannot remember ever watching a complete episode of the *Sullivan Show*. He always struck my younger self as the most unlikely of television stars: short, shrunken, almost the epitome of the grumpy old man trying to be polite for the cameras.

In contrast, Walt Disney and his show were Sunday night interlopers, having only arrived on the scene in the fall of 1961 (but remaining a Sunday night staple until 1982). *The Wonderful World of Disney* aired on NBC opposite *Sullivan* from 7:30 to 8:30pm.

In the prime of my childhood years, the show was preceded at 7:00pm by *Mutual of Omaha's Wild Kingdom*, hosted by St. Louis Zoo curator Marlin Perkins (almost as engaging a television personality as Walt Disney). Along with his game assistants Stan Brock and Jim Fowler, Perkins took us all over the world in search of nature's beauties and dangers. His laconic narration was known for its ability to combine facts about nature with plugs for his title sponsor: "A lioness in Africa will go to the ends of the earth to protect her children from all dangers. Mutual of Omaha will do the same for you."

The 9:00pm slot on the schedule belonged to *Bonanza*. The show followed the adventures of Ben Cartwright (Lorne Greene) and his grown sons (Parnell Roberts, Dan Blocker, Michael Landon) as they tried to manage their huge Ponderosa ranch outside Virginia City, Nevada, in the late 19th century. This was another long-running show, a mainstay of the NBC schedule from 1959 to 1973, and for most of that time it ran on Sunday nights. NBC's decision to air this show in color is what started the trend toward Americans buying color TV sets. Disney's color show joining the Sunday night line-up accelerated the pace.

Starting in 1971, *Bonanza* moved to another night to make way for *The NBC Mystery Movie*, another anthology series featuring the rotating police dramas *Columbo* starring Peter Falk, *McCloud* starring Dennis Weaver, and *McMillan & Wife* starring Rock Hudson and Susan St. James.

Regardless of whether it was *Bonanza* or *The NBC Mystery Movie*, my mother would only allow me to watch the opening credits of the show (featuring classic theme songs by Jay Livingston and Henry Mancini, respectively), then off to bed for me.

No doubt about it, from 1961 to the late 1970s, NBC Sunday nights was our TV viewing of choice and at the center of it was Disney.

A Show by Any Other Name

The TV show I am calling *The Wonderful World of Disney* went through many changes over the course of its run. Between 1954 and 1983, it switched networks, nights of the week, and show titles even as it fundamentally remained the same show. (For simplicity, I'll refer to it as *The Wonderful World of Disney* throughout this book.)

When it debuted on ABC-TV in 1954, the show was called *Disneyland* and it aired on Thursday nights. It was called *Disneyland* because Walt wanted to promote the new amusement park he was in the process of building (and which ABC had bought a partial interest in). This is the period when the show aired classic episodes like *Davy Crockett* and *Johnny Tremain*, the "Man in Space" science shows that helped spur America's space program, and animation themed shows like "The Plausible Impossible" and "Where Ideas Come From."

In 1959, the title changed to *Walt Disney Presents* (because ABC sold its interest in the park). This is the period when the series relied on a rotating collection of serialized dramas built around characters like Texas John Slaughter (Tom Tyron), Elfego Baca (Robert Loggia), the Swamp Fox (Leslie Nielsen), and Zorro (Guy Williams).

After two seasons, NBC-TV persuaded Walt to bring his show over to their network. They promised him complete creative freedom in episode selection (Walt felt ABC interfered too much in this area) and the chance to broadcast his show in color. Starting in 1961, the show began airing Sunday nights and the title was switched to *Walt Disney's Wonderful World of Color*. When today's Baby Boomers look back and cite their favorite episodes from the series (*The Horse Masters*, *The Scarecrow of Romney Marsh*, *Gallegher*), they are usually episodes from this period.

After Disney's death in 1966, the title was changed again to *The Wonderful World of Disney* and it held that name the longest, from 1968 to 1980. For its last three seasons, the title was changed one last time, to *Disney's Wonderful World*.

A Kaleidoscope of the World

The Wonderful World of Disney was an anthology show. Outside of Walt acting as the host, there were no recurring cast members. One week could be a nature show where viewers might find themselves anywhere from the Amazon jungle to the plains of the American West. The next week could be a period drama set during the American Revolution or the Civil War. The week after that could be another drama set in Europe or the South Seas. And the week after that could be an animated show to teach viewers something about science or music under the tutelage of the show's absent-minded animated scholar Professor Ludwig Von Drake. Or best of all, Walt might take us out to Disneyland to preview its latest ride or attraction, or walk us around his studio and give us a preview of one of his upcoming movies.

In its prime, the show was PBS, Cartoon Network, Nickelodeon, the Travel Channel, the History Channel, Animal Planet, the Discovery Channel, Arts & Entertainment, the Science Channel, the NASA Channel, E! Entertainment, HBO, and MTV all rolled into one. We literally never knew what was going to be on from week to week and the possibilities kept us coming back.

And at the heart of it all was Uncle Walt, as he was commonly called.

Each week's episode would begin in the same fashion. It would fade in with a teaser scene from the night's episode designed to grab our attention, set the stage, and perhaps even leave us in suspense about the outcome. A quick fade out and then the opening credits would begin. A shot of Disneyland's Sleeping Beauty Castle would appear. Fireworks would fill the sky above. And out of the bursts would fly Tinker Bell from *Peter Pan* (1953). With her magic wand, she filled the screen with bursts of color like an artist painting a picture.

That would give way to seemingly random shots: sweeping plains, the crystalline white of snow-covered mountains, Dutch children running hand in hand past a twirling windmill, animals in nature, a spectacular sky at sunset. Running under this would be the theme song written by Disney's favorite songwriters at the time, Richard M. and Robert B. Sherman, promising us that the world was a marvelous place filled with all kinds of wonder and that we were about to spend the next hour seeing a part of it. The opening would conclude with a montage of kaleidoscope shots (they literally attached a kaleidoscope to the end of a camera) while the show title appeared and the opening song came to an end in a booming crescendo like a symphony orchestra concluding a concert.

The cynical among you will shake your heads and say that these breathtaking shots were only designed to sell RCA color TV sets—and you would not be wrong—but like most things in life, their use had multiple intentions. Which one you choose to believe says more about your outlook on life than about the show's aims.

As a child taking this all in, the opening was mesmerizing. It was like the entire world was being displayed before us. We could go anywhere, see anything, and, by implication, do anything. It truly was a wonderful world and we were getting shown how we could be a part of it.

At this point, Tinker Bell would make one more appearance. Announcer Dick Wesson would introduce the title of tonight's episode and introduce our master of ceremonies: "And now your host, Walt Disney."

Uncle Walt

The scene shifted to Walt Disney's office (actually a set on a sound-stage). Walt would look at the camera and smile and welcome us to tonight's show. And we would instinctively smile back. Unless it was an episode where he hosted the entire show, Walt's introductions were only two or three minutes long. And yet they did a marvelous job of setting the stage for what was to come.

What was it about this middle-aged man that instantly captured our attention, made us relax, tickled our imaginations, and opened us up to what was to come like a master storyteller getting ready to tell us a tale?

Walt Disney connected with us children for a number of reasons:

- His child-like enthusiasm. You could see it in the way he walked around the office, the way he spoke to us—he had something fun to share and he could not wait to show it to us. His enthusiasm was infectious.

- He did not talk down to us like so many adults do to children (even more so in those days than now). He rightly assumed that if he could understand something then we could, too. It didn't matter if he was talking about a moment out of American history, the complexity of science, the process of animation, or the intricacies of nature's ecosystem. At the same time, Walt had a way of speaking where he could take these complex subjects and boil them down to a simple analogy, an analogy which would open the door to the wider subject, because if we could under-stand that then we could understand the entire thing. It was all very empowering decades before that term had been coined.

- Walt used these segments to share what he was interested in. And since most of what he was interested in was cutting edge (pushing the boundaries of animation, movie-making, robotics, theme park design), we kids were interested in them as well. And if it was not clear why we should be excited, Walt was able to demonstrate in his intros why we should be.

The message that we eagerly took in with our youthful eyes and ears was that the world was a marvelous place filled with adventure and beauty and love. The past was an intriguing time populated by people who helped make our today possible. Nature was something to experience and treasure and keep safe. The future was here and it was going to be better than today. And, most important of all, we children could be a part of it all. All we had to do was dream.

He smiled. He laughed. He made us laugh. He made us feel at ease. He made us feel welcomed. It was like coming over for a fun weekly visit with a treasured relative, which was why we all called him "Uncle Walt".

He was ready to show us Baby Boomer children the wonders of Disney's world and we were happily ready to come along for the ride.

CHAPTER TWO

A Carousel of Color

Animated Fun and Learning with Von Drake

In retrospect, it is hardly surprising that Walt Disney decided to lead off *The Wonderful World of Color*'s NBC debut in the fall of 1961 by doing an entire show devoted to exploring the virtues of color. "An Adventure In Color" was simultaneously designed to show off the advantages of color TV and to also explain the usefulness of color in our everyday life.

An Adventure in Color /
Donald in Mathmagic Land (1961)
TV Premiere: September 24, 1961

Walt opened the show by standing against a black-and-white background and giving us a crash course in the development of animation, reminding us how just a little over thirty years ago the movies had been black and white as well and, worse, without sound. Just black-and-white images projected onto the screen in our neighborhood theater. If a character wanted to say something, their words appeared in a thought bubble or in a separate title card. If a filmmaker wanted us to feel something, they were beholden to the theater organist playing along with the film.

Walt reminded us that that had all changed, mostly thanks to him, with the creation of the first synchronized sound cartoon *Steamboat Willie* (1928) starring Mickey Mouse. That led to his Silly Symphonies series which combined animation and music in new ways that pushed animation further forward. And that led to the first color cartoon, *Flowers and Trees* (1932), and just eight short years later to the lyrical beauty of *Fantasia* (1940) with Walt screening a segment from the water lilies dance.

As Walt beams out from the TV, he reminds us that, "Dreams have a way of coming true" and "Color looks pretty good, doesn't it?" And watching on our RCA Victor TV, I had to agree with him.

From there, Walt introduced the show's new resident scientific expert Professor Ludwig Von Drake, an animated and educated duck (and distant relative of Donald Duck), to "tell us about the wonderful world of color." Von Drake has always been one of my favorite Disney characters. I particularly liked him when I was little because I knew that when he came on the show, I was going to have fun and I was going to learn something. He may lose his train of thought or get a bit confused, but that was only because his head was so full of facts and he was so intent on sharing them with us that they inevitably would come out in a bit of a jumbly mess.

Von Drake spent the next few minutes explaining the color spectrum. While his presentations may have been blustery and a little confusing, his scientific facts never were. I remember being surprised to learn that humans only see one octave of the available color in the world. What were the rest of them like? I also remember being amazed at how easy it was to combine the basic colors to get all the rest.

Inevitably, just like in this episode, Von Drake would get himself confused and resort to song to make his point. In this case, he sat down at a piano and illustrated his point by singing "The Spectrum Song." This is the moment when I fell in love with Ludwig Von Drake. The song, penned by Richard and Robert Sherman, did what Disney songs do best: take a difficult concept and present it in a way that not only explained it but hung it on a catchy tune. The "I'm No Fool" and "Encyclopedia" songs from *The Mickey Mouse Club* did the same thing. Once inside our heads, they never left.

Two inspired moments stick with me from "The Spectrum Song." After running through it once, Von Drake decides to sing it again, except this time in black and white for those who don't yet have a color TV. He then proceeded to recite the lyrics, but rather than reeling off the different colors, he just sings "black, white, grey, white, black, black, black, grey, black, white" ad nauseam. It was a clever way to gently nudge the recalcitrant black-and-white audience to embrace color—much like how we are now always being chided to purchase the latest iPhone or marvelous electronic creation. The song gets interrupted by the NBC peacock who struts off stage while showing off his feathers of many colors. A perturbed Von Drake confides that "he dyes his feathers."

An attempt to explain how color TV works forces Von Drake to give up again and resort to song. In this case, it is the full opening credits song which again not only illustrates color but also promises "the wonders to be told" in the show ahead. Viewers were hooked whether they were watching in color or black and white, and I am sure a number of children turned to their parents at that moment and began demanding they buy a color TV. I was glad that my own family already had one.

The second half of the show, *Donald In Mathmagic Land*, found Donald dressed as a hunter, but finding himself a stranger in a strange land where every tree or animal was some kind of geometric shape or mathematical formula or measuring device, and the footprints they leave are all numbers. I remember finding it particularly humorous that the trees all had "square roots."

"What kind of crazy place is this?" Donald wonders.

And yet he is assured by the narrator (the ubiquitous Paul Frees) that this—the pursuit of knowledge—is the "True Spirit of Adventure."

"Ah, that's for eggheads!" Donald responds, but the show takes him by the hand and does what Disney educational films always did that worked for me. They took us back in history to the origins of how things got started (in this case, ancient Greece). They took the abstract concepts and applied them to everyday life so we could understand their relevance. Here, they explained the connection between math and music and how it helped develop the musical scale, thus bringing the whole thing full circle to where the show began with Von Drake. Donald became convinced of the importance of knowing this and so did we.

There are a few clunky moments in the show. It turns out that the magic words for turning Walt's workers in the paint and ink department from black and white to color are "NBC color TV." "Bibbidi-Bobbidi-Blue" only turns them into the blue, yellow, and red elements of Technicolor. Later on, when introducing "Donald In Mathmagic Land," Walt loses his train of thought while explaining math because of all the "attractive figures" of the female workers in Paint and Ink.

But the moment that stuck with me and would, like "The Spectrum Song," be something I referred back to through the rest of my childhood and into my adult years was when the narrator takes a tour of Donald's head to see if he is ready for understanding the wonders of math. Unfortunately, he discovers that Donald's brain is already too cluttered, and that both he (and we) need to first clean out our minds and dispose of the "antiquated ideas," "false concepts," "superstitions," and "confusions" that prevent us from comprehending something new.

I also took away from the episode that "the mind is the birthplace for all of man's scientific achievements," that "the mind knows no limits when used properly," and no piece of paper was "large enough to hold all your ideas." As the show's final quotation (from Galileo) proclaimed, "Mathematics is the alphabet with which God has written the universe."

At the very end of "Mathmagic Land," Donald finds himself in a corridor of doors that are all locked. When he complains to the narrator, he is informed that these are "the doors to the future" and that "the keys to opening them are mathematics." It remains an oddly stirring moment for me and, even as a youngster staring at that screen, I knew that mathematics were not the only keys for opening the future (just like humans can only see one octave of color); the other keys were the arts: music and literature and painting and sculpture. And those keys could be mine if I worked to understand the history of what happened before and then applied it to my life. Yes, indeed, mathematics (and the rest of education) was magic and also key.

Pretty heady stuff for a children's show. And *The Wonderful World of Color* was just getting started!

Ludwig Von Drake hosted so many episodes in the next five years that Walt Disney began to joke that the professor was the co-host of the show. Von Drake even picked up an animated co-host of his own: Herman the Beetle, who seemed to be both a colleague and a rival.

Sometimes they hosted shows designed to explain the absurdities of human nature like *The Hunting Instinct* (1961) or *A Square Peg in a Round Hole* (1963). Other times the shows were meant to be educational, like in *Fly with Von Drake* (1963), a primer on aviation history illustrated by clips from *Victory Through Air Power* (1943), or *Kids Is Kids* (1961) about proper parenting, with clips from a Goofy or Donald Duck cartoon, or music appreciation in *Music For Everybody* (1966). *In Shape with Von Drake* (1964) taught the value of exercise illustrated with generous clips from classic Goofy cartoons like *How to Play Baseball* (1942), *How to Play Football* (1944), *How to Play Golf* (1944), and *The Art of Skiing* (1941).

Sometimes Von Drake became a travel guide taking us down to South America in *Carnival Time* (1962) where I first got exposed to the wonders of Brazil and Rio and Carnival and the samba, or to sunny Spain for *Von Drake in Spain* (1962) which featured an introduction to Flamenco dancing, or a *Mediterranean Cruise* (1964). But only two episodes really stand out for me and helped mold how I would see the world.

Man Is His Own Worst Enemy (1962)

TV Premiere: October 21, 1962

Like the others, this typical Ludwig Von Drake episode was built around classic Disney shorts and yet for this impressionable child it did a wonderful job of helping me understand both the power and the dangers of emotions—how they can, if kept in check, help us to enjoy and appreciate life to its fullest, but, if we let them have the driver's seat, they can potentially ruin our lives.

This was perfectly illustrated in the episode's first short, *Reason and Emotion* (1942). I loved how it showed that when we are children, emotion is all we know and so we act on any impulse that crosses our minds without regard to consequences. As we grow older, reason joins emotion in our brains and helps balance out emotion's potentially harmful impetuousness. The short concludes by illustrating how emotion plays a key part in helping us date and fall in love, and how sometimes against our better judgment we let emotion get the better of us. Given the circumstances, this can be a good thing when done in small amounts. It can be highly dangerous if we let our emotions dictate our daily activities.

I did not find out until years later that the short contained a second half not included in the Von Drake special. The second half showed how Adolf Hitler used fear, sympathy, pride, and hate to manipulate the emotions of the German people. It had been removed because its timeliness was no longer valid and yet it remains illustrative of the dangers of what can happen when an entire country lets their emotions overrule their reason. For me, it remains one of the best illustrations of how to recognize when any politician or public figure is pulling these levers of emotion to get us to do something we should not, and which may lead us into further danger.

The second short in the episode hammered that point home even more. *Chicken Little* (1943) is an uncommonly dark interpretation of the familiar tale. It powerfully illustrates how listening to gossip and unfounded rumors can result in the total downfall of a society. In this retelling, the chickens all live safely in the barnyard behind a strong fence and a locked gate. Cocky Locky is mayor. Henny Penny passes her days playing cards with the gossip crowd, Turkey Lurkey sips tea with the intellectual set decrying how horrible things are. The Jitter Birds—young people interested only in having a good time with no social responsibilities—spend their days at the club while Goosey Loosey and his boys spend the day drinking at the bar. They are absolutely in no danger. There is no way that the devious Foxy Loxy can get to them, so he decides to use psychology to manipulate them right into his hungry hands.

"I'm not a fox for nothing," he tells the audience.

"To influence the masses," he reads, "aim first at the least intelligent."

That turns out to be our "hero," Chicken Little, identified as a playboy and yo-yo champ,

"If you tell them a lie," Foxy Loxy reads, "don't tell them a little one, tell them a big one."

Foxy Loxy tries to convince Chicken Little that the sky is falling. Chicken Little then tries to warn the rest, but Cocky Locky immediately steps in and disproves the threat by showing it is not a piece of the sky, just a wooden star.

Foxy Loxy ups his game for the next step: "Undermine the faith of the masses in their leaders."

He hurries around and whispers through holes in the fence exactly what will set off each group. "Suppose he is wrong," he tells Henny Penny and the gossip crowd. "And if he is wrong, we will all be killed." "Cocky Locky is trying to dictate to us masses," he tells Turkey Lurkey and the smart set. "I hear Cocky Locky has been hitting the mash lately," he slurs to Goosey Loosey at the bar.

The whispering campaign boomerangs throughout the yard. Soon enough, it reaches Cocky Locky and starts to undermine his own faith in himself.

"By the use of flattery," Foxy reads, "insignificant people can believe that they are naturally born leaders."

Foxy talks up Chicken Little who burnishes his newfound belief in himself into a messianic zeal. Chicken Little rallies the birds who no longer believe in Cocky Locky's leadership. He takes on Cocky Locky in a debate. Chicken Little still appears to be losing when Foxy Loxy throws another wooden star that hits the mayor in the head. The sky IS falling. The world IS ending. Emotion is definitely not listening to reason. Chicken Little urges them all to open the locked gate and leave the safety of the barnyard for the supposed safety of the nearby cave (another idea Foxy Loxy planted in his brain). They promptly do and Foxy Loxy traps them all in there.

"Don't worry, folks," the narrator assures us, "it all turns out alright."

Only it doesn't. In a surprisingly dark turn, we venture inside to discover that Foxy Loxy has eaten every single one of them. They are all dead and his nasty smile at the final fade out would haunt my dreams for years to come.

It also gave me a checklist to use as a child and as an adult to understand and recognize when anyone—politician, religious leader, radio entertainer, or political commentator—was using psychology to manipulate me into "running for the cave." It has proven to be one of the best and most useful civic lessons the *World of Disney* ever taught me. And it served to illustrate that man IS his own worst enemy.

The Truth about Mother Goose (1963)

TV Premiere: November 17, 1963

This episode strived to tell the origins behind a trio of our popular nursery rhymes. Since these were songs I was already singing in school (my elementary school teachers were big into trying to teach us the glories of song), I found it fascinating that the rhymes had deeper meanings beneath their simplistic lyrics. As the opening title song by the Page Cavanaugh Trio in the episode stated, "Nursery rhymes from olden times are really part of history."

And so we were walked through the origin stories for:

- "Little Jack Horner" originated from 16th century England. It was really about a disobedient servant who stole a royal gift from the pie he was meant to deliver to King Henry VIII. The act haunted him for the rest of his life.

- "Mary, Mary Quite Contrary" was really a condemnation by her subjects of the airs and extravagances and thoughtlessness of Mary, Queen of Scots, who, as the narrator informed us, proved to be "quite contrary" and ultimately paid for it by losing her head, literally, in 1567.

- "London Bridge Is Falling Down" emerged from the 17th century and told the story of the original London Bridge, the first span across the Thames River when it was completed in 1209. It was not just a bridge but also contained large buildings within its span that included shops and luxury apartments for the rich and for well-to-do artists. It was practically a city within a city. It hosted carnivals and entertainments and tournaments and was THE place to be seen for centuries. But after being badly damaged in the Great London Fire of 1666, the bridge began to crumble and collapse—causing people to begin to sing the song. After centuries of further decay, the bridge was finally torn down.

The Truth about Mother Goose was filled out to an hour by a showing of *Mickey and the Beanstalk* from *Fun and Fancy Free* (1947). Von Drake and Herman took over the narrator chores from original storytellers Edgar Bergen and Charlie McCarthy. A very loose retelling of the classic fairy tale with Mickey Mouse, Donald Duck, and Goofy filling in for Jack, this version has its funny moments. Willie the Giant from *The Brave Little Tailor* (1938) makes a humorous, non-threatening giant. This adaptation is remembered mostly as the moment when Walt Disney stepped aside as the voice of Mickey Mouse to be replaced by Jimmy MacDonald. The moment when Goofy and Donald are trapped in a large jewelry box is a highlight. After Mickey fetches the key, Donald Duck tells him, "Let me have it, Mickey," leading to the monstrous key bursting through the hole and smacking Donald in the face.

But the biggest lesson I took away from *The Truth about Mother Goose*, one that has motivated me down through the decades, was to not accept the surface explanations for anything in history. I needed to delve deeper and look behind stories and myths to the original sources of a song or story. This was in an age when we were still being taught in school that George Washington threw a dollar coin across the Rappahannock River and that he chopped down a cherry tree before confessing the deed to his mother. I learned that communal stories we tell each other may have no basis in truth or they may be, in the case of the songs, an attempt to express rebellion by the populace against a ruling monarch or government. It was the first forming of a healthy skepticism that I have applied since to government explanations, confessions of feckless politicians, religious doctrines, or official histories. Learning *The Truth about Mother Goose* served me well in the era of Watergate and countless political scandals as our generation began to look beneath the surface of what we were taught and to not just accept what we were told.

It's Tough to Be a Bird (1969)

TV Premiere: December 13, 1970

This episode originally began as a theatrical short released into theaters in 1969. Directed by Disney animator Ward Kimball, the short was paired with the feature film *The Computer Wore Tennis Shoes*, a prescient movie in its own way that will be discussed in chapter 10. I am including this episode here because, even though it was not hosted by Ludwig Von Drake (a bird of another feather), it has the same plan of attack that the Von Drake shows had: introduce a problem, give us the history of how we came to this point, and offer up ways we can help. Again, the plans are attained through education and awareness.

In this case, the problem is the poor shape the birds are in due to human involvement. Narrated by an animated bird (though the movie is a mix of animation and live action), it succeeds by helping us to see things through the birds' point of view and give us the perspective of the victim in this centuries-old story.

Like *Donald In Mathmagic Land*, the wonder of animation sends us back to ancient times where we learn how birds evolved into the species they are today: one hundred thousand years compressed into less than a minute. Everything was fine until humans came along. Our bird narrator reminds us of all the good things birds have done, from serving as navigators of the ocean (helping Noah's ark find land or helping Christopher Columbus and Leif Ericson discover America) to helping settle disputes before a battle (if a chicken from one army ate the corn offered by the opposing army, they would not fight that day, thus the origin of the phrase "to chicken out").

The show asserts that we humans seem to envy the birds because we have spent so many centuries trying to fly like them (becoming successful only in the last century). It also highlights the grandiosity of man—the hubris of him wanting to fly, trying to fly, but not succeeding.

But it is on the subject of hunting that the bird narrator sounds the most despair.

"I guess you must desire for us to be extinct," sighs our avian narrator. To reinforce his point, he shows us examples of bird species that humans hunted to extinction, such as the passenger pigeon and the great auk. He then shares a list of bird species under the threat of extinction: the whooping crane, trumpeter swan, California condor, and bald eagle. He closes the segment by emphasizing that time is running out.

For possible ways the audience could help, our trusty narrator recommends the National Audubon Society as well as bird watcher groups. He also encourages us not to focus solely on the pretty birds, but to find beauty as well in the "ugly" birds like the buzzard. To illustrate, the movie takes us to the buzzard festival in Hinckley, Ohio, where they celebrate the annual spring return of the buzzards.

The short closes with a montage that reaches back into the past and forward into the future. The closing comes with our narrator thanking us for helping to save his kind by using a closing line attributed to George M. Cohan in *Yankee Doodle Dandy* (1942): "My father thanks you. My mother thanks you. My sister thanks you. And I thank you." It was a closing that used to be part of our pop culture vernacular back in the day, only here he is literally thanking the audience (in advance) for saving his species. Animator Kimball then launches into an animation montage that appears prescient in its style—a rapid fire collage combining drawings and photographs, its anarchic style a dead ringer for the cartoons Terry Gilliam made for *Monty Python's Flying Circus* (a TV series that debuted in Britain the same year as *Birds*). Even the NBC peacock and Mary Poppins get into the act.

To put a final emphasis on their plight, our bird narrator is literally gunned down right in front of us, an event that would be traumatic to small children if he didn't continue talking to us while literally pushing up daisies from his grave.

It is not surprising that Disney made this kind of film at this particular time. Like many things Disney did in the 1960s, it caught the zeitgeist of the time (just like the notion that computers were about to enter our everyday lives). As the 1960s gave way to the 1970s, environmentalism was on everyone's mind. The ecology movement was on the rise. Earth Day became a holiday six months before the show aired. It was the same year that Iron Eyes Cody famously paddled his canoe down a river littered with pollution. Becoming aware of man's damage to the planet was, for the first time, emerging in the national consciousness.

What strikes me as significant is that all the endangered species featured on the bird's list were ultimately saved. Through the concerted efforts of science and public awareness, people worked to save the birds' habitats by prohibiting urban growth and helping to reestablish natural habitats, helping to ban destructive pesticides like DDT that compromised the shells of the birds' eggs, and working to improve breeding. *It's Tough to Be a Bird* did not do this single-handedly, but it certainly was part of the effort that brought the problem to public attention.

Hall of Fame Fun and Learning Episode

From All of Us to All of You (1958)

TV Premiere: December 19, 1958

Few episodes of *World of Disney* were more anticipated and aired more often than this semi-annual Christmas special. In fact, it is the only episode that has outlived the show. It continues to be aired annually at Christmastime in European countries, particularly in Scandinavia. It has become so identified as a part of the holiday that attempts through the years to stop airing it have met with mass outcries and protests from the general public, forcing the broadcasters to back down. *From All of Us to All of You* is alive and well and still spreading its traditional yuletide joy.

The format of the show has not changed much. It is essentially a compilation of great Disney moments, a "clip show" as we like to call it. The original 1958 episode opened with an introduction from Walt that got eliminated in later years to make room for a section promoting the latest Disney release. What good is a Christmas special if not for making some money? Walt then turned the show over to our holiday host, Jiminy Cricket, who was joined by Mickey Mouse on piano playing the episode's rousing theme song that always got us singing and tapping our toes.

From there we took a quick trip up to the North Pole to view Santa Claus' final preparations. We did this by seeing the 1932 Silly Symphony cartoon *Santa's Workshop*. The cartoon remains hilarious as the camera patrols the toy factory and we get to see the bizarre, ingenious, and impossible ways that Santa's elves make toys. The cartoon has been censored through the years as it contains a few moments that are no longer considered socially acceptable. At one point an elf is giving their dolls a final check and if they are ready to go he raises their skirts and stamps a big "OK" on the butt of their white panties. At another place in the factory, Santa is also checking out dolls. If they can say "Mama" back to him then they are ready to be boxed up. Everything is fine until one doll comes down the conveyor belt in black face, drops to her knees, and belts out, "Mammy!" (an obvious ode to Al Jolson). Santa collapses in laughter. There are also a few inside jokes in the cartoon if you have a quick eye, like the Mickey Mouse doll in Santa's bag as they load it on the sleigh. By the end of the cartoon,

Santa is on his way and children can sit and relax knowing it is only a matter of time before he arrives at their house.

From there, Jiminy brings on Chip 'n' Dale to explain how they celebrate Christmas. They decide it is better to show rather than explain (since they are both talking over one another) and that leads into a cartoon. Originally, it was the Donald Duck short *Toy Tinkers* (1949) where the two chipmunks spy Donald cutting down a tree for Christmas and follow him home. A battle of wills follows that is not much in the spirit of Christmas, but totally in keeping with the many battles between the hotheaded duck and the resourceful rodents. As usual, Donald loses; his house is in a mess, and Chip 'n' Dale end up with the goodies and the presents.

In the 1970s, the short was replaced with *Pluto's Christmas Tree* (1952) which had essentially the same story. Mickey Mouse and Pluto are out getting a tree for the season when Mickey accidentally cuts down the tree the chipmunks live in. Once the tree is set up and decorated, the chipmunks discover the fun and goodies of the season while Pluto goes berserk trying to convince Mickey that their home has been invaded. In the end, Pluto is proven right but only after the tree and decorations have been ruined. Mickey remains unfazed by it all and offers to let the chipmunks stay for the holiday. The short ends on a lovely note as Minnie Mouse, Donald Duck, and Goofy stop by to serenade them with the Christmas carol "Deck the Halls."

The part I always enjoyed most was the next section, where Disney characters sent viewers a Christmas card containing favorite moments from their movies. Later generations have to remember that VCRs, VHS, or DVDs did not exist, so these clips were the only way we could relive these amazing moments from our favorite Disney films. It was totally enchanting to watch Peter Pan, Wendy, and the boys take off for Never Land while singing "You Can Fly" from *Peter Pan* (1953) and Thumper teach Bambi how to ice skate in *Bambi* (1942). Or see Pinocchio perform "I've Got No Strings" from *Pinocchio* (1940), and Tony and Joe serenade Tramp and Lady with "Bella Notte" from *Lady and the Tramp* (1955), the mice making Cinderella's ball gown in *Cinderella* (1950), and the dwarfs entertaining Snow White by singing the raucous "Silly Song" from *Snow White and the Seven Dwarfs* (1937).

Because it was the yuletide season, several of the lyrics jumped out at me in ways they wouldn't the rest of the season, such as in "You Can Fly" when the chorus encourages the children to "think of Christmas, think of snow, think of sleigh bells. Off you go." Or the Bambi on ice segment because my sisters and I often skated at a pond in the woods near our house just like the one in the film. Even as a boy, the romantic in me loved "Bella Notte" and how brilliantly the animators caught that moment when Lady is totally swept away by the mood and emotions of the evening and falls in love with Tramp. That moment became the touchstone for me when I experienced similar moments on some of my favorite dates as a teen or an adult (while always being sure to keep reason firmly in control over emotion).

The next-to-last segment of the show would be reserved for a scene from the latest Disney animated film, whether *The Sword in the Stone* (1963), *The Jungle Book* (1967), *The Aristocats* (1970), *Robin Hood* (1973), or finally, *Pete's Dragon* (1977). The juxtaposition of great Disney moments with a segment from the new film helped to convey the notion that Disney animation was alive and well and made us want to see the new film as badly as we wanted to watch the classics.

Finally, the episode would end with Jiminy sharing his favorite moment, singing "When You Wish Upon a Star" from *Pinocchio*. He would introduce the song by telling us that it "symbolizes faith, hope, and all the things that Christmas stands for...something that can make Christmas every day if you just believe."

He belts out the song in that gorgeous Cliff Edwards voice (to my mind, one of the loveliest songs ever sung) as all of the great Disney characters gather around in the light of their Christmas tree: Alice from *Alice in Wonderland* (1951), Pluto, Goofy, Donald, Huey, Dewey, Louie, the Three Little Pigs, the Seven Dwarfs, Br'er Bear and Br'er Rabbit from *Song of the South* (1946), the mice from *Cinderella*, and the forest animals from *Snow White* and *Bambi*.

I can see why the special became and remains so beloved. It is a perfectly pitched balance of great Disney moments that put us in the proper holiday mood for the season while simultaneously empowering us to feel we can do anything in the new year as long as we believe in both the power of Christmas and the power of wishing. After all, "If your heart is in your dream, no request is too extreme." As a child, those sentiments made me want to wish to make it so. Speaking as an adult, I can tell you that that formula is all you need to make your dreams come true. I have used that very same method to make a number of my adult dreams come true (including this book you hold in your hands).

A big thank you to Ludwig Von Drake and Herman and Donald Duck and Goofy and Mother Goose and all the animated characters who taught me well in my early years. They prepared me for greater adventures to come as I started to step out of the early years of childhood and delve into the vast landscape of American history and folklore.

CHAPTER THREE

A Carousel of American History

Heroes of Folklore and Literature

Whenever I talk to people about the heroes in their favorite episodes of *The Wonderful World of Disney*, their faces will light up as they burst out with, "Johnny Tremain!" "Texas John Slaughter!" "Elfego Baca!" "The Swamp Fox!" and, most frequently of all, the King of the Wild Frontier himself, "Davy Crockett!" Some will even get a bit confused and blurt out "Zorro!" even though that was a different Disney show. Others will yell "Daniel Boone!" even though they are confusing Daniel Boone with Davy Crockett, probably because Fess Parker played both frontiersmen, Crockett for Disney in the 1950s and Boone on the popular CBS western series from 1964–1970.

I also find it interesting that all but one of these characters predate the World of Disney years. Davy Crockett and Johnny Tremain were the first big hits of the *Disneyland* years (1954–1959) while Texas John Slaughter, Elfego Baca, and the Swamp Fox were part of a revolving set of continuing serials that made up *Walt Disney Presents* (1959–1961). Equally interesting for me is that, while Walt regularly re-ran episodes of the show every couple of years, only Davy Crockett and Johnny Tremain were ever re-run during the World of Disney years. The other characters, popular in their time, were left to languish on the Disney vault shelves even as their exploits remain vividly in the minds of the boys and girls watching.

It is no surprise that these figures loom large in the imagination of Baby Boomers. Growing up in the 1950s and early 1960s, children obsessed over tales of the American West in the same way that today's children are mesmerized by science fiction and superheroes. We kids lived, ate, and breathed the American West. We dreamed of owning our own horse, strapping on our own six shooter, and setting out for parts unknown, even if it were only the far reaches of our backyard.

And I was no different. So Disney was only mirroring the American mood, one that would last until the first space rocket blasted off from Cape Canaveral in Florida. To quote Stinky Pete in *Toy Story 2* (1999), "Two words: Sput-nik. Once the astronauts went up, children only wanted to play with space toys."

As a boy growing up around the farms of rural Indiana and then the cramped river valleys and towering mountains of West Virginia, the wide open plains of the American West that I saw on TV were like a dream: majestic and daunting and beautiful. Set before them rode heroes and heroines from our past—some real, some fiction—but all embodying the spirit and the beliefs that helped make America into the country we know today.

Looking back I was pleasantly surprised at how multi-cultural many of these heroes were, and how *World of Disney* introduced me to key aspects of minority culture. At the same time, the episodes exposed the darker side of America's manifest destiny: the tragedy of the Native Americans, the horrors of the Civil War, and the stain of racism that has colored and tainted our society. *World of Disney* introduced me to a balanced view of our American past to absorb and learn from.

Tales of the Revolutionary War

In my youth, the Revolutionary War between Great Britain and its American colonies was portrayed as the ultimate underdog tale. The Americans were a ragtag collection of poorly trained citizen soldiers going up against the British Army, which then enjoyed the reputation of being the best in the world. Of course, we had lots of external help, particularly from the French, that contributed to our surprise victory, but to our child-like eyes in the twentieth century, it was the perfect example of Yankee grit, determination, and resolve—traits of the American character that we could always call on. And the best place to start was with the "Shot Heard 'Round the World."

Johnny Tremain (1957)
TV Premiere: November 21, December 5, 1958

Based on the Esther Forbes novel, *Johnny Tremain* had a circuitous route to the small screen. Walt originally conceived it as a two-part episode for the show, but after the budget climbed higher than expected, he packaged it for theatrical release. Appropriately enough, it premiered in theaters on July 4, 1957, then made its TV debut the following autumn around Thanksgiving. The movie is dedicated "to the youth of the world...in whose spirit and courage rests the hope of eventual freedom for all mankind."

The movie tells the tale of Johnny Tremain, a teenaged boy (Hal Stallmaster) working in colonial Boston before the war broke out. He is apprenticed to a silversmith and has dreams of becoming the top silversmith in town. Johnny is arrogant and cocky and quite sure of himself.

"You can keep your politics," Johnny tells his fellow patriots. "I'll stick to my own trade and mind my own business."

"When the meek inherit the earth," the silversmith's pretty daughter Priscilla (Luana Patten) grumps, "I doubt you'll get one square inch of sod."

One Sunday, Johnny defies the law against working on a Sunday to fulfill a rush order for a rich client. In the process, he mistakenly burns his hand. His fingers fuse together, rendering the hand useless. Dismissed from his job, Johnny soon discovers that nobody else in town will hire a man with only one good hand.

The only people to take him in are the local Sons of Liberty organization. He strikes up a friendship with fellow teen Rab Silsbee (Richard Beymer) and finds himself in a budding romance with Priscilla. At the same time, revolutionary patriots like James Otis, Samuel Adams, Dr. Joseph Warren, and Paul Revere take him under their wing.

"But I'm a nobody," Johnny says when the Sons of Liberty offer to let him join.

"We're all nobodies," Samuel Adams says, "when we're standing alone. It's when we fight together that counts. And we happen to believe that we must fight just as hard against small tyrannies as against big ones."

Against his better wishes, Johnny soon finds himself embroiled in revolutionary politics as tensions between the colonists and the British soldiers occupying Boston build to the breaking point. It all climaxes with the Boston Tea Party, Paul Revere's ride, and the first battles of the war at Lexington and Concord. In the end, Dr. Warren restores Johnny's hand and he goes off to fight as campfires of the patriots surround the beleaguered British in Boston, foreshadowing their defeat to come.

Johnny Tremain served as my primer for not only the Revolutionary War but also what to expect in American society. It made me aware of the discrimination by class, something that was there right from the beginning and embodied in the character of Squire Lyte (Sebastian Cabot). The rich in this country could have it their way anytime they wished. They could warp the justice system to suit their own ends. And at the bottom of it all, their interest in a political cause was only related to how much money they could make from it. Only after they are shown the financial benefits of embracing the new system (or are surrounded and realize they have no choice) will they change.

The other new thing the movie exposed me to for the first time was the heartbreak of disabilities. Johnny Tremain was the first fictional character I knew with a handicap. And while it may not be a serious disability in this day and age, it was enough for me to identify and wonder how I would fair if I were in Johnny's position. His hand is scarred and ruined, but that doesn't mean he has nothing to contribute. The merchants of Boston can only see what his body can contribute. They find no value in the person inside. It taught me that what makes a person is not the abilities of their physical body but the spirit and resilience of their personality within. The merchants look down on Johnny as useless and inferior just as England looked down on its American colonies. Only the Sons of Liberty see Johnny's potential, so he gladly gives himself to the cause. When Johnny's hand is repaired at the end, it represents not only the rebirth of Johnny Tremain the person but also the birth of the American character and the spirit that he personifies.

The movie is also one of the few American films to put us at the opening moments of the Revolutionary War. American students are taught about the first skirmishes on the greens of Lexington and the legendary "shot heard around the world" at Concord, but *Johnny Tremain* puts us in the middle of that action. We see the United States coming to vibrant, bellicose life as this ragtag collection of farmers and merchants barely trained as a militia unit makes their first stand against the British. Lexington is a quick loss, but the news of the loss motivates hundreds of other men to grab their guns and join the fight. They manage to turn the British back at Concord, then harass them all the way back to Boston. You can practically see the American spirit rising, and the sequence is rightly stirring.

The last thing *Johnny Tremain* taught me was the rush of being part of a movement, especially a movement aimed at improving the lives of all. The Sons of Liberty is an egalitarian organization, welcoming and employing all: old, young, male, female, doctor, lawyer, clergyman, farmer, merchant. It made me realize that the most successful groups employ all members of society. The Sons of Liberty's philosophy is best expressed in their rallying song, "The Liberty Tree," sung throughout the movie. At first a few, then dozens sing it. By the end of the movie, with Boston surrounded by patriot campfires, thousands are singing it.

As the commanding British officer says to his men, "You see those campfires, gentlemen? Yesterday we ruled over Boston. Tonight we are besieged in it. And still they come from every village and farm. Tonight ten thousand. Tomorrow, perhaps twice ten thousand. We've experienced more than a defeat, more than a mere misfortune of war. We have been vanquished by an idea, a belief in human rights."

Through *Johnny Tremain* we witness the birth of the United States.

Ben and Me (1953)

TV Premiere: November 15, 1964

This cartoon short chronicled the exploits of Amos the Mouse (Sterling Holloway) and taught the lesson that behind every great man, in this case Benjamin Franklin (Charlie Ruggles), there was a great mouse. When the two first meet, Franklin ("just call me Ben") is a struggling printer in colonial Philadelphia with bill collectors gathered at his door. Amos takes him under his wing. By sharing his knowledge as a friend, he helps Franklin invent the stove and bifocals. He shows Ben how to go about publishing a successful newspaper and utters many of the truisms that end up in *Poor Richard's Almanac*. More than that, Amos teaches him the etiquette and sophistication necessary to get Franklin noticed in Philadelphia society.

The friendship is not perfect. The movie shows Franklin's cruel side as he teases and taunts Amos and pulls practical jokes that lead to physical harm. Franklin is happy to accept Amos' help, but he is equally happy to accept all the credit from the public. It is no surprise that when Franklin seeks to resume their partnership at the end of the episode, he sees it as the renewal of a friendship while Amos sees it as more of a business deal and comes with paperwork in hand that needs to be negotiated and signed. When Amos threatens to quit, Franklin pleads that he meant no harm and that it was no big deal, just like any schoolyard bully. In the end, the moments of humiliation prove too much for Amos and he walks out, though he continues to watch Franklin's career from afar as tensions build and the Revolution approaches.

The lessons I learned from *Ben and Me* were to treat the official version of events with skepticism. There is always more to tell and the people written out of the story are probably the ones who made the major contributions.

The Swamp Fox (1959–1961)

TV Premiere: October 23, 1959

The Swamp Fox was an eight-part serial that ran on *Walt Disney Presents*. It chronicled the true adventures of Francis Marion (Leslie Nielsen) aka the Swamp Fox. During the closing years of the Revolutionary War, he led a fighting unit that harassed and troubled the British throughout South Carolina which ultimately contributed to the American victory. He is described by Walt in his introduction as the "Robin Hood of the Revolution," hero, patriot, and guerrilla fighter. The serial is an old-fashioned, rip-roaring adventure yarn. The announcer promises us "adventure to take you out of the world of reality" and "action that is new, different, exciting." But underneath the exciting action were several dark sides of the emerging American character that I realized I was going to have to keep an eye on in the world around me.

The first and foremost was this obsession we have about deciding who is and who is not an American. The characters in *The Swamp Fox* live in a war situation where it is hard to tell whose side people are on. About half the people in the area favor the British and half favor the Americans. A person is just as likely to get shot for wearing a Continental Army jacket as a British redcoat. This uncertainty breeds fear and fear breeds suspicion and violence. People who support the Americans are called "Americans" and anyone who does not support their cause, even if they were born in America, are called "foreigners."

Mobs of angry citizens roam the countryside confronting anyone they suspect of supporting the British. Anyone suspected will suffer the indignity of seeing their house and farm burned to the ground, or worse. It made me realize that, given the right circumstantial evidence, anyone could be accused of being a traitor. With the episodes premiering a mere five years after the McCarthy era (and while the blacklist was still in force in Hollywood), I am sure the connection was not accidental.

It also made me appreciate the dangers of mobs and how they can be easily swayed in the heat of the moment. The country people have the laudable motive of wanting to ferret out the traitors, but they prove to be easily misled by a loud-spoken leader who may just want to get revenge on a brother or neighbor, usually by generating an emotional reaction out of the crowd.

I could not help noticing that the mobs targeted outsiders whose only crime was not socializing with the community as much as others. They also targeted the rich more out of envy than out of true suspicion of traitorous activity. Yes, mobs could be swayed both for good and bad. I remember the scene where Marion confronted one such mob on its way to burn the house of his wealthy girlfriend and was finally able to turn them aside using reason, but only after allowing the emotionalism of the moment to dissipate.

Bad lessons aside, *The Swamp Fox* also communicated some quite progressive values for its time. Toby, Marion's slave who joins him on his raids, is rarely treated as a slave but more like an equal. He usually rides at Marion's right side, a spot usually reserved for the second in command. When the men are hiding out in the swamp, he serves as the group's doctor, cook, and morale booster (he is the one who comes up with the catchy theme song and serenades the men when they are feeling low).

Even women are treated more like equals. Mary has several

opportunities to move to safety, but prefers to remain working as a spy in her British-sympathizing parents' home. She proves a useful conduit for information to Marion and his men. There is a funny moment when Marion visits a local school just as recess is beginning. In a satire on celebrity, the children are so intent on playing the Swamp Fox that they fail to notice that the real Swamp Fox is among them. And the girls want to play war as much as the boys.

"The girls still want to be generals?" asks the male school teacher.

"Why not?" replies his daughter and fellow teacher. "They're smarter than the boys."

But the biggest jolt *The Swamp Fox* gave me was when Marion's nephew Young Gabe is gunned down by Tory sympathizers at the end of episode three. This was a real shocker for me because major characters (just like our own friends and neighbors) were not supposed to die in TV wars. It didn't help that Tim Considine, the rugged, athletic, good-looking star of *Spin and Marty* and *The Hardy Boys* played Young Gabe. He was a strong, outgoing guy, the kind who effortlessly ended up quarterback of your high school football team and most popular guy in your class. He was someone most boys aspired to be and most girls hoped to date. The death of Young Gabe proved to me that war was not some young boy's adventure (even in *Johnny Tremain* all the major characters survived), and that even young people could pay war's ultimate price. I no longer saw war as something glorious, but something that should only be resorted to when absolutely necessary.

But, hey, what a catchy theme song!

The Legend of Sleepy Hollow (1949)

TV Premiere: October 26, 1955

Washington Irving's early 19th century tale of an itinerant school teacher and his run in with the ghostly Headless Horseman is not a true story of American history, but it is one of the first stellar examples of American literature. Disney had adapted it as a short film and released it theatrically in 1949 paired with a classic of British literature, *The Wind in the Willows*. The movie was called *The Adventures of Ichabod and Mr. Toad* and it marked the return of the Disney studio to serious animation after nearly a decade of producing educational films, army training films, live-action films with animated sequences like *Song of the South* (1946) and *So Dear To My Heart* (1948), and the so called "package films" (feature films consisting of many short cartoons) like *Fun and Fancy Free* (1947) and *Melody Time* (1948).

As a young boy, I knew none of this. I only knew that, for a time, *Sleepy Hollow* was a Halloween staple on *World of Disney* and a fittingly scary one at that. The story is really a battle of wits between Ichabod Crane, the smart but decidedly plain schoolmaster, and Brom Bones, the handsome but vain man about town. Their object is the fair hand of the lovely Katrina Van Tassel, the daughter of the wealthiest farmer in the area. Ichabod may be smart, but he has a weakness for ghost stories and superstitions and, while riding home on Halloween night, he has a fateful encounter with the area's top specter, the Headless Horseman.

For all his popularity with the townsfolk, Brom Bones is just a big bully and bullies always need to be stood up to, not by meeting them on their own ground, but by playing to your own strengths like Ichabod does. I also learned to ask myself if the woman I am pursuing is worthy of pursuit. It becomes clear early on that Katrina is only using Ichabod as a pawn to enrage Brom's jealousy. She laughs at Ichabod behind his back and fakes affection for him in public. In the end he gets his heart broken by a callous, manipulative woman (a point made clearer in the original story) before the Headless Horseman appears.

When they do cross paths, Ichabod's encounter with the Headless Horseman is a masterpiece of building dread. Riding home late at night through the hollow, the superstitious schoolmaster begins to imagine that all the innocent sounds of nature have ominous portents. Crickets chirping become the screams of ghosts, bullfrogs croaking in the night are calling out Ichabod's name or that of the Headless Horseman. The sound of galloping horses are just reeds being pounded against the side of a log by the wind. And a crow overhead warns him to "Beware! Beware! Beware!" It is almost a relief when the Horseman arrives.

The chase through the forest grabs me every time. It is a mad chase both comic and horrific toward the safety of a covered bridge (which the Horseman cannot cross) while avoiding the ghost's sword bent on chopping off Ichabod's head. Once again, Ichabod succeeds against the odds and he and his old horse, Gunpowder, manage to cross the bridge to safety. Unfortunately, having done so, he makes the fatal mistake of looking back and that presents the Horseman with the chance to finish him off by hurling a fiery pumpkin at him. Final lesson learned: don't look back!

Sleepy Hollow is burned in my brain because it was a part of one of the most horrific nights of my childhood: October 31, 1965. That was one of the first times my parents took me out trick or treating. Actually, Dad took my sisters and I while Mom stayed home to hand out candy. We hadn't been out too long when I saw a boy dressed up as a scary devil. The only problem was that I thought he was a real devil. I cried and screamed and got so hysterical that my father had no choice but to bring me back home. He left me with Mom and went back out with my sisters. Not more than five minutes later, our doorbell rang and there was that kid dressed up like the devil standing at our front door. He had only come for our candy but to my young eyes, he had deliberately followed me home to steal my soul. So I proceeded to have one of the biggest freak-outs of my young life right there in our living room. Mom eventually got me to settle down and then she plopped me in front of the TV to watch *Sleepy Hollow*! I still remember the horror of that night. And how scary *The Legend of Sleepy Hollow* was.

Go West, Young Man!

With the Revolution won and the 18th century giving way to the 19th century, the United States began looking west to expand beyond the original thirteen states. Trappers and settlers crossed the forbidding Appalachian Mountains that hemmed in the young country and started settling the Ohio River valley as well as the upper Midwest and the new states of Kentucky and Tennessee.

As a country we started celebrating the mountain men who helped blaze those trails and led us to these new lands: Daniel Boone, Kit Carson, Jim Bridger.

In 1845, a newspaper editor named John O'Sullivan coined the phrase "Manifest Destiny" to explain how it was our country's mission and its God-given right to settle those plains beyond the Mississippi River and bring the land all the way to the Pacific Ocean within our country's borders—which we promptly set out to do, as long wagon trains made their way to the far-off lands of Oregon and California.

Westward Ho the Wagons! (1956)

TV Premiere: February 19, 26, 1961

As a 1960s kid raised on TV westerns, the sight of a wagon train heading west was as familiar as that of a rocket lifting off into space. *Westward Ho the Wagons!* (1956) served as a good introduction to such a journey. The movie works almost as a kid-sized adventure since it is the children of the wagon train who drive the drama forward. The movie stars Fess Parker, fresh off his Davy Crockett fame, as Doc Grayson, a scout leading a party of settlers along the Oregon Trail. Populating the train are familiar actors like George Reeves (*Superman*), Morgan Woodward, and Disney character actor Jeff York. Mouseketeers Cubby O'Brien, Karen Pendleton, Tommy Cole, and Doreen Tracey play the children of the train, as well as *Spin and Marty* star David Stollery.

As the movie opens, the wagon train arrives at Chimney Rock, a popular landmark along the trail that marked the end of the prairie and the beginning of the western desert. The settlers stop and rest for a few days before moving on. As a result, they fall victim to a Pawnee Indian raid that steals several of their horses. David Stollery gets kidnapped by another Indian party but manages to escape. That provokes an attack that the settlers are able to repel only by releasing their extra horses for the Indians to take.

The second half finds the wagon train arriving at Fort Laramie, another famous Oregon Trail landmark. They befriend a French trading post operator (Sebastian Cabot). A party of Sioux Indians is also camped there. When their medicine man (Iron Eyes Cody) takes an interest in young, blonde Cora (Karen Pendleton), he tries to buy her. When the settlers refuse to sell her, the Indians are offended. Things worsen when the chief's son is gravely injured while playing. It is looking like the settlers will be massacred until Doc Grayson (who knows a little bit of medicine) steps in and cures the boy. The settlers have now made friends with the Indians, who offer to guide them safely to Oregon.

Westward Ho the Wagons is an exciting children's tale—short on plot but long on action. The gaggle of Mouseketeers proves why they were selected for the show as they come across as natural, average children, something difficult to achieve on screen. Fess Parker makes a good scout leader. Like Davy Crockett, he is all-knowing in the ways of the west and even sings a couple of nice songs. Jeff York basically repeats his blustery characterization of Mike Fink from the Crockett shows.

If there is a villain in the piece, it is the self-centered and pompous businessman Spenser Armitage (Leslie Bradley) who is more willing to put the wagon train in danger than shed some of his business assets (horses to sell). When they reach Fort Laramie, it is his ignorance of the Indians' intentions and customs that leads to the showdown. He taught me the importance of always getting to know the person or the culture you are interacting with so that you can find some common ground. Armitage also taught me never to put business ahead of the personal. In contrast is the character of Bissonette, another businessman but one who believes in getting to know the culture and language of his customers in order to do business with them with dignity.

Westward Ho the Wagons may have a child's point of view regarding the adventures they encounter (the dangers of the journey or the possibility of death in the various battles never comes up), but it also illustrates how the children shall lead in bridging the gap between the two cultures in conflict: whites and Native Americans.

The children on both sides are not hung up on differing languages and customs. They can look beyond the color of each other's skins and the differences in clothes to see the person inside. In that sense, the medicine man is correct. Cora is a goddess. She becomes the key to bridging the widening chasm between whites and Native Americans.

By the end of the movie, the two groups have resolved their differences and they head west together, father riding beside father, child riding beside child. It is a hopeful vision at the beginning of the western expansion; one that won't last, despite our hopes.

The Adventures of Bullwhip Griffin (1967)
TV Premiere: January 17, 24, 31, 1971

In its time, few episodes had such a profound effect on me as *The Adventures of Bullwhip Griffin*. I was already familiar with the era of the California Gold Rush, that mad race by land or by sea by the 49ers, as they were called, eager to strike it rich. I had seen that time and place dramatized in other movies like *How the West Was Won* (1962), so I did not come into *Bullwhip Griffin* ignorant of the subject matter.

The movie tells the tale of two rich Bostonian siblings, Jack (Bryan Russell) and Arabella (Suzanne Pleshette), who discover after the death of their grandfather that they are destitute. Everything must go, including the house they live in to pay their debts. Already fired up by the tall tales of gold in California, young Jack stows away on the next ship sailing west. Griffin (Roddy McDowall), the family butler who quietly pines for Arabella, manages to sneak aboard just before it sails and the two are on their way. While aboard ship, they meet Quentin Bartlett (Richard Hayden) who claims to have a map to the mother lode, and the thieving Judge Higgins (Karl Malden) who will do anything to get his hands on that map.

Once they reach San Francisco, Judge Higgins manages to steal the map and flee. Griffin and Jack raise money for their grubstake by giving haircuts. That draws the ire of Mountain Ox (Mike Mazurki), a properly named mountain of a man with the legend of being the toughest guy in Frisco. Ox works as the bouncer at a saloon owned by Sam Trimble (Harry Guardino). When he hears that Griffin managed to knock Ox out with one punch (aided by a bag of gold in his hand) and earned the nickname "Bullwhip" for his fighting prowess, Trimble wants to stage a fight between the two.

Griffin declines and the trio head to the gold fields. Eventually, they strike it rich and return to San Francisco, only to have Higgins steal their gold and render them destitute once again. Griffin also discovers that Arabella has followed them west and is now a singer in Trimble's saloon. Jealous and needing the money, Griffin agrees to fight Ox one more time. It turns into the biggest match in San Francisco, with massive fortunes riding on the outcome.

Looking back on the movie, it remains a fun film but I am struck by how episodic it is. The troubles with Judge Higgins would be easily resolved if they would just hold onto him for a few minutes more, but I suppose that is the appeal of the adventure. The movie is told through Jack's eyes and that is also probably what I found thrilling about it as a youngster. It really is a boy's eye view of the California Gold Rush—all of the thrills and none of the dangers. It didn't hurt that Jack was played by Bryan Russell who also played Emil in *Emil and the Detectives* (1964), another Russell character I greatly identified with (see chapter 9).

Like the dime novel tales of gold and adventure that Jack dreams over at the beginning, *Bullwhip Griffin* filled me with a desire to head west. I wanted to find gold and sail on a clipper ship and maybe even win the hand of a fair maiden some day. I remember playing *Bullwhip Griffin* around the house. Grabbing a toy pick and shovel and journeying from the safety of my bedroom to the far-off land of our basement family room where I "dug" for gold in our linoleum floor and fought Mountain Ox until my loud play caused my mother to stomp down the stairs and demand to know what I was doing. Embarrassed, I could only hang my head and give that rote boyish answer, "Nothing."

I bought the novel *By the Great Horn Spoon!* (1963) by Sid Fleischman that the movie is based on and found it very different but still thrilling. It got me interested in the subject of the Gold Rush and clipper ships, the swiftest sailing ships of their day aimed at getting passengers to the gold fields as fast as possible. I read the American Heritage books *The California Gold Rush* (1961) by Ralph Andrist and *Clipper Ships and Captains* (1962) by Jane D. Lyon, both of which brought that era even further alive for me.

In the end, *Bullwhip Griffin* turned out to be just a phase, but it opened doors in my imagination and my knowledge and isn't that what a movie should do? It didn't hurt that when it aired on TV, *Bullwhip Griffin* was one of those rare three-part episodes. Even rarer, the last episode did not fill its entire hour. The final half hour was devoted to *Project Florida* (1971), a progress report on the building of Walt Disney World down south in the sunshine state. It was another thing that would open my eyes and open yet another door, this time to the future (see chapter 13).

Tales of the Civil War

No historical event in American history has a greater hold and a greater allure than that of the Civil War, or the War between the States as it is known down south, which broke out in the middle of the 19th century. A complicated conflict that started as a disagreement over states' rights and ended up as a battle to eliminate slavery, the Civil War has inspired more literature and more movies and TV shows than any other event in our country's history. More than the Revolutionary War, even more than World War II, it is the Civil War that helped form the modern United States that we live in today. And *World of Disney* did not pass up the opportunity to portray this vivid and tragic chapter in our American tale.

Interestingly, when *World of Disney* sought to tell stories set during the war, they did not go for those with epic scope or sweeping battles. They kept the war down at a simple level, one that children like me could relate to; they kept it about children and they kept it about family.

Johnny Shiloh (1963)

TV Premiere: January 20, 27, 1963

Johnny Shiloh was the first *World of Disney* episode to tackle the Civil War and it did so in a way that its youthful audience could identify with. It tells the true story of John Clem (Kevin Corcoran), the youngest drummer boy to serve in the Union Army during the war. Corcoran was a smart choice to play the part. Arguably the most popular Disney male child actor at the time, Corcoran excelled at playing the younger brother roles. He had first achieved stardom playing Moochie in the *Spin and Marty* serials on *The Mickey Mouse Club*. Moochie was the younger brother or the kid hanger-on that older siblings wished would go away and stop hassling or embarrassing them when all he wanted was to be a part of what everyone else was doing. He went on to play a variation of that character in movies like *Old Yeller*, *The Shaggy Dog*, *Swiss Family Robinson*, and *Babes in Toyland*. As the youngest in my family who seemed to always be running after my older sisters and cousins, I had no trouble relating to Corcoran's characters.

At the beginning of *Johnny Shiloh*, ten-year-old John Clem is very much in the Moochie mold. A Union platoon called the Blue Raiders (in reality the 22nd Michigan Infantry) has been drilling in their unnamed small town getting ready for the day when they will be called up to join the army. Young John Clem has been drilling right beside them as a drummer boy even though his fellow soldiers regard him more as a mascot than a regular soldier. When word comes that they are to leave town and head for the war, Johnny has it in his head that he will go along and nothing any of the officers say, including second-in-command Jeremiah Sullivan (Darryl Hickman) and Sergeant Gabe Trotter (Brian Keith), can dissuade him. Even the unit's new commander, Captain MacPherson (Skip Homeier), cannot talk Johnny out of his desire to go along and take part in the great fun of the war.

When the platoon leaves town, Johnny smuggles his way onto the train. Attempts to send him back home end with him running away and returning to the unit. Gabe's attempts to expose him to the hard life of a soldier are unsuccessful as well. In the end, Johnny wears them all down and they let him to join the army.

Johnny's notions about the "fun" of war are quickly destroyed during his first battle, the bloody Battle of Shiloh that raged for two days in Mississippi in early 1862. Shiloh saw more casualties in two days than in all the American wars combined up until that time. In the heat of battle, Johnny sees his friend and commanding officer Jeremiah cut down right in front of him. Though scared and crying, he does not panic and instead uses his drum to rally the Blue Raiders to stand firm against the Confederates and drive them back. His bravery is witnessed by General George Henry Thomas (Edward Platt) who nicknames him "Johnny Shiloh," a nickname that earns him national fame.

In the second half of the show, Johnny and Gabe have been promoted to scouts on Thomas' staff. While delivering a message during the Battle of Chickamauga, Johnny gets captured and held in a Confederate camp. While there, he befriends his equivalent on General Wheeler's staff, a boy named Billy Jones (Eddie Hodges). Johnny soon learns that the Confederates are no different from his unit on the Union side. Both sides believe in the rightness of their cause. Both sides are brave and would do anything for their fellow soldiers. And both sides have lost friends and loved ones in the conflict that have left them bitter and emotionally scarred. Even though he eventually escapes and returns to the Union side, he has completed his journey as a character.

Johnny starts out with every young boy's belief in the glorious heroics of war, that it is all about charging and sword-rattling and defeating the enemy with little to no bloodshed. Soon enough, he realizes that war is not a glorious thing. It involves real dying by real people, some of them our friends. And that the enemy we are fighting are not some unthinking fanatics but real people just like us who happen to believe in a slightly different thing. *Johnny Shiloh* does a lovely job of depicting the education of John Clem to the realities of war, and by doing this, the filmmakers educated young viewers as well. It helped contribute to us questioning the worthiness of any war and its personal costs.

Willie and the Yank/Mosby's Marauders (1967)

TV Premiere: January 1, 15, 22, 1967

Willie and the Yank (or *Mosby's Marauders* as it was known when released as a movie overseas) continues the notion of the Civil War as a personal feud between families. Just as *Johnny Shiloh* starred "every boy" Kevin Corcoran, this episode—another rare Disney three-parter—stars the new "every boy" of the late 1960s, Kurt Russell as Willie. At the beginning, Willie Prentiss and his buddy Lomax (Robert Random) are teenaged Confederate soldiers guarding a forgotten backwater of a river crossing in a forgotten corner of the war. They and their Yankee counterparts on the other side view the war as more a game than a real conflict. Willie has even struck up a friendship with a Yank soldier, Henry (James MacArthur). Both sides regularly cross the river to share supplies or engage in good-natured shooting contests. The good times come to an end when a superior officer, the legendary cavalry commander John Mosby (Jack Ging), stops by for a surprise visit. Scared of being caught fraternizing with the enemy, Lomax attempts to shoot Henry. Willie tries to stop him, but ends up wounding Mosby instead. Afraid of being hung for shooting an officer, Willie runs away.

Soon enough, he is captured and by Mosby's own unit. It turns out Willie did not kill the legendary commander. He just wounded him. But the wound has left Mosby bitter against Willie and more than willing to hang the boy. Fortunately, Willie is able to talk his way out of a hanging and prove himself to be a good scout worth keeping around. He becomes a valued member of Mosby's unit.

Things get complicated when Henry the Yank rematerializes as part of General Sheridan's division fervently seeking Mosby's men. Henry gets captured. Rather than sending him off to a POW camp, Willie takes Henry home to the Prentiss farm. There, Henry falls in love with Willie's older sister Oralee (Peggy Lipton) while not revealing that he is a Yank. A wedding date is set and both sides invite their friends and superior officers—only Willie and Henry realize that they have set up a social event that will be attended by Yankee and Rebel soldiers alike. The Union commander sees this as a way to capture Mosby and his men. A trap is set, but in the end things turn out fine. Willie and his family are able to convince both sides that the war is really just a spat between a large, extended American family and, like any family, the rules should be bent to insure long-term family harmony. Mosby and his soldiers are allowed to go free. Henry marries Oralee. And Willie has grown into a man.

Willie and the Yank was the first original episode aired after Walt Disney's death and its message is one I am sure he could relate to. It has a lot to say about compromise and how much of what makes this American nation function is our willingness to compromise and to see ourselves as part of one big family rather than "us vs. them". If Willie and Henry can find a way to put their differences aside for the purposes of friendship and love, then the rest of us should be able to do so as well. It was an interesting message to convey when the episode aired at the beginning of 1967, the year of the "Summer of Love" but also national protests against the Vietnam War and race riots in major cities like Detroit.

Menace on the Mountain (1970)

TV Premiere: March 1, 8, 1970

Menace on the Mountain returns to the dramatic device of seeing the War Between the States through the prism of a family. Jed McIver (Charles Aidman) volunteers to join the Confederate army, leaving his teenaged son Jamie (Mitch Vogel) behind to take care of farm and family: Jamie's mother Leah (Patricia Crawley), his brother Mark (Eric Shea), and his sister Suellen (Jodie Foster).

Like so many Disney boys on the verge of becoming a man, Jamie finds himself a bit in over his head with little help from his siblings. Once again, he is expected to solve these difficulties on his own "like a man" and half of his struggles involve earning the respect of the adults around him who believe "having a boy in charge" means the farm is free for the picking.

The story is unique in that it takes place in the dying days of the war when the Confederacy is on the verge of losing. It also takes place far from the action, on the home front as they used to call it, in a small Appalachian community in the western part of Virginia. The war is less of a concern to the area citizens than a mountain lion that has been terrorizing the local farms.

The villain is another imposing mountain of a man named Poss Timberlake (Albert Salmi). He abides by no law and takes what he wants with pretty much everyone else in the town too timid to stand up to him. He is kind of like Brom Bones without the looks and the swagger. And what Timberlake wants is the McIver farm and Jamie's pretty mother. Jamie doesn't like the way Timberlake talks about his mother and the farm and he particularly doesn't like the way the mountain man laughs about his father being dead.

When Timberlake announces to the town that he is going to bag the mountain lion for its $35 bounty so no one else better try, Jamie is more than ready to try, partly because the family needs the money and partly to show up Timberlake. While out hunting for the big cat, Jamie stumbles on a wounded Union cavalry officer (Richard Anderson) who he brings home. His mother wants to nurse the man back to health, but Jamie can't see past the blue uniform and regards all Yankees as complicit in the murder of his missing father. In the end, Jamie's hardened exterior can't hide the fact that he still has a good heart and he lets the officer go.

When he succeeds in killing the lion, Jamie takes his first step toward becoming a man in the town's eyes. But he also then has to pay the price of Timberlake's vengeance and that price is a public whipping. Jamie is prepared to stand up to Poss. None of the men in town seem prepared to stop him, but it all gets interrupted when lawmen ride into town to arrest Timberlake for deserting the army. Poss flees and begins running with a gang of bushwhackers—a motley crew of soldiers from both sides bonded by their love of pillage and plunder. The first thing they do is seize the McIver farm and kick the family out.

Near penniless and now homeless, the family moves in with a neighbor (Dub Taylor) who had his farm burned by the bushwhackers. Things can't seem to get any worse. Fortunately, a ray of light appears in the form of Jamie's returning father who wasn't killed in the war but spent most of it in a POW camp. He rallies the few Confederate vets in the area and some of the townspeople to charge up the mountain and take back his farm. Unfortunately, their single shot muskets are no match for the Spencer repeating rifles that the bushwhackers have, freshly stolen from the Union Army.

Jamie tries stealing a cache of the rifles from a nearby Union camp but gets captured instead. The commanding officer turns out to be Major Galt, the same wounded officer they nursed in their home. He agrees to help Jamie. His soldiers and artillery join Jed's ragtag group of Confederates and, together, they are able to defeat the bushwhackers.

Menace on the Mountain is a rather serious film for *World of Disney*. The dangers encountered are real and so are the consequences. The scale of the story is small. There are no battle scenes between the Union and Confederate armies. The episode is less interested in causes and more in how war dehumanizes us so that we fail to see the individual behind the uniform. When Jamie first sees the wounded Major Galt, all he can see is the uniform and what it symbolizes, not the man inside. And yet Jamie's decision to be kind and let the man escape rather than turning him in to the authorities is what allows him and his father to save the family farm.

I find it interesting that, by the end, the lines between North and South have not just been blurred but obliterated. Timberlake's bushwhackers are made up of both Union and Confederate deserters, proving that there were good and bad soldiers on both sides. And, in the end, the force that retakes the mountain and the McIver farm is also a combination of northern and southern troops.

When the combined forces retake the mountain, they also symbolically retake and reunite our nation as well. When Galt and Jed shake hands, the war's wounds are officially healed. This is confirmed when Galt asks to visit the McIver's the following summer and bring his son along, and the McIvers heartily agree. The war is over. It is time to heal, and the best way to heal is through family.

I found this episode particularly interesting back in 1970 because my own family had just moved to West Virginia, not too far from the film's setting. I was just beginning to appreciate the Scotch-Irish roots of Appalachian culture which was based less on laws passed by faraway governments and more on family and kin. Pride, honor, and reputation were the things most prized, usually because a family had few other material things to call their own. It was a different way of looking at the world and this episode, though set during the Civil War, helped me to understand it better and to make me feel more at home.

The Civil War was over. North and South reunited. The California coast was now part of the country. All that remained was the settling of the Great Plains.

Lawmen of the West

Considering how popular they were in their heyday, it is surprising how Disney's Zorro (Guy Williams), Texas John Slaughter (Tom Tryon), and Elfego Baca (Robert Loggia) have faded from the public imagination. How popular were they? Well, in the *Disneyland* TV special celebrating the park's fifth anniversary, all three of the characters portrayed by the actual actors themselves rode in the parade along with the cast of *The Shaggy Dog* (1959) and the classic Disney cartoon characters.

These characters along with the Swamp Fox dominated the *Walt Disney Presents* period of the show (1959–1961). Elfego Baca had eight episodes. The Swamp Fox also had eight. Zorro had his own TV series on ABC, but four episodes were filmed for the *World of Disney* show after the series went off the air. Texas John Slaughter had sixteen episodes. When you consider the fact that Davy Crockett only ever appeared in five episodes. then you can see how outrageously popular these characters were back then.

I admit that this era of the show predates me and, because none of these episodes were re-run during the *World of Disney* era, I had little personal connection with them. Zorro is probably the closest. All of the episodes are available on YouTube if you wish to acquaint yourself.

The Tales of Texas John Slaughter (1958–1961)

TV Premiere: October 31, 1958

By far the most popular of the *Walt Disney Presents* serials, this one told the true tale of Texas John Slaughter, a man known for his distinctive white hat and pearl handled revolvers. Returning to Texas after the Civil War, Slaughter is only interested in settling down on a small ranch of his own, raising some cattle, and getting married. Unfortunately, he has chosen to settle in an area known for its lawlessness and rustlers. When his herd gets stolen and his hired hand murdered, Slaughter joins the Texas Rangers to bring law and order to his town. Once he accomplishes this, he marries and starts a new life. Eventually, his itching foot causes him to move farther west and Slaughter becomes a rancher outside Tombstone, Arizona. Soon enough, the legendary lawlessness of Tombstone and Slaughter's known reputation as a lawman cause him to be hired as the town sheriff and he helps clean up Tombstone. With law and order established, Slaughter can hang up his guns for good.

Texas John Slaughter is based on a real lawman who lived both in Texas and Arizona in the late 19th century and is winningly played by Tom Tryon in his star-making role. Disney has tidied up the man's life story a bit, although the inevitable theme song sung in each episode implies that Texas John Slaughter may not have been the nicest of men.

"Texas John Slaughter," as the song goes, "made them do what they oughta or else he'd shoot them dead." Wow. One of his contemporaries described the man as "the meanest good guy you ever met."

The series does get into this aspect of his character once he moves to Arizona. The closing episodes find the citizens of Tombstone questioning Slaughter's ruthless methods of bringing bandits to justice. He seems to be just as hard and mean as the criminals. He also finds himself on the outs with local businessmen when, once Slaughter's reputation gets around, outlaws and bandits start avoiding the town in such numbers that business slumps. They begin to wonder if Tombstone wouldn't be better with the outlaws back freely spending their ill-gotten gains rather than the lower profits of law and order. The stable economics of a respectable town, and the fruitfulness of Slaughter's methods, are soon enough proven when people from the east start settling in the town and boosting its economy. John also sees the error of his ways, that he is becoming the thing he is trying to eliminate, and reforms. All's well that end's well, as they say.

Looking at the episodes today, it is interesting how "un-Disney" they feel. They look less like a Disney show and more like a Republic Pictures serial that a child like my father would have seen at a 1940s Saturday morning matinee. Perhaps they feel that way because the episodes are populated with veteran Republic actors like Harry Carey Jr. and directed by veteran Republic director Harry Keller. There is a hardness to the tales, an edginess not usually found in Disney. And yet it also has a pulp fiction feel like a bunch of old cowboys sitting around and telling tall tales years after the fact. As the newspaper editor so wisely spoke in *The Man Who Shot Liberty Valance* (1962), "when the legend becomes fact, print the legend." The real Texas John Slaughter lived in quiet retirement until his death in 1922. Like other historical figures in this chapter, it was only after his death that his legend began.

The Nine Lives of Elfego Baca (1958–1960)
TV Premiere: October 3, 1958

This series is based on another famous lawman. Elfego Baca lived in New Mexico at around the same time as Texas John Slaughter. He gained his reputation when he took the law into his own hands and arrested some outlaws the local sheriff would not take on. To get back at Baca, the rest of the gang surrounded his house and spent the next 33 hours pouring close to 4000 bullets into the building. Baca emerged unhurt and thus developed the nickname "The Man Who Couldn't Be Killed." The incident triggered comparisons to being like a cat, hence the name of the series, *The Nine Lives of Elfego Baca*.

In the wake of his survival, Baca became a sheriff. He developed a national name for defending the rights of Mexican-Americans and his unconventional law enforcement method. When a known criminal came to his town, Baca would write them a letter informing them who he was and politely asking them to come down to the sheriff's office and turn themselves in. Because of Elfego Baca's reputation as "The Man Who Couldn't Be Killed," all but one of the outlaws did just that.

Years later, when he saw the limits of reforming law enforcement, Baca became one of the first Latino lawyers in America. He represented downtrodden clients and took on unpopular cases that challenged powerful but corrupt interests like judges and ranchers. The real Elfego Baca went on to be a major political leader in New Mexico all the way up until his death in 1945.

Elfego Baca is more Disneyesque in its approach than *Texas John Slaughter*. Once again, the title character is winningly played, this time by Robert Loggia, and the series comes across as surprisingly progressive for the 1950s. The fact that Disney decided to champion a Latino character in a decade known for its lack of diversity and convention of relegating Latino characters to the role of comedy relief speaks volumes. While not well remembered today, in his time Elfego Baca was as beloved a Disney character as Davy Crockett or the Swamp Fox. He is a forgotten Disney character well worth rediscovering.

Zorro (1960–1961)

TV Premiere: October 30, 1960

By far the most long-lasting and popular Disney serial character and the one I am most familiar with is another Latin legend, although this one is fictional. *Zorro* is a rare Disney property that actually predates its Disney version. Based on a 1919 novel, the character of Zorro previously appeared in several American movies. Douglas Fairbanks starred in *The Mark of Zorro* (1920) and its 1925 sequel *Son of Zorro*. Tyrone Power starred in a 1940 remake, and there were numerous B-movie serials made by Republic Pictures in the late 1930s and early 1940s set in modern times, featuring various actors as the descendants of Zorro.

Set in the small backwater town of Los Angeles in the years prior to the Gold Rush when California was just an outlying province of Mexico, Disney's *Zorro* tells the tale of Don Diego, a man society used to call a "dandy" because he was considered too weak and effeminate to be labeled a "real man." Don Diego is a rich man who deliberately cultivates the reputation of a weakling and a coward. In truth, he is the bandit Zorro who dons his mask and cape and comes to the aid of anyone victimized by the corrupt Mexican regime symbolized by the local commander (Britt Lomond). Zorro is part Robin Hood and part Scarlet Pimpernel, another literary bandit (this time in England) masquerading as an effete gentleman.

Zorro was a popular Disney show independent of *Walt Disney Presents*. Once it was cancelled by ABC in 1960, Disney made a feature film out of it then produced four hour-long episodes for *Walt Disney Presents* featuring prominent guest stars like Ricardo Montalban, Rita Moreno, Gilbert Roland, and Disney's own Annette Funicello. In rapid succession, Zorro must deal with another outlaw gang in town, a bride who does not wish to be married, and an arch enemy who has learned his secret.

I became familiar with *Zorro* because the series continued in afternoon syndication well into the 1960s. Zorro/Don Diego is played by Guy Williams who I knew better as Prof. John Robinson on another favorite TV series of mine, *Lost In Space* (1965–1968). He is supported by two wonderful character actors: Gene Sheldon as Don Diego's mute major-domo, proving that a person can still speak volumes without saying a word, and Henry Calvin as the bumbling Sergeant Garcia whom Zorro always seems to get the best of.

The stories are fun and easily digestible. All I know is that they made me want to don a mask and pick up a toy sword and slash "Z"s into any kind of clothes I could find, a task made futile by the fact that all my toy swords had dull tips. Still, *Zorro* helped me understand that the values and attitudes society considered proper for a "real man" to display were just surface gimmicks and no real indicator of a man's true strength. Men like Don Diego refuse to prove their manhood through pointless displays of strength. They prefer to prove their worth with quiet acts to those truly in need. It helped me decide to forgo empty public acts of manhood (and be wary of those who did them) and concentrate instead on proving my worthiness through quiet acts.

The Dark Side of Manifest Destiny

The settling of the West had its unforgivable dark side as well. The spread of American democracy, society, and culture from the Mississippi River to the Pacific coast between the years 1840 and 1890 massively displaced the Native-American tribes who claimed that land as theirs. Through occupation, disease, and military conflict, the United States destroyed their lifestyle and demonized them as horrible savages. American society always needs an "other" to set themselves apart from and give themselves meaning whether it be immigrants or socialists or communists or terrorists. For much of the 18th and 19th centuries, that "other" was the Native American.

World of Disney has been criticized in recent decades as a program that showed only the "white man's" version of manifest destiny. But a closer look reveals that even in the 1950s the show was trying to bridge the gap between the races and get whites like me to identify with the non-white victims of manifest destiny. No two episodes exemplified this more than these two Disney movies aired on the show.

The Light in the Forest (1958)

TV Premiere: November 12, 19, 1961

Set in western Pennsylvania during the time between the French and Indian War (1754–1763) and the American Revolution (1775–1783), *The Light In the Forest* tells the story of True Son (James MacArthur), a white male captive raised among the Delaware Indians led by Chief Cuyloga (Joseph Calleia). As part of a treaty to settle land disputes in the river valleys around Pittsburgh, both whites and Indians are required to surrender their captives. That includes True Son who has spent the majority of his life as a Delaware. Mountain man Del Hardy (Fess Parker) agrees to escort True Son back to his real family and stick around to see that he is able to successfully make the transition back into white society.

The early going is rocky. True Son resists giving up his Delaware name and heritage. He rejects his former identity as Johnny Butler. His mother Myra (Jessica Tandy) and father Harry (Frank Ferguson) are patient and understanding and just glad to have their boy back. But

True Son finds the going tougher with his white neighbors, in particular Wilse Owens (Wendell Corey) who believes the old adage "the only good Indian is a dead Indian." It doesn't help that True Son has caught the eye of Wilse's indentured servant Shenandoe (Carol Lynley) whom the married Wilse has his own lustful eye set on.

Wilse is the very symbol of male entitlement and never misses the chance to taunt and humiliate True Son in public, hoping he will lose his temper and reveal himself as the true savage he is, or engage Wilse in a fight that will finally allow the bigoted landowner to kill him. True Son's precarious place in the white community is exposed when his Delaware friend Half Arrow (Rafael Campos) attempts to visit only to be shot by settlers fearing he is part of an Indian raiding party.

True Son flees back to the Delawares, but finds himself no more at home there than among the settlers. His adopted father has fallen under the influence of Niskitoon (Dean Fredericks), a Native American just as bitter and bigoted as Wilse. Niskitoon has seen how the whites are already violating the newly minted treaty by settling on lands given to the Indians and believes the only good white man is a dead white man. He and his like-minded braves begin to raid and kill the illegal settlers. The whites see only rampaging Indians and prepare to take up arms to rid themselves once and for all of these troublesome savages. When True Son refuses to take part in the attacks, he is banished from the village.

He returns to the white settlement and challenges Wilse for the murder of Half Arrow. Combining his newfound knowledge of white fist fighting with his learned Indian wrestling skills, True Son defeats Wilse, destroying the tough man's standing in the community and winning the love of Shenandoe. The two of them leave to settle alone by a gorgeous waterfall on land that they call their own.

Based on the popular novel by Conrad Richter, *The Light in the Forest* is an enlightened view of racism and how it corrupts all peoples. White and Indian cultures are presented evenhandedly with both their good and bad sides on display. Wilse Collins is just as bigoted as Niskitoon—neither one is able to see past the skin color of their enemy.

The white settlers allow Wilse to speak and act in bigoted ways because challenging him will inevitably lead to a fight and no one has the ability to defeat him. Niskitoon holds a similar standing within the Delaware tribe. Chief Cuyloga lets him have his way because Niskitoon has the support of the younger braves who long for war. Challenging him would only lead to Cuyloga's removal as chief.

The movie again made me aware that I need to evaluate people not by the color of their skin but in the words of Martin Luther King Jr., "by the content of their character," and that any time a person is defending their views through violence, those views are either not held by the majority of the society or they are on their way out. It only requires one person to challenge them to inspire others to challenge them as well, but that one person must be careful because a bully willing to defend his threatened beliefs through violence is a person who will have no problem killing to defend those values. Lastly, it taught me that whatever emotional pains one may suffer at the hands of others (whether suffered by True Son at the hands of the whites or by the indentured Shenandoe at the hands of her master), it can be healed through the cleansing power of love, symbolized by the waterfall at the center of True Son's land.

Embodying the values and traditions of both cultures, Johnny Butler has, in fact, become the "true son" of both these worlds, the one best positioned to become the mediator to bridge the gap, even if neither side is interested in talking. It is the beginning of the war between whites and Indians that won't find an ending until the final showdowns on the plains of the Dakotas over one hundred years later.

Tonka/Comanche (1958)

TV Premiere: February 18, 25, 1962

I vividly remember the first time I saw *Tonka* (or *Comanche* as it was called for the show) on the *World of Disney*. For most of my childhood, I had been hearing about the Battle of the Little Bighorn, or Custer's Last Stand, as it was still being referred to in the early 1970s. Perhaps it was through elementary school history or perhaps due to the popular Johnny Horton song of the period, but I was already well aware of the tale of the cavalry horse Comanche, billed in pop culture as the lone survivor of Custer's Last Stand, an inaccurate honor. There were hundreds if not thousands of survivors of the Battle of the Little Bighorn: the thousands of Indian warriors who battled Custer's 7th Cavalry and the other columns of the 7th who fought separately in the engagement (only Custer's column was wiped out). Comanche wasn't even the lone horse survivor from Custer's obliterated column. But it still makes a popular legend—"when the legend becomes fact..."

Anyway, *Tonka* tells the story of Comanche, a wild stallion running the plains of the Dakotas in the 1870s. He first catches the eye of a young Sioux brave named White Bull (Sal Mineo) and his best friend Strong Bear, played by Rafael Campos from *The Light In the Forest*. When White Bull fails to capture the horse, he loses his standing in the village and is humiliated by his rival Yellow Bear (H.M. Wynant). Wishing to reclaim his honor, White Bull sets out to find the horse. He discovers it trapped in a canyon and spends the next few weeks nursing it back to health and winning its trust. He calls the horse

Tonka. During training, the horse and rider catch the eye of a passing cavalry officer, Captain Myles Keogh (Philip Carey).

When White Bull returns to his village with Tonka, Yellow Bear takes advantage of his warrior standing to claim Tonka as his own. The village elders do not agree, but see no way to prevent it. Yellow Bear turns out to be a horrible owner, whipping and abusing the rebellious Tonka who refuses to let his new owner ride him. Unable to listen further to the horse's cries, White Bull sets him free. Tonka's restored freedom doesn't last long as he is soon caught in a U.S. Army round up. He catches the eye of Captain Keogh who buys him and nurses him back to health. He names the horse Comanche and his strong but compassionate treatment soon wins the horse over.

As tensions between the whites and the Indians mount, Keogh and Comanche are assigned to General Custer (Britt Lomond)'s famous 7th Cavalry. Keogh is at first honored to be serving under the famous general, but his admiration is soon dashed when Custer turns out to be a vain, egotistic martinet with particularly bigoted views of the Indians. When White Bull is sent to scout the army's strength, he spies Tonka and steals inside to visit him. Keogh discovers him there. Their mutual animosity is soon displaced by their common love for the fabulous horse they share. They part as friends, hoping to never meet on the field of battle.

Of course, their hopes are soon dashed. Custer and the 7th Cavalry are dispatched to locate Sitting Bull's village along the Little Bighorn River. Custer is under specific orders to just locate the village and wait for the rest of the army before attacking, but the ambitious officer has other plans. He forces his unit to race toward the Little Bighorn, hoping to get there before anyone else. When he locates the village, he moves ahead with plans to attack even though that is against orders. Afraid that they have been spotted and not taking the time to scout out the village, he separates his command into three columns and launches the attack.

Considering this is a 1950s Disney film, its depiction of the resulting Battle of the Little Bighorn is surprisingly accurate. The topography of the land is very similar to the actual battlefield. Major Marcus Reno's column is sent to attack the village head on. Captain Benteen's column swings left to catch any Indians who may flee. Custer takes his column of 275 men and swings around the hills to attack from the rear. In hindsight, it was a huge mistake. Sitting Bull's village housed 10,000 people and nearly 3,000 warriors. Rather than fleeing, they charge out to attack, concentrating their forces on the hated Custer. Custer's column is quickly surrounded and wiped out, done in by their commander's own arrogance, vain glory, and lack of preparation. Keogh is killed along with the rest of Custer's command. White Bull and Strong Bear are in Sitting Bull's forces, engaged in their first battle. Strong Bear is killed and White Bull badly wounded.

When the rest of the army arrives the next day, they find the bodies of Custer's fallen men. No one seems alive until the injured Tonka/Comanche forces itself to its feet. The soldiers are prepared to put the horse out of its misery when wounded White Bull also forces himself to his feet to save his horse. In the end, Comanche is honored as the battle's sole survivor. The army declares that he is never to be ridden again and treated as special. His new army caretaker is White Bull, recovered as well from his wounds. The friends are reunited.

Tonka was an eye opener. It was the first time I realized that Custer's Last Stand may not have been the heroic attack that the history books had taught. It also taught me the hazards of blindly following a leader without question. Major Keogh and his fellow officers know they are probably riding to their doom, that Custer is a commander not to be trusted, but they also know that a junior officer cannot question a superior officer in the army. All Keogh can do is quote Alfred, Lord Tennyson's "The Charge of the Light Brigade" and follow orders, hoping against hope that the outcome will not be as bad as he fears it will be.

The movie reinforced my desire to not accept official versions of a story and to delve down to find the truth. It also taught me again that people are people regardless of their skin and their culture. All we can do is try and connect with a person face to face as a human being. Following of bigoted leaders will only result in our own deaths.

Tonka went a long way toward destroying my respect for Custer, but that didn't stop me from closing my analytical eye when sitting down to watch, by far, the best American history episode in the show's run. So don that coonskin cap from your closet and get out those buckskins your mother made you and that toy musket as we take on the most popular figure in the history of the show. Facts be damned! Let's enjoy the legend.

Hall of Fame American History Episode

Davy Crockett (1954–1955)

Premiere: December 15, 1954

If there is one character who made the *World of Disney*, it was Davy Crockett. Whenever I ask Baby Boomers to name their favorite character, the answer is almost always Davy Crockett. They then usually lapse into his catchy theme song. It is difficult to communicate to later generations how much of a phenomenon Disney's backwoods frontiersman was to 1950s America. Simply put, while teenagers were going nuts for Elvis Presley and rock and roll, we children were going gaga for Tennessee's folk hero.

For the show's first season, Walt approved the filming of three episodes, each built around a significant moment in Crockett's life. "Davy Crockett, Indian Fighter" dramatized Crockett's involvement in the Florida Seminole War (1816–1819) and his first run-in with General Andrew Jackson. "Davy Crockett Goes to Congress" chronicled his turbulent years as a congressman in the House of Representatives (1827–1831 and 1833–1835) and his clashes with President Andrew Jackson. The last episode, "Davy Crockett at the Alamo," followed his travels to Texas and his legendary death at the 1836 Battle of the Alamo. At Davy's side through all of these adventures is fellow frontiersmen Georgie Russell (Buddy Edsen).

The shows proved such a ratings phenomenon that Walt wanted to make more. Unfortunately, he faced the irreconcilable problem that his hero had already died. So Walt decided to go back to an earlier time in Crockett's life to create more tales. "Davy Crockett's Keelboat Race" found Davy and Georgie going up against another frontier legend, Mike Fink (Jeff York), as they raced down the Mississippi River to New Orleans. Crockett and Fink then teamed up in "Davy Crockett and the River Pirates" as they attempted to rid the river of a known band of criminals robbing boats while masquerading as Native Americans.

I was not alive when Crockett first swept the country. Instead, I got to watch the episodes when they were re-run in the 1960s. I already knew Fess Parker from the western TV series *Daniel Boone* (1964–1970). Buddy Ebsen may have been a song-and-dance man back in the 1930s, but I knew him then as Jed Clampett on *The Beverly Hillbillies* (1962–1971).

So what was it about the Davy Crockett episodes that caught the public's imagination? Why are they held in such high regard even today? Why is Davy still the "King of the Wild Frontier"?

Davy is resourceful, rugged, independent, a deadly shot with a weapon, practically unbeatable in a fight. He has an innate sense of right and wrong. He may tell some tall tales about his own accomplishments for fun and entertainment, but he can also tell when someone else is fibbing for their own advancement, especially politicians, generals, and businessmen. And he has no problem pointing that out. He is, as they used to say, "plain spoken." He has a sense of humor about himself and the world around him.

The episodes work because they are funny, the action is suspenseful, and Davy and Georgie represent the qualities American males wish to see in each other. He is one of the quintessential American male icons reflecting how Americans wish to see themselves, from Natty Bumpo to Davy Crockett, Abraham Lincoln, Buffalo Bill, Horatio Alger, Will Rogers, John Wayne, and Clint Eastwood.

Was Davy really King of the Wild Frontier? Does it really matter?

All I know is that when the episodes came on, I felt good about myself. I felt good about my country, and I relished the fact that I was part of a progressive history that produced individuals—part history, part legend—like Johnny Tremain, the Swamp Fox, True Son, Johnny Shiloh, Elfego Baca, and Major Keogh, and that when I was grown, I would try to emulate their example.

I couldn't wait.

CHAPTER FOUR

Adventures in Nature

The Marvels of Earth, Sea, and Sky

Just as *The Wonderful World of Disney* broadened my knowledge of American history, it also expanded and sparked my interest in the natural world and the creatures sharing this planet with me. The early nature episodes on the show were simply screenings of Walt's Oscar-winning documentaries like *Seal Island* (1949), *Beaver Valley* (1950), and *Nature's Half Acre* (1951). Soon enough, the studio began making original nature episodes for the show, usually narrated by either Winston Hibler or Rex Allen. I came to understand the beauty of the outdoors and the fragile ecosystem that supported all life on Earth. For a while, I contemplated becoming a forest ranger in one of America's national parks. That never came to fruition but I retained both a love of and respect for nature that continues to this day. Highlighted in this chapter are the episodes that affected me the most.

The Yellowstone Cubs (1963)

TV Premiere: September 19, 1965

Few episodes got re-run more often during my childhood than *The Yellowstone Cubs*. Perhaps because it was only one hour long, the episode could get plugged into the schedule whenever the producers had a hole to fill. It aired four times in ten years which is more than twice the number of times other episodes aired. As such, I became intimately familiar with this tale of wandering bear cubs, and yet I never grew tired of it.

It probably had a lot to do with the fact that it was set in Yellowstone National Park, a place I have dreamed of visiting but never have to this day. My family vacationed there the summer before I was born. Whenever I suggested going back, my father would shake his head and say, "Sorry, we've already been there," and plan a family vacation somewhere else. So whenever this episode aired, I viewed it as my only chance to visit Yellowstone.

Of course, no Disney nature documentary was worth its salt unless cowboy star Rex Allen was narrating. There was something about the tone of his voice, at turns comforting and then irreverent, that made him perfect for these stories. It communicated that this was going to be fun. And so we sat back and enjoyed.

Allen was in fine form narrating the tale of two bear cubs, Tuffy and Tubby, and their mama bear Necomus. The story opens with them waking up and Allen's narration does a lovely job of establishing the cubs' personalities in a sentence or less. Tuffy "never saw anything without wanting it and seldom wanted anything without getting it" while Tubby is described as wanting "just two things: food and sleep."

After some early morning run-ins with a skunk and a mouse, their mother leads them down to the public roads where, despite the clearly posted signs asking visitors to not feed the bears, the general public does precisely that. As Allen snickers, the bears find their usual spot and "the big mooch is on." All so visitors can get a funny photograph of them feeding a bear—proof positive that dangerous selfies existed long before cell phones.

Unfortunately, the cubs crawl inside a family's trailer and get trapped there when they drive off. Necomus sets off in hot pursuit. When the family arrives at the campground, the cubs escape. Necomus shows up to find them, but the public and rangers think she is just a marauding bear. She gets tranquilized, marked as a troublesome bear with a swatch of yellow paint, and the rangers relocate her to the high country—far away from the public. If she comes back again, she will be shot. Necomus doesn't care. She heads back to find her cubs.

The bear family spends the summer apart. Left on their own, Tuffy and Tubby roam Yellowstone. They visit Geyser Park and other landmarks. They take an accidental ride on a motorboat. Their adventures were always motivated by two things: appetite and curiosity. Meanwhile, Necomus still searches. It all comes to a climax at the Old Faithful Inn.

Tuffy and Tubby sneak into the kitchen and help themselves to a delicious combination of dough, pies, hot dogs, and creme topping. Necomus enters through the front door and terrorizes the guests while looking for her cubs. The rangers are called. Since Necomus is a marked bear, they prepare to shoot her. At the last moment, the cubs reunite with their mother. The rangers now understand. Mother and cubs are chased back into the woods and the happy family heads up into the trees, leaving humans behind.

The Yellowstone Cubs is a fun show that expertly conveys both the fun and the danger of animals and the contradiction at the heart of our national parks. For some reason, humans think the animals they encounter inside the park are somehow tame, like a dog or cat. The danger that the humans get into has more to do with their own disregard for the rules than anything the animals have done. They are just behaving like bears do. It is the humans' expectation that the bears are going to behave like people that gets them into trouble.

The two families at the heart of *Yellowstone Cubs* make an interesting contrast. The human family are in Yellowstone for a vacation and a vacation means forgetting the rules and restrictions for a while. The children want to feed the bears? They feed the bears. Even though they are camping outdoors in the woods, they treat their campsite like their kitchen back home and don't put everything away. Why would it attract hungry wild animals? And then they are shocked when the bears get angry at them for not giving all the food in their hand. Or they run for the hills when they find that their campsite has been invaded.

In contrast, the bear family has simple needs and gives off a simple vibe. They just want to eat and explore and stay together. Someone offered us food? We are going to follow you till the food is gone. You kidnapped my cubs, even accidentally? I am going to follow you (and their scent) until you give my cubs back.

Mediating between the two families are the park rangers. In this episode that is Ranger Joe. He is initially confused by Necomus' behavior because he does not know that the bear has given birth. He thinks she is too old to have cubs, so he believes she is just causing trouble. He has no choice but to follow the rules, even though he knows that the animals are just paying the price for human infractions.

The episode taught me that it is important to enjoy nature, to get out and experience it in any national park that I could convince my family to visit (other than Yellowstone). Enjoy it and embrace it, but also follow the rules and respect the animals in that park. They are not your garden-variety cat or dog. They can hurt you (or worse) if you cross the line and get too close.

Run, Light Buck, Run (1966)

TV Premiere: March 13, 1966

One of my favorite episodes during the heyday of the show, I found this tale of the little pronghorn antelope captivating. Maybe it was seeing the antelope depicted in *The Vanishing Prairie* (1954) or the frequent appearances of the species on *Mutual of Omaha's Wild Kingdom*, but antelope struck me as both fun and majestic.

Light Buck is a young antelope that gets scared by a storm and ends up tangled in some vines. A kindly old prospector comes along and rescues him, then takes him down to his cabin at the bottom of the

Grand Canyon. There, Light Buck spends the winter. He becomes a part
of the man's sparse household. He befriends the prospector's testy
mule and has fun adventures while cut off from the outside world. In
the spring, the man takes Light Buck back up out of the canyon and
sets him free. The antelope soon meets up with a female antelope and
they head off together. Happily ever after.

Like *Yellowstone Cubs*, *Run, Light Buck, Run* was another one-hour
episode; it aired three times in ten years. Out of all the episodes pro-
filed in this book, this was one of the few I could not locate and watch
again. So I am relying on my memory here. What I remember most
is enjoying the grace and beauty in Light Buck's leaping ability as he
hurried through the prairie grass. I remember the multi-colored coat
the prospector wore, almost a cross between a Hudson Bay jacket and
Joseph's coat of many colors from the Bible. I already wanted to visit
the Grand Canyon and take the pack mules down to the bottom. So
seeing the prospector living down there seemed like a dream, a chance
to combine my longing to visit a place with my own Robinson Crusoe
wishes to live apart from the rest of the world—only needing a few
animals to share my life with. I probably wouldn't choose a pronghorn
antelope or a mule, but they served for this story.

The biggest thing I remember from the episode is how readily the
filmmakers got me to identify with young Light Buck. Even though
I was just a human boy of elementary age and Light Buck was an antelope, I recognized the same eager nature to explore the world in him
that I had. It helped me to better understand growing up and how
some day I would do the same. There were always dangers in the world
that I had to watch out for. But, usually, there would be someone there
like a parent or the old prospector to help me through. Life was an
adventure and I had a part to play in it. Run, Richard, Run!

The Boy Who Flew with Condors (1967)

TV Premiere: February 19, 1967

Not a nature documentary, per se, but one I remember very vividly, *The
Boy Who Flew with Condors* opens with teenager Chris Jury (playing
himself) on the hillsides observing California condors in flight. This
was a rare thing at the time because the condors were an endangered
species. Chris smiles and admires the way they glide and dive along
the air currents and wishes, like millions of people before him, that he
could do the same thing. Suddenly descending into his life is a glider
piloted by a pretty teenaged girl, Margaret Birsner. Margaret has just
completed her first solo flight. Soon enough, Chris is in love—though
it is hard to tell whether he is in love with Margaret or the glider.

Chris sees the beauty of gliding like the condors. Margaret introduces him to Fred Harris, a sailplane instructor. Chris finds there are definite ups and downs to gliding. His first solo flight ends with him landing in a pond. A second flight ends on the fairway of a local golf course. But Chris soon learns the ropes, becomes an accomplished pilot, and is ready for his distance solo flight that will confirm his abilities as a glider pilot.

In the middle of Chris' training, Fred introduces he and Margaret to NASA test pilot Milton Thompson who takes them out to Edwards Air Force Base for a tour of the latest planes he and his fellow pilots use to train for space. He shows them the X-15, still the fastest and highest-flying plane ever built, capable of climbing to the very edge of space. They see a demonstration of the Lunar Landing Research Vehicle the astronauts used to learn how to fly the strange spider-like Lunar Module craft they will use on the moon. And we see the M2-F2 lifting body, sort of a high-altitude space glider that foreshadowed how future spaceships (like the space shuttle) would return to earth.

When this episode first aired in 1967, it was less than a month after the tragic fire that had killed the Apollo 1 crew during their final training exercise on the launch pad at Cape Canaveral. That was to have been the first Apollo mission. Now, the entire moon program was on hold while NASA figured out what had gone wrong. It looked like the Russians were going to beat us to the moon.

Though obviously filmed before the tragedy, this episode helped me to understand that America's space program was going to continue. We would eventually return to space and also land on the moon. We would still beat the Russians there. From a TV perspective, I realize today that the M2-F2 lifting body is the same plane crashed by Steve Austin (Lee Majors) in the opening credits of *The Six Million Dollar Man* (1974–1978). His injuries turn him into the world's first bionic man.

Like many of you, I dream of being able to fly. I have no illusion of soaring like a bird, but I have always wanted to fly a plane. This episode introduced me to the world of sailplanes and gliding. I was fascinated by the differences between flying a plane and flying a sailplane. I was excited by the notion of attaching a glider to a cable and having another plane tow it into the air, then learning how to use the air currents to stay aloft in much the same that a sailing ship uses the wind to travel the seas, or a bird uses them to fly. It made me want to look into doing the same, and helped me to appreciate the beauty and design of condors. I came away from the episode ready to learn how to be a pilot, although outside of reading a few books on the subject like *Ann Can Fly* (1959) by Fred Phleger, I never did more. I was also eager to save birds like the condor and not have them go the way of the passenger pigeon.

I am happy to say that scientists in the decades since have pulled the condors back from extinction and they are thriving today.

So while not truly a nature documentary, *The Boy Who Flew with Condors* opened my eyes to what it was like to be a bird, something *It's Tough to Be a Bird* (1969) built on. It helped me to appreciate the abilities other species have that humans did not. But I also appreciated our ingenuity to use mechanical means to adopt those abilities for ourselves, whether the astronaut-training vehicles or the sailplanes. We too could soar like the birds and then fly even higher to the stars.

Run, Appaloosa, Run (1966)

TV Premiere: October 22, 1967

The success of *Run, Light Buck, Run* triggered a trilogy of nature episodes on the show all with the word "Run" in the title. Maybe the show's producers recognized this as sane advice to give any wild animal. Maybe it reflected something in the pop culture of the era—there was a successful Saturday morning series called *Run, Joe, Run!* that aired around the same time. Maybe it is just a cool title we connect with—as in *Run, Lola, Run* (1998).

Run, Appaloosa, Run, narrated by Rex Allen, tells the tale of a horse named Holy Smoke. While still a colt, a cougar kills his mother. Nez Perce Indian Mary Blackfeather (Adele Palacios) takes the orphan home. A champion horse trainer, Mary teaches the colt all he needs to know. She finds the Appaloosa bright but a bit of a handful.

Once he grows up, the tribe's chief decides to sell him. The tribe needs the money and no one goes against the wishes of the chief. Like many Disney horses, Holy Smoke has trouble finding an owner who will treat him with compassion. Reduced to being part of a rodeo clown act, Holy Smoke is eventually rediscovered by Mary who buys him back.

To show off both his skill and hers, she enters the Hell's Mountain Suicide Race, sort of a cross-country triathlon for horse and rider. The race has been the domain of men for quite awhile and white men in particular. Undeterred, Mary and Holy Smoke take them all on and with the help of her dog Silver, rides to victory. Her win brings honor to both herself and her tribe.

Run, Appaloosa, Run was the first time I had seen a woman battling horse to horse and elbow to elbow with men and winning, or at least proving that she was the equal of a man. It caused me to rethink not only a woman's role in the world (maybe she could do more than be in the kitchen), but also the roles of minorities like the Indian. In the year of 1967 when race riots and civil rights marches would dominate the news, this episode seemed a very forward statement on the part of Disney to get children thinking about what we could and could not do. Maybe social barriers were as easy to overcome like Mary and Holy Smoke leaping over a jump.

Run, Cougar, Run (1972)

TV Premiere: November 25, December 2, 1973

The last installment in the unofficial "Run" trilogy, this nature movie took the novel approach of forcing me to see the world through the eyes of a "killer"—in this case, the eyes of the cougar or mountain lion. They had frequently been cast as the villain in so many Disney episodes. What I learned in this episode is that this animal is no better or worse than any of the other animals that inhabit the American West.

The main character in this drama of nature is Seeta, a cougar raising her three cubs with the help of her mate in the Redrock Mesa section of Utah. The cougar family has a pretty good life until a hunter (Stuart Whitman) kills Seeta's mate. Seeta decides to relocate her family, but first she must dodge the hunter who sees the entire cougar family as evil and strives to wipe them out. The lone human exception is a friendly shepherd (Alfonso Arau). He befriends the widow cougar and welcomes her nightly visits to his campfire.

Run, Cougar, Run does a wonderful job flipping our perspective on who is the good guy and who is the bad. Seeta is portrayed as a caring and sensitive animal. She loves her children and is simply trying to do what is best for them. Yes, she hunts and kills, but is that any different from us meat-eating humans? Her cubs grow up and learn the skills they need to survive, even if their first prey is a frog with bad-tasting skin. They also learn that they can be the hunted when a hawk attempts to snatch one of the small cubs by dive-bombing out of the sky until Seeta intervenes. The approach works. We find ourselves rooting for the cougar against the hunters.

"She was not meant for you or for me," says the theme song. "Let her wild heart live on. Keep her free."

It was a powerful ecological message for its time. It helped me to step back and see how Nature has been designed so that every species has a role to play in keeping ecosystems in balance. The only species that seems to not fit in and sees no problem with that are humans. Like the hunters, we believe we can do what we want, shoot what we want when we want to, and believe there will be no consequences.

Only the shepherd has achieved a harmony with nature. He is able to appreciate Seeta for who she is, even though she is just as likely to knock off one of his lambs in the dark (but doesn't). He tries reaching out to the hunters, but they dismiss his attempts to humanize their prey. They want to see the cougar strictly as a prize, something they can mount on their wall and brag about to friends. In the end, Seeta is able to evade the hunters and their dogs. She says goodbye to the shepherd and leads her cubs out of the valley to a newer and hopefully safer clime.

Fire on Kelly Mountain (1973)

TV Premiere: September 30, 1973

Phil Mallory (Larry Wilcox) is a new forest fire lookout in California's El Dorado National Forest. When a fire starts, Phil hopes to be included in the squad of rangers battling to put it out. Instead, his boss (Andrew Duggan) opts to leave Phil behind in his observation tower atop Kelly Mountain. Mad at not being included, Phil passes the time sulking in his tower until a lightning strike starts a fire on Kelly Mountain. Unable to call for help because of a broken walkie-talkie, Phil must battle the growing blaze alone. Just when it seems the fire will get out of his control, Phil's girlfriend and his boss' daughter (Anne Lockhart) notices the increasing smoke from her own post and alerts her father. Disaster is averted and Phil is praised for his solo efforts.

Fire on Kelly Mountain was another frequent re-run on *World of Disney*, again most likely due to its one-hour length, but I made a point to watch it each time it aired. Gorgeous nature photography and stunning scenes of the firefighters battling the blaze aside, I once again connected with the solitary nature of Phil's job. I loved the notion of spending hours, if not days, alone in a tower with the aim of keeping nature safe. It seemed like a good life, complete with a pretty, like-minded girlfriend (who just happened to be played by the daughter of June Lockhart who played the mom on both *Lassie* and *Lost in Space*).

I dutifully began pretending that the back porch at our West Virginia home was an observation tower. Our backyard including the trees, bushes, and hedges lining our property was the forest. I borrowed my father's binoculars and spent a few days sitting in a lawn chair on the porch watching the yard, spotted a few pretend fires, and rushed down to put them out. It was all very dramatic and fun and totally in my head. The only problem was that Anne Lockhart never dropped by to bring me a sandwich or help me put out those fires. And eventually the notion of being a forest ranger faded away (though it still has its allure).

With my exposure to all these nature shows, I began to feel at home in nature. I began to understand it and identify with it. I came to see the beauty of it, the feeling of connection one gets when you become a part of something greater than yourself. And I came to see the importance of learning that what happens in nature allows us humans to continue to survive. We are not separate from nature. We were not above it. We were just as much a part of it now as we have been for centuries. Disney's nature episodes helped me to see the importance of that connection at a time when technology and progress seemed to be pulling us away from it. It is a connection I have not forgotten.

Nature as Pets

Probably no *World of Disney* sub-genre was as popular as children befriending a wild animal and bringing it home, sometimes with parental approval and sometimes not, to try and turn it into a domesticated pet. And then, over the course of the story, the children (and sometimes the grown ups) learn that keeping a wild animal is just not a good idea. The best thing they can do is return it to nature.

The episodes mostly follow the same template and the best ones work as lovely metaphors for the role pets play for young viewers. They are our first children. We learn to love them and care for them. They teach us our first hard-life lesson that it is best to let them go to pursue their own way in the world. It is our way of acknowledging that they have grown up and we have, too.

Sammy, the Way-Out Seal (1962)

TV Premiere: October 28,& November 4, 1962

This episode is the prototype for those that follow. The Loomis family has spent the summer at a rented beach house. Unbeknownst to their parents, brothers Arthur (Michael McGreevey) and Petey (Billy Mumy) have befriended an injured seal. They call him Sammy and spend the lazy summer days nursing him back to health then having fun with him through an endless serious of romps. By the end of the summer it is time to go home, but they can't bear to part with their new friend. They sneak Sammy into the family trailer (why is it always trailers?) and take him back home. Once there, the brothers have to figure out how to keep Sammy cool and wet while working up the nerve to tell their parents (Robert Culp, Patricia Barry) what they have done. Arthur and Petey soon learn that Sammy can't be kept in their bathtub so they convince their tomboy neighbor Porsche "Rocky" Sylvester (Ann Jillian) to let Sammy spend time in her family's pool. She is all for that and the children have lots of fun romping in the pool with Sammy. Of course, they can only hide Sammy's presence for so long and soon it all comes to light in the most publicly embarrassing way possible.

For the most part, *Sammy* is just a fun family episode. The problems of keeping a real seal in the house are rather glossed over. A great deal of the show is spent showing the children frolicking with Sammy in Rocky's pool. The parents are portrayed as clueless, too wrapped up in their adult worries to notice what is running around, literally, under their noses. There are a lot of pratfalls and a lot of accidental plunges into the pool. An extended scene where the boys take Sammy downtown hidden in a baby carriage and it rolls into an office building elevator is particularly funny. In the end, the boys have the opportunity to keep Sammy, but they decide it is best to return him to the ocean, where he quickly falls for a girl seal.

Sammy was the first of many Disney episodes starring child actors Michael McGreevey and Billy Mumy, usually playing brothers. They have a natural chemistry together. Ann Jillian fits right in and it is too bad she wasn't featured in more Disney works (other than *Babes in Toyland*, this was her only Disney credit). The show doesn't delve too much into the consequences of the boys' actions, but that is appropriate for this kind of episode.

Charlie, the Lonesome Cougar (1967)

TV Premiere: November 2, 9, 1969

Perhaps reflecting the naturalness of its setting, *Charlie, the Lonesome Cougar* is one of the best "nature as pets" episode. Set in the Canadian wilderness and narrated by Rex Allen, it tells the story of Charlie "the cougar who didn't know he was a cougar." Orphaned as a cub, he is found by Jess Bradley (Ron Brown) a worker at a local lumber mill. Jess names the cub "Good-Time Charlie" and brings him home to raise. Allen makes it clear that Charlie is filling the gap in Jess' lonely bachelor life. As Charlie grows, Jess takes him everywhere and the lonesome cougar becomes the unofficial mascot of the sawmill and its employees. Still, Charlie never misses a chance to get into trouble and the problems he causes on a log drive down river prove particularly frustrating to Jess.

Once Charlie becomes fully grown, the mill's bosses view his antics as less than adorable and much more costly. Jess is ordered to keep Charlie at home from now on. Charlie dislikes the cage Jess builds for him and soon enough escapes into the wild. For a while, he finds the going tough, since Jess taught him no hunting skills. But Charlie proves a quick learner and soon masters the skills of an adult cougar. After months away, Charlie returns to the sawmill where his former buddies fail to recognize him. They corner Charlie and plan to shoot him until Jess steps in and recognizes his former pet. Charlie is saved. Jess and his new fiancée return Charlie to the wild where he soon meets up with a female cougar of his own and the story ends happily ever after for Jess and Charlie alike.

Rascal (1969)

TV Premiere: February 11, 18, 1973

Rascal is based on the best-selling memoir from author and jour-nalist Stirling North recounting the summer of his twelfth year (in Wisconsin, 1917) when he rescued a baby raccoon. This was not the first time Disney adapted the works of North. Back in 1948, one of his books had served as the basis for the classic movie *So Dear to My Heart* (1948). Walt had seen his own past in the recounted childhood of North. *Rascal* holds that same fascination for me.

It helped that young Stirling was played by Billy Mumy. Mumy had been one of the top child actors of the 1960s. He not only starred in a number of shows for Disney, but also in some classic episodes of *The Twilight Zone*. I also recognized him as Will Robinson on *Lost in Space*. Billy was an audience surrogate for me up on screen and he continued to be after *Lost in Space*'s prime-time run. And here he was in *Rascal* making me long to be up there on the screen taking his place again.

As portrayed in the movie, Stirling is a lonely boy largely living on his own. His mother has recently died and his distant father (Steve Forrest) is away from home a lot as part of his job as a traveling sales-man. Stirling has his dog Wowser, a lovely golden retriever, but it is when Stirling finds the baby raccoon that he makes the friend who will fill the emotional hole in his life. The key to appreciating the story is found in the subtitle of the original book: "A Memoir of a Better Era." The rose-colored glasses are in full tint for this nostalgic look back. The movie, ably directed by the under-rated Norman Tokar, captures those lazy summers in our childhoods before the hormones start kicking in to drive the teenage years (emotion over reason!) and before the demands of adulthood fill our days with responsibilities.

Even from my vantage point in the early 1970s, Stirling North's year with Rascal looked really good. I did not have a pet of my own then. I was still having to make due with my stuffed animals and my imagination. Having a cute wild animal like Rascal, a perfectly named pet, seemed like just the ticket. And if the adults around Stirling were less than enthused by the cute raccoon's destructive tendencies, well, too bad. It was our way of showing up those stuffy adults, all focused on money and such. And yet as the summer comes to an end, Stirling must face the fact that his best friend is also growing up. Rascal is no longer a pet but a wild animal. Like Jess Bradley before him, Stirling must face the notion of keeping Rascal in a cage for the rest of his life or setting him free. He opts for the latter. He takes Rascal on a canoe ride out into the woods and lets him go. It remains one of the saddest, most bittersweet moments I have experienced on the *World of Disney*.

It is that moment when Stirling discovers the change in Rascal, when he unexpectedly bites Stirling, and Stirling looks into the raccoon's eyes and no longer sees the pet he loves but a wild animal, that lingers with me. Before I ever had human friends to call my own, *Rascal* introduced me to the horrible notion that animals and best friends change. Growing up is about separation and saying goodbye to those we love. It is also about recognizing when it is time to let go. *Rascal* is set in the summer of 1917 because that was the last "innocent" summer before World War I transformed our country. The movie helped prepare me for the losses and change I would have to face, the many loved ones (human and animal alike) I would have to welcome and say goodbye to over the course of my life. And yet, I would also have the memories to relive deep in the unvarnished and unaffected corners of my mind where they will stay fresh forever until I am only a (hopefully cherished) memory in somebody else's mind.

Inky, the Crow (1969)

TV Premiere: December 7, 1969

This appears to be a largely forgotten episode in the Disney canon and yet it has stuck with me for almost fifty years. On the surface, the episode seems to be just another "teenager bonds with animal" story. Carol Lee (Deborah Bainbridge) is a shy 13 year old who befriends a crow she finds covered in yellow paint. She nurses it back to health, but the crow she names Inky turns out to be a very mischievous bird. His antics draw the wrath of a local farmer who swears he will shoot it.

Both Carol Lee and the farmer are two shy souls. Carol Lee has given up trying to fit in with classmates, and has turned to nature to fill the void in her life. The farmer has developed a "get off my lawn" reputation because he drives the local kids out of his orchard. Inky becomes the unlikely catalyst to bring the two of them back into the world and find meaning again in their lives.

This was another episode I could not locate and so I have to rely on my memories. I mostly remember the scenes between Carol and Inky. The antics of the crow were amazing and a coup for the filmmakers. Over the years, Disney cameramen had gotten quite good at capturing the behavior of all kinds of species, from seals to beavers to otters to lions, and filming them in a way that personifies human emotions and relations. But nobody had been able to do that with birds and particularly small bird species like crows. Inky turned out to be not only a gifted prankster but also able to convincingly portray human emotions. It didn't make me want to own a crow, but it did make me appreciate the gift of this crow to change people's minds and lives. I wish I could see it again.

The Boy Who Stole the Elephant (1970)

TV Premiere: September 20, 27, 1970

I admit that this is not the best Disney episode and yet it remains vivid in my mind. It tells the story of a turn-of-the-century circus run by Colonel Rufus Ryder (David Wayne), a fast-talking operator with a weakness for gambling. When his bedraggled circus arrives in a small town, their equipment is falling apart, the tent is starting to rip, and he already owes money to many people in the town. With rain starting to fall, those people are the only customers who show up.

The thing I most remember is the horrible performance that follows. The falling rain has created a muddy mess around the entrance to the big top. The ripped tent has allowed a big mud puddle to form in the center of the ring. Their star bareback rider's shoes get so muddy that once on her horse, she cannot stand on its trotting back. She keeps slipping down into a sitting position before she slides off and belly flops into the mud puddle. The aerialists' trapeze set breaks apart and they fall into the clowns' arms. Then the whole tent rips apart and collapses, soaking everyone inside. The performance is over.

Colonel Ryder's only true believer is his adopted grandson Davey (Mark Lester). The troupe's fortunes begin to turn around when Ryder accepts the gift of an elephant, Queenie, from friend and rival circus owner Molly Jeffrys (June Havoc). The elephant energizes the other acts and soon the new tent is filled with customers who are now both laughing and entertained. A special bond develops between Davey and Queenie. The happy period ends when Ryder succumbs once again to his gambling demon and he ends up gambling Queenie away. Aghast at this news and disillusioned with the colonel, Davey steals the pachyderm and starts traveling cross-country to return her to Molly. The journey is not as easy as Davey thought. Queenie seems to have a gift for meeting the wrong people at the wrong time and they leave a widening trail of destruction in their wake.

One of the things I most enjoyed about this episode was the cast. Mark Lester was hot off his star-making turn in the Oscar-winning musical *Oliver!* (1968). He does an okay job, though his Englishness is never adequately explained. Joining him are fellow child actors Chris Shea (the voice of Linus in the original *Peanuts* holiday specials) and Susan Olsen (Cindy in *The Brady Bunch*). Whitney Blake (the mom on the TV sitcom *Hazel*) plays their mother. The rest of the cast is sprinkled with venerable character actors like Richard Kiel, Dabbs Greer, Parley Baer, and others. There are even a couple of genuine old-time showbiz people. The buyer from the zoo is played by Tom Drake, Judy Garland's beau in *Meet Me in St. Louis* (1944) while Molly is played by

June Havoc, the real life sister of Gypsy Rose Lee and one of vaudeville's last stars.

In the end, Davey learns the same lesson that our other Disney heroes learned: no matter how much we love them, keeping a wild animal as a pet is just not practical. All agree that Queenie belongs in a zoo. And orphan Davey decides it is best to give up the vagabond life of the circus to live with Chris Shea and Susan Olsen and their mother, to embrace a normal structured life and go to school—much as the rest of us made that same choice (or had that choice made for us) when it was time to begin our own formal education. As much as we may love the notion of journeying across the country in a circus or riding on a stolen elephant, adulthood calls and the best place to get ready for it is in school.

Nature in the Human World

Even when we decide that humans belong with humans and nature belongs with nature, the two are inevitably going to collide as long as we continue to travel into nature's domains, and as long as our cities continue to sprawl outward, taking over more and more of nature's habitats, thus forcing nature to continue visiting us. Sometimes the encounters are humorous and sometimes they are downright dangerous. For me, the two best examples of nature in the human world are the two episodes below.

A Country Coyote Goes Hollywood (1965)

TV Premiere: December 19, 1965

This is another classic Disney nature episode, part drama and part documentary. Produced by Winston Hibler and narrated by Rex Allen, it tells the story of Chico, an itinerant coyote living in California's Mojave Desert. One day, he is minding his own business when he finds himself on the run, chased by a pack of greyhound dogs and thoughtless humans marauding in a dune buggy. They are not out to kill Chico; they're just chasing him because it seems like a fun thing to do on a boring afternoon. But Chico can't tell the difference and so he runs for all he is worth. Fortunately, he comes to a moving van pulled over on the side of the road. He leaps in the back and soon enough Chico is on his way down the highway and out of harm's way. What he doesn't know is that he has hitched a ride to Los Angeles. Once the truck arrives in the City of Angels, Chico makes a break for it.

Instinct sends him to the high country and soon he finds himself in the Hollywood Hills. He rests a bit in Griffith Park while watching some humans play golf. He steals a few golf balls, but finds they aren't too tasty. After that, Chico wanders into the hills below the Hollywood sign. He also discovers he is not the only coyote living in Hollywood. A pack of city-dwelling coyotes welcomes him and shows him around town. Chico learns that, while country coyotes like him live off the land, city coyotes live off the land owners. He is taught the fine arts of cracking open a bottle of milk or going through garbage cans or stealing from the local dogs.

It seems like a fun, care-free life until the Santa Ana winds whip up a brush fire that endangers them. Chico and the coyotes seek safety in a metal storm drain on Mulholland Drive, but the raging fire forces them to escape up the hill pursued by a fire that quickly outraces them. Fortunately, fire-fighting planes make a chemical drop extinguishing the fire. The coyotes scramble to safety.

Chico decides he has had enough of city life and looks for a way out of town. His departure is delayed when he encounters a lovely female coyote. The two hit it off. It looks like the beginning of a beautiful romance until it turns out she already has kids: three pups. Soon enough she is heading down the road leaving Chico to babysit. He tries running away from his newfound responsibilities, but finds himself trapped in a cage. A sympathetic human gives Chico a ride back to the Mojave, but once he gets there, he finds the place boring compared to the glitz of city life. Fortunately, yet another moving van is stopped on the side of the road. Chico leaps aboard and books himself another free ride, this time to New York City.

Country Coyote is a perfect example of what Disney's nature films did best: exposing kids to the lifestyles of the animals while at the same time giving them human reactions and characteristics that made them relatable. Chico has the personality of a silent film comedian—an innocent who finds himself constantly reacting to bad situations he stumbles into. Along the way the filmmakers provide a bit of funny social commentary. When describing the wildlife in Hollywood, the narrator mentions the thunderbirds and jaguars, all the while showing those very makes of cars. There are jokes about the footloose male, the wiles of the sexy female who turns out to be a single mom (a rather uncommon occurrence in the 1960s), and the unspoken horror of men getting trapped with children who are not their own. Chico's first foray into a mansion of the rich and famous finds him trashing the residents' sculptures, lawn furniture, fancy trees, groomed hedges, and private swimming pool, and the audience is encouraged to laugh at all of it.

The episode proved so popular that a sequel of sorts, *The Nashville Coyote*, aired in 1972. Beneath the humor, though, *A Country Coyote Goes Hollywood* does an excellent job dramatizing the dangers that happen when humans and wild animals cross paths with each other, this time on human terrain. We may expect them to act like humans, but they do not. We may think animals are beneath us and not worth our concern, but that would be wrong as well. While animals do not act like humans, sometimes humans act like animals, as our next episode illustrates.

A Tiger Walks (1964)

TV Premiere: March 20, 27, 1966

Love it or hate it, and I know people who feel both ways, *A Tiger Walks* has a lot of "un-Disney" things to say about people, politicians, the press, and the public. There are few of the usual Disney characters inhabiting this story and a couple of popular Disney actors play very dark versions of characters they usually play in other Disney fare.

A Tiger Walks is set in the small California town of Scotia. Sheriff Pete Williams (Brian Keith) is running for re-election. He is popular and expected to win. The state's governor (Edward Andrews) has targeted Pete for defeat. Pete lives a rather quiet life with his wife Dorothy (Vera Miles) and his teenage daughter Julie (Pamela Franklin). On the surface, it appears to be another of those likeable and picturesque Disney towns we are used to seeing Disney movies set in. The familiarity is increased by the movie having been filmed on the studio backlot.

One day, a traveling circus pulls into town, not to give a show but because they have a flat tire on the truck that hauls the tiger cages. Tiger trainer Josef Pietz (Theodore Marcuse) is a drunkard and a braggart—a fake man hung up on showing how manly he is. When he opens the cage door to show off his tiger-handling skills, the male tiger named Raja bolts past and runs away. The entire town is terrified that a tiger is on the loose. It is up to Sheriff Williams to restore order. This becomes increasingly harder to do as events start to spin out of his control. When Pietz charges off with a rifle to take Raja down, the tiger lashes out and kills the abusive trainer. The state's reporters flock into town looking for a big story and playing up what a dangerous man-eater Raja is.

Developments bring out the darker side of the town's residents. Mrs. Watkins (Una Merkel) operates the local hotel. She starts charging triple the going rate for the dozens of reporters and state officials who descend on Scotia. Aspiring writer Bob Evans (Doodles Weaver) is more interested in using the event to further his journalism career than in helping the sheriff. The governor sends in the National Guard in a cynical ploy that is all about politics and little about public safety. If the soldiers (who have orders to shoot to kill) get the tiger, the governor will look like a good law-and-order man. It will also make Pete look bad to area voters and lead to his defeat in the election. None of the key players are interested in seeing Raja captured alive. They have too much invested in shooting the tiger dead.

The one person thinking about Raja is Pete's daughter Julie. She doesn't believe he is a man-eater mostly because when he first escaped, Raja had a chance to kill the fallen Julie. They stared eye to eye for a second and the tiger chose to walk away. Raja spared her life and Julie believes she owes him the same. With the zeal only a passionate, idealistic fourteen-year-old girl can possess, Julie takes advantage of the media circus in town to go on TV and argue her view that Raja is harmless. The adults dismiss her plea as naïve, but it connects with children around the country. They send money so Julie can buy Raja and his tiger family and give them a home in a zoo. The "Save That Tiger!" campaign becomes a national sensation, but it only compounds Pete's problems when the press and politicians warp the message into making it seem Pete cares more for the tiger than for the town's safety. His re-election hopes begin to fade.

In *A Tiger Walks*, Disney and director Norman Tokar present a surprisingly bleak vision of what lies ahead for the USA. It is almost unique among Disney films in that the adults are motivated more by self-interest and less by what's good for the community. Politicians are portrayed as deliberately manipulating the public's fears and emotions for their own personal gain. Reporters come across as a ravenous mob more interested in twisting a story to sell more newspapers than in communicating the truth about what is going on. The guard officers feel they have no choice but to follow orders and the guard soldiers are portrayed as clueless yokels out for a lark and looking to get famous by being the one who kills the tiger. In tone, this movie is more like Billy Wilder's dark, cynical *Ace in the Hole* (1951) than *Sammy, the Way Out Seal*.

The only person talking sense is Julie and the more she pushes her agenda to save the tiger, the more the adults push back and try to discredit her. When I saw this movie as a boy, I totally sided with Julie. Why wouldn't adults want to work to capture Raja and move him and his family to a zoo? Julie's youthful idealism will not consider any ambiguity or extenuating circumstances to her position regarding this complicated public hazard. The only thing that sticks with her is that moment when Raja spared her life. Viewing the movie as an adult, I identify more with her father Pete. I now recognize the conflicting forces he needs to deal with. The situation is not quite as black and white as his daughter insists, and her refusal to consider anyone else's viewpoint but her own is both frustrating and off-putting. No wonder the adults dismiss her.

And yet, in Julie's strident appeals I can hear the beginnings of the hippie counter-culture that will soon explode across the 1960s. Authority is questioned. Why do we have to mindlessly go to war? Why do we have to see animals as unthinking, unfeeling creatures? I also see the first rumblings about how circuses are bad and should be outlawed for the way they treat their animals, although 21st century youth would even bristle at Julie's solution of moving the tigers to a zoo. The film is an early example of how the youth of the country can create social change if they band together.

A Tiger Walks made me a fan of Pamela Franklin, known more today for her work in the horror classics *The Innocents* (1961) and *The Legend of Hell House* (1973) and as the rebellious student in *The Prime of Miss Jean Brodie* (1969). *Tiger* cemented my affection for Brian Keith as the perfect on-screen father, not to mention Vera Miles as the perfect on-screen mom. Her character even shared my mother's name of Dorothy.

The movie also made me wary of politicians and reporters, or anyone who will manipulate the public's emotions for their own gain. I decided that from that moment on I would not allow myself to be swayed by any town leader looking to scare the public into making emotional snap decisions. I was going to be on the side of the Julies of the world, especially when it came, above all else, to nature.

Hall of Fame Nature Episode

One Day at Teton Marsh (1964)

TV Premiere: November 8, 1964

Out of all the Disney nature shows that aired, the one that affected me the most is this simple documentary portraying one day in the lives of the animals who populate the Teton Marsh outside Jackson Hole, Wyoming. Narrated by Sebastian Cabot, it follows the residents of the marsh, prey and predator alike, as they go through the hopes and dangers of another day in the life.

The film's motley collection of animal stars includes an osprey, otters, a wolverine, a porcupine, trumpeter swans, beavers, muskrats, and assorted fish.

The story begins at dawn with the osprey surveying his kingdom from a treetop. It is a late autumn morning so the air has "a touch of chill in it." The bird goes for an early morning flight and the sweeping point-of-view shots of the valley from the bird's perspective immediately sucked me into the story. The beauty of the American West lies below, the snow-capped mountains reflected in the mirror surface of the crystal lake. And yet a series of uncommon events begin to mark this as an unusual day. The osprey misses the fish he is trying to catch. Surprised, the bird focuses on a mother otter who has caught a fish. They battle for the fish and the osprey wins.

The focus shifts to the rest of the otter family, described as "probably the happiest and hungriest creatures on earth." The baby otters set off on a journey with no destination in mind. They set off down the river. After swimming for a while, they pause to rest on a warm sandy riverbank. Far up the hillside, a loose rock triggers a landslide that slides down and buries the three otters before they know what happened. Only one escapes. The beautiful morning has a sad ending.

The surviving otter heads back upstream to locate his mother. Cabot describes the otter's emotional state as an "overwhelming sense of emptiness" and how "loneliness can destroy the will to live" in an animal. The otter spends the rest of the day trying to find a suitable replacement for his family. He tries a porcupine, but that ends with the frightened animal making a decided point. He checks out a flock of trumpeter swans on the pond. They cannot fly because they are in their molting period. Seeing these endangered birds back then, I marveled at their white beauty. Watching the film now, I am so glad to know they are no longer endangered.

By mid-afternoon, the otter arrives at the beaver pond only to discover that beavers don't care for otters. Our hero persists and follows the beavers into their lodge. The underwater shots in the beaver pond are still stunning after all these years. Eventually, the otter gives up and swims on, but a female beaver shows up. The two bucktoothed lovebirds commit to their match in an instant and spend their "honeymoon" gathering food for the winter. The otter's loneliness ends with the return of his family, not only his mother but his brothers supposedly lost in the rockslide. They are a family once again.

But the marsh's peace is quickly broken by the arrival of a late afternoon thunderstorm. Its swift ferocity brings to mind similar storms in *The Old Mill* (1938) and *Bambi* (1942). The music even calls to mind Oliver Wallace's "April Showers" song from the latter film. Lightning strikes a tree and it topples, ripping open a hole in the beaver dam. The beavers scramble to repair the damage even as the otters hinder progress by riding what appears to be a natural waterslide.

As the storm passes and sunset arrives, the animals feel a chill in the air. Autumn is almost over and soon the "full brunt of winter" will be at hand. For the animals, it is time to either migrate or hibernate. As they bed down for the night, "a sense of peace" returns to the valley. Life is once again triumphant and undefeated. It was "a good day to be alive."

One Day at Teton Marsh captures all the elements that made the Disney nature shows great. The animals are portrayed as they are with a minimum of human personification. The simplicity of the animals' lives helped me understand what their existence would be like if they were just left alone with no traces of "man in the forest" (to quote from *Bambi*). At the same time, the movie helped me to appreciate my own life. The animals live in the moment, relishing the simple pleasures of life whether it be the industriousness of the beavers or the sense of family of the otters or the majestic soaring of the osprey. If it doesn't take much for them to find fulfillment in life, why must it sometimes take so much to make us feel fulfilled?

I walk away from *Teton Marsh* reveling in the beauty and wonder of nature, how so much of what the animals feel is very close to our own emotions, and feeling a connection to the natural world that makes me want to preserve it, to make myself a good steward of the land. Although I never fulfilled my childhood ambition of becoming a forest ranger, these shows made me want to seek out nature by traveling to our national parks and working to preserve what we have in the face of overpopulation and unrelenting human progress. They are lessons I remember to this day.

Making Mom's Pizza

My mother was a fine cook, but she was a recipe follower, not an innovator. She didn't like to experiment with sauces or make dishes from scratch. She preferred to follow the recipe. When it came to food items, she would search around for a brand that she (and we) liked best, then stick with that brand until it was no longer available. Her cooking bibles were the *Betty Crocker Cook Book* and other popular cooking books from the 1960s. She may not have originated her recipes, but she executed them well.

Her pizza was much the same. It started off with a crust mix. It could either come from a box or a bag. I believe initially in the 1960s it came from a Chef Boy-Ar-Dee pizza kit. Back then, we bought separate kits for a sausage pizza or a cheese pizza or a pepperoni pizza. Everything we needed was inside: crust mix, a tall can of pizza sauce with the pepperoni or sausage included, and a small can of grated cheese.

Each Sunday night, Mom would make up two different pizzas. One of them was always cheese because my sisters insisted on it. The other alternated weekly between sausage and pepperoni. We only had two pizza pans: one round and the other rectangular. Mom would cut each pizza into small squares of about three inches. I suppose she cut them that way to ensure the two pizzas fed our family of five. A large bowl of popcorn augmented the meal.

As the years passed, Mom started adding real pepperoni or real sausage rather than using the chopped-up stuff that came in the mixes. She substituted real mozzarella cheese for the powdered flakes found in the boxes. Soon, she stopped buying the pizza kits at all and just bought the dough.

But the breakthrough on Mom's pizza came when she found "her" pizza sauce recipe. I know she did not create it. I believe she got it from a family friend. But once we started using it, it was so much better than what we used before that we (and the adult me) have been using it ever since.

Pizza Tomato Sauce

6 ounces tomato paste
½ cup water
½ teaspoon garlic salt
½ teaspoon salt
½ teaspoon sugar
½ teaspoon oregano
¼ teaspoon pepper

Mix and spread on dough. Add meat and shredded mozzarella cheese. Bake at 425 degrees for 10 to 15 minutes.

By the time I was in my teen years, Mom had handed off the making of the pizza to me. It became one of my specialties and I have been making it ever since. As an adult, I don't make pizza every Sunday night, but I do still make it on special occasions, and I usually find a reason for a special occasion about twice a month.

CHAPTER FIVE

Life Lessons and Journeys with Our Pets and Horses

Throughout the history of humans, no three animals have been by our side more than the holy trio of dogs, cats, and horses. They have served us as hunters, workers, companions, friends, and family members. For children, they are the first ones to teach us about friendship, love, and loss. They also teach us about empathy: the right and the wrong ways to treat our fellow human beings. How we treat our animals says a lot about who we are. If we can learn to love and care for a dog or a cat or a horse, we can learn to love and care for anyone, including ourselves.

And no *World of Disney* episodes made that clearer than the ones dealing with pets and horses. Even before my parents allowed us to have a dog or a cat (never a horse), Disney showed me the ropes on how to treat them right.

Seeing through Their Eyes

Little Dog Lost (1963)

TV Premiere: January 13, 1963

Few episodes have lingered in my mind as much as this one. It tells the story of Candy, a Welsh Corgi who has been given to two young children, Bud (Dennis Yanglin) and Katy (Priscilla Overton). They love the idea of having a puppy but their parents, while nice enough in that stoic 1950s way of parenting, have a definite old-fashioned way of disciplining a pet. Candy gets relegated to the basement at night. During the day, he sleeps next to the kitchen stove. Mother (Margaret Gerrity) doesn't seem that pleased to have a dog. She complains that he is always under foot and in the way. One day, she loses her temper. She trips over Candy and breaks several breakfast dishes. Naturally, she blames Candy. She leaves the door open to the laundry room. Candy goes in and chews on Mother's stockings. Naturally, Mother views this as Candy's fault. In a horrifying scene shot from the dog's point of view, Mother grabs a broom. She whacks Candy and herds him into a corner then uses the broom to trap him there overnight. She doesn't mean to leave him there. She simply forgot, which is worse. The ordeal traumatizes Candy. He now associates brooms with beatings and getting locked up.

A trip to visit the children's grandfather gets interrupted when the family station wagon suffers a flat tire. Candy and Katy play by a creek. But when a broom discarded along the shore whomps Candy on the head, he flees in panic. A sudden rainstorm forces the family to move on before they can locate their scared dog. Abandoned, Candy wanders the countryside for months and develops a fear of all humans. A couple of times when it seems he might have found a new home, a broom comes out for whatever reason and Candy is on the run again.

He steals food from local farms. One of those farms belongs to an old man named Carlson (Hollis Black) who has recently suffered the twin losses of his wife and his favorite dog. Of course, it turns out that Carlson is the grandfather of Bud and Katy. When Mother brings them to visit, they recognize Candy and want to take him home. Carlson reluctantly agrees. Candy is not pleased. On the trip back home, Katy notices Candy's distress and lets him go. Candy runs back to Carlson who is finally able to help him overcome his fear of brooms and its association with pain and rejection.

Narrated by Winston Hibler, *Little Dog Lost* taught me everything about how not to treat a pet. I always wondered why the parents got Candy in the first place. They don't really seem to want him. Mother is always carping about him being underfoot. Father puts in a less-than-adequate search for Candy along the creek before deciding they have looked enough, herds everyone back in the car, and half-heartedly promises to look for Candy "some time." After Candy is lost, Father disappears from the story. Perhaps he is like the other 1950s men, too busy at work to interact with his family. Only Carlson seems to understand what a dog needs or how a dog thinks. Only he figures out why Candy is reluctant to bond with people.

Most of the episode is filmed from the dog's perspective. We get to experience it first-hand from Candy's view. We understand how terrifying it is to have those towering humans chasing you, how large and scary and hurtful objects like brooms can be. How confusing humans can be: friendly and loving one minute, then mean and yelling at you the next. How disorienting to have someone there for you one minute then gone the next, forcing you to live on your own. In many ways, a dog's perspective is not too different from a child's. *Little Dog Lost* taught me to be mindful of my actions and to recognize the scarring effects they can have on others: not just dogs or pets, but on children and friends.

The Three Lives of Thomasina (1963)

TV Premiere: November 14, 21, 28, 1965

Consequences and loss are at the heart of this Disney classic as well. Based on the Paul Gallico novel, *The Three Lives of Thomasina* tells the story of a veterinarian named Andrew McDhui (Patrick McGoohan). Andrew is not a bad man, but life's hurts have made him hard, especially the recent death of his wife. He keeps his emotions to himself and tends to neglect his daughter Mary (Karen Dotrice). Mary has reacted to her father's remoteness and her mother's death by pouring all her love and attention onto her beloved cat Thomasina. The film is told from Thomasina's perspective and narrated by her as well; she rightly believes she is the center of the world because Mary has made her feel that way.

When the cat falls ill, Mary takes it to her father to cure. Her timing proves poor as her father is already in the middle of an operation to save the local blind man's dog. By the time he can turn his attention to Thomasina, the cat is beyond help and dies. Word gets around that McDhui has failed to save his daughter's own cat. The news confirms what the town gossips have already implied: he doesn't love animals and he doesn't love his daughter. It turns the town against him. Even Mary refuses to acknowledge his presence and proclaims to all who will listen that her father is dead. McDhui tries many things to reconnect with Mary, but she stubbornly sticks to her notion that her father is dead to her, even telling it to his face with a hardness of expression that is downright chilling.

Only the town children fully understand her loss. They band together to give Thomasina an elaborate and public funeral. The sight of the children's procession through town further hardens the residents' opinion of McDhui. When the children attempt to bury Thomasina in the woods, the local "witch" of the forest named Lori (Susan Hampshire) interrupts the service. The children flee in horror.

Lori turns out to be less a witch than a hermit content with keeping the world at bay. She does this more out of shyness than out of any sense of loss or pain. An examination of Thomasina's body reveals that the cat is not really dead. Lori takes her back to her cabin in the woods where she nurses Thomasina back to health. It turns out that the "magic" Lori employs to heal her many animal patients is just good old-fashioned love and caring.

McDhui visits Lori to stop her unlicensed healing of animals, but soon finds himself falling under her spell as well. When Mary believes she has seen the ghost of Thomasina (really the wandering, recovered cat) outside her window, she frantically chases it into the rain and catches pneumonia. Traditional medicine fails to save her and Mary appears on the verge of death. Desperate and guilt-ridden, McDhui pleads with Lori to use her "magic" to save his daughter. At the height of the crisis, Thomasina appears again outside Mary's window, this time with plenty of witnesses to see her. Mary sees her too and the sight of her father opening the window and bringing Thomasina safely inside simultaneously brings Mary (literally), her father (symbolically), and Thomasina (who really never died) back to life. Magic, indeed. The story ends happily with McDhui and Lori married and Mary and Thomasina reunited.

When I saw *Thomasina* as a child, I considered it almost a horror film. It had a cat that died and became a ghost, it had a witch in the woods like "Hansel and Gretel," and it had visions of the afterlife that did not correspond with any Judeo-Christian notions of Heaven that I was aware of. Thinking of watching it sent chills up my spine and yet it was that delightful kind of chill that contains more anticipation than fear, and affords us the chance to touch the supernatural without suffering the consequences. Viewing it as an adult gives me an entirely new perspective.

The Three Lives of Thomasina is a powerful exploration of the destructive power of grief. How it can be as messy as a divorce. How grief not acknowledged becomes grief misdirected. If we don't resolve the hurt inside ourselves, we will take it out on someone around us: a child, a father, a neighbor.

The death of a pet is usually a child's first encounter with grief. Since it is our first experience with a powerful negative emotion, we find it overwhelming. And we cannot understand why the rest of the world can't see how hurt we are. We haven't yet learned that adults hide their emotions. They do not wear their moods on their sleeves like children do. We confuse self-restraint with hardness. Mary believes her father does not care how she feels. She doesn't understand that Andrew has learned to bury his grief behind a façade of uncaring. Both Mary and her father can only bridge the gap between them by learning to love again.

Thomasina was also the first time I had been exposed to the concept of reincarnation and near-death experiences. Each time she passes, Thomasina ascends a grand staircase to cat heaven. There, she meets the great cat god surrounded by cat angels, even though she hasn't technically died. The concept that Thomasina would reincarnate into a new life opened new religious questions that I would ponder for years to come.

Long before I had personally suffered any kind of loss, *The Three Lives of Thomasina* helped prepare me for its devastating effects. And while it did not lessen those harsh pains when they came, it did help me to understand what was happening to me. It also taught me the healing power of forgiveness to bridge the gaps between us and how love is not possible without forgiveness.

Big Red (1962)

TV Premiere: December 6, 13, 1964

Big Red is another Disney movie that uses animals to deal with forgiveness. While the movie is named after the big red Irish setter they both love, the primary characters in this drama are Rene Dumont (Gilles Payant), a teenage French-Canadian drifter, and James Haggin (Walter Pidgeon), the dog's wealthy owner. Big Red is an award-winning show dog whom Haggin has recently purchased. He has ambitions of using Red to win the Westminster Dog Show, the most prestigious canine competition in the world. Haggin buys the dog, then turns him over to his trainer Emile (Emile Genest) to get him ready for the show. Into all three of their lives walks Rene, an orphan looking for a job.

Despite Rene's brashness and lack of English (he is French-Canadian), Haggin sees something promising in the boy. He hires Rene as an assistant and dog walker. Soon enough, Rene has taken to the job and to Big Red in particular. The bond between the two grows and they soon become inseparable. For the first time, Rene has a companion to go anywhere with and, for the first time, Red has someone he can just be a dog with and do the things a dog does (run, hunt, dig, lay around) rather than the more restrained life of a show dog.

As the weeks go by, Haggin grows to resent the closeness between dog and boy. He orders Red to stay with him in his big mansion up on the hill and forbids Rene from seeing Red. The separation is painfully difficult for both dog and boy. The night before Red leaves for Westminster, Rene breaks the rules and hurries up to the mansion to say goodbye. He doesn't enter, but says farewell to Red through a glass patio door. All Red sees is a boy he cannot reach and when Rene turns to go, Red can stand it no longer and leaps through the glass to get to him. The shattering glass leaves Red badly injured. Haggin orders the dog put to sleep. Unable to face another loss and blaming himself for Red's injuries, Rene steals the near-death dog and escapes into the mountains to nurse him back to health. It soon becomes apparent that Haggin and Rene are both suffering from previous losses in their lives. It will take losing Big Red to finally convince each one to come to terms with their loss, to learn to forgive life, each other and themselves.

Big Red is a big, beautiful film shot in and around La Maibaie, Canada, just north of Quebec City. Director Norman Tokar was an unsung master of dramatizing the beauty of the natural world and showcasing the interaction between humans and animals. *Big Red* was his first chance to really show off his skills and he pulls out all the stops.

As a boy, I identified with Gilles Payant as Rene. He perfectly embodies the forthright certainty and stubbornness only fifteen year olds can have. He knows what needs to be done. He knows what is right. Why can't the others see that?

Now as an adult, I relate more to Walter Pidgeon as Haggin. This was the aging star's only Disney movie and he does an admirable job of portraying Haggin's surface coldness that age and experience bring while still hinting at the hurt and affection lying just underneath. He may resist revealing that hurt, but it still manages to poke itself out through a wry glance or his slumped posture as he walks away. Like Andrew McDhui, life's hurts have caused Haggin to keep life at bay, something a rich man can more easily do on a large country estate.

And lastly, I have to compliment Big Red himself. The Irish setter playing him does an admirable job conveying the dog's changing emotions as he transitions from hardworking show dog to a canine discovering the simple joys of being a dog just hanging out with the person you love. After healing from his wounds, Red becomes the healing force that brings man and boy together.

Of course, the scene everyone remembers from this film is the harrowing one where Big Red leaps through the glass window to be with Rene, probably because we all can identify with the pain of being separated from the one we love. Most humans can mask that emotion in their day-to-day lives, but a dog cannot, and Big Red's palpable distress at seeing Rene through the glass but not being able to reach him is almost unbearable, worse than if Rene had followed his instructions and not come to see him at all.

So when Red leaps through the glass with all the desperate ardor of someone trying to reclaim a lost love, he is simply acting out something we humans fantasize about doing at least once in life, usually in our teenaged years when we, like young Rene himself, are so certain we have found exactly the life and first love that will last the rest of our lives that we will sacrifice ourselves to hold onto it. Red's leap is an affirmation of adolescent love eternal, one we must make once in our lives in order to grow. The dog becomes a symbol of our "Big Red" heart that humans grow to deny, but a dog will always display with the earnest sincerity of a teenager who has just discovered their first love whether it is a dog or a boy.

The Incredible Journey (1963)

TV Premiere: October 23, 1977

Besides the big hearts that our dogs possess, they also have an unswerving loyalty to their owners. Dogs know who they belong to and when they are not with "their" humans, they will do anything to go back to them. That is the premise of *The Incredible Journey*, based on the classic Sheila Burnford novel. The Hunts, the family in the story, have three pets: a Labrador retriever named Luath, a bull terrier named Bodger, and a Siamese cat named Tao. When the Hunters leave to visit England for a few months, the animals are left with family friend John Longridge (Emile Genest). Longridge lives about 300 miles away from the Hunters in a stone cottage in the country. When he subsequently leaves on a hunting trip, the pets believe they have been abandoned so they start walking cross-country to get back to their home.

Making their way through rural Ontario, the domestic pets encounter all kinds of dangers, from a mother bear to a hungry lynx to a swollen river. When a collapsing beaver dam sweeps Tao away, the lonely daughter of a farm family nurses the cat back to health. In their brief time together, the cat and the girl bond. She has a companion to share her day, help her with her chores like setting the table, and play with. Their time together is all too brief, but we get the impression that it is a life-changing experience for both of them.

Even the dogs grow over the course of the journey. Luath learns to trust humans a little more, as when the dogs befriend another farm couple so that the farmer can pull the porcupine quills from his face.

The Incredible Journey is an amazing movie combining all the skills Disney learned making the True Life Adventure series with the studio's storytelling skills. Even though they never say a thing in the course of the film, the three animals' thoughts and motivations are perfectly communicated through their actions and by narrator Rex Allen.

This movie was a Disney holy grail for me. I heard about it for years, but it never got aired on the Sunday night show or re-released into theaters. Tired of waiting, I eventually bought the book through my elementary school book club and read it. It made me want to see the film even more. When I finally did get to see it during my early high school years, it did not disappoint.

The film also taps into one of the worst fears we have as a child: that our pets might be lost and there is almost nothing we can do to find them. It makes us want to hold our pets closer, to demonstrate our love more, to make them feel even more appreciated than they are now.

The Ugly Dachshund (1966)

TV Premiere: November 3, 10, 1968

The Ugly Dachshund dramatizes a comedic canine battle of the sexes that starts among the household dogs and grows into a heated rivalry between husband and wife. Mark Garrison (Dean Jones) is a success-ful artist who has recently married Fran (Suzanne Pleshette). She brings her pregnant award-winning dachshund named Chloe to live with them. When Chloe has puppies, Fran dotes on them as if they were her children and dreams of turning them into award-winning dogs like Chloe. Feeling a bit left out, Mark adopts a Great Dane puppy named Brutus. Like the title namesake, the ugly duckling, Brutus finds himself ostracized by the other dogs because of his looks. The dachshunds gang up on him much like the cats Si and Am set up Lady in *Lady and the Tramp* (1955). Like Aunt Sarah in the former, Fran believes Brutus can do no right and her dogs can do no wrong. Mark gets it in his head to train Brutus and try turning him into a blue-ribbon winning dog so he can show up Fran.

Never one of my most favorite Disney comedies, I still find *The Ugly Dachshund* relatable because as a child I often felt the same as poor old Brutus. While not exactly ganged up on, I frequently felt outvoted by my two sisters. They had a habit of using their two votes in our family with three children to get what they wished whether it be selecting what TV show to watch (except on Sunday nights) to choosing the family activity of the day (usually shopping). So I can relate to how Mark and Brutus could feel like outcasts in their own home. And while I may not have been competitive, I was bound and determined to take the ridicule I received from sisters and classmates to turn myself into some kind of award-winning something.

The movie also taught me the futility of inter-relationship rivalries. They usually ended up proving nothing and leaving the players (outside of dogs who harbor no grudges) with hurt feelings that take years, if ever, to heal. It is always better to support each other in whatever endeavor your spouse or child wishes to pursue and to genuinely celebrate when they win. Only then will you have a harmonious household, at least until the children start arriving.

Atta Girl, Kelly! (1967)

TV Premiere: March 3, 12, 19, 1967

Another favorite and moving episode, *Atta Girl, Kelly!* stuck with me through the years for a number of reasons. It tells the story of Kelly, a German shepherd raised to be a seeing eye dog for the blind. This was a big-deal Disney production. It was produced with the cooperation of The Seeing Eye training school in Morristown, New Jersey, the first school to specialize in training seeing eye dogs. The show is another rare three-part episode so we can sense the importance that Walt (one of the last TV episodes he oversaw) put on this production.

Part one introduces us to Danny (Billy Corcoran), the young boy looking to train a dog as part of his 4-H project. He gets assigned Kelly and his task is to raise and train the puppy while keeping track in a journal of all the good and not-so-good things she does. His father (James Broderick) is a bit of a grouch about the whole thing (almost a running trope by now in Disney), but his mother is supportive. And since it is his first dog, Danny can't help falling in love with Kelly, even as she displays annoying habits like running off. Usually she has good reasons for doing so, like looking for Danny when he is at school or saving a lost lamb who has run off. Unfortunately, Kelly's journeys lead her to cross paths with Paul Durand (J.D. Cannon), the head of training at The Seeing Eye. He is a firm, almost cold man. When it comes to his job he seeks nothing but perfection from his dogs. Kelly's indiscretions make him doubt whether Kelly is capable of becoming a guide dog. In the end, Kelly passes and Danny must return Kelly to the school as planned. It is tough for boy and dog, but he knows it is time to move on.

Part two chronicles Kelly's training at the school under the guidance of Matt Howell (Beau Bridges). He is a junior trainer and Kelly is his first dog. Unfortunately, Kelly pines for Danny and her former life. Matt is sympathetic. Durand is still dubious of Kelly's abilities and it doesn't help when she jumps the fence at the school and runs home to Danny (who dutifully returns her, even though he doesn't want to).

Over the next few weeks, Matt works with Kelly. He teaches her how to trust and accept him as a friend. She begins her training around town learning the things that seeing eye dogs must: how to recognize curbs, how to cross streets in traffic, recognizing overhanging obstacles, riding on buses, going shopping, and using revolving doors and elevators. All of this is done under the skeptical eye of Durand who still fears (as does Matt) that Kelly has not made a thorough emotional break from Danny and still longs to go back to him. Their worries turn out to be unfounded and Kelly passes with flying colors (as does Matt as a trainer).

Part three finds Kelly paired up with a blind person and going through final training before they leave the school. Evan Clayton (Arthur Hill) is a middle-aged lawyer who has returned to the school for his new dog, having recently lost Jenny, his first seeing eye dog. Clayton's roommate Chuck Williams (James Olson) is a man who has just recently become blind and is still overcoming his bitterness at this life development.

Clayton, a lonely single man, has his own issues to work through. While physically ready for another dog, he has not gotten over the emotional loss of Jenny. That lingering grief prevents him from bonding with Kelly. It mars their training and threatens to end Kelly's career as a seeing eye dog before it has begun. It all comes right when Clayton and Kelly get lost in a thunderstorm and Kelly must lead Clayton through a set of downed power lines (a harrowing sequence I remember well fifty years after seeing it). Durant finally sees Kelly as worthy. She and Clayton are ready to spend the rest of their lives together.

Atta Girl, Kelly! has stuck with me through the decades for a number of reasons. First, it helped me to better understand the episodic and transitional nature of life. Matt and Durand emphasize over and over how hard it is to be a seeing eye dog because it requires a dog to learn to love over and over again. They must not turn bitter and pine for the past. I learned that that is true for humans as well as dogs. At first, Danny has a very hard time letting Kelly go, but he does so because it is the right thing to do. As Kelly leaves the school with Clayton, we learn from Durand that Danny has contacted the school and asked to receive another puppy to raise. The cycle goes on. Matt is a bit more stoic about losing Kelly, but he too has a hard time watching Kelly transfer her affections to Clayton. After all, she is the first dog he has trained. It is a bit like watching an old girlfriend or boyfriend fall in love with someone else. And lastly, Clayton must learn to get over the loss of his beloved Jenny in order to love (and live) anew with Kelly, just as Chuck Williams must learn to accept his life as a blind man and move on. Life is about recognizing and embracing the transitions that come with being alive and accepting those changes even if we don't necessarily like them. It was a message I applied to my own life as I grew up and experienced moving, the loss of friends, parental divorce, the end of relationships, and other emotionally draining events.

As mentioned earlier, Walt Disney seemed to have taken a particular interest in this story. His intros find him wearing a blindfold as Kelly leads him around the studio and helps him locate his office. Unlike most TV episodes which were filmed at the studio or out at the ranch, *Atta Girl, Kelly!* was filmed on location at The Seeing Eye's facilities in Morristown, NJ.

The episode was made extra poignant because Walt's introductions aired three months after his death. Like millions of others at that time, I was still going through my own grief over the loss of "Uncle Walt" (see chapter 8). The theme and lessons of *Atta Girl, Kelly!* helped me through that as well.

Years later, I would find myself living in Rochester, Michigan, just down the street from Leader Dogs for the Blind, another top training school. As I strolled around town, I would see trainers and clients out with their dogs. For a moment, it made me feel as if I were an extra in *Atta Girl, Kelly!* and it made me smile.

Greyfriars Bobby (1961)

TV Premiere: March 29, April 5, 1964

The undying faith and love of dogs has never been better portrayed than in this lovely film that tells the true story of Bobby, a Skye terrier living in 19th century Edinburgh, Scotland. When his master dies and is buried in a pauper's grave, Bobby returns each night to sleep on the grave. At first the elderly cemetery caretaker (Donald Crisp) tries to shoo Bobby away, but after all his attempts fail, he comes to accept, and even like, the dog. Bobby, in turn, becomes a favorite of the children in the town. Soon a local restaurant owner (Laurence Naismith) begins feuding with the caretaker as to who now owns Bobby. The conflict escalates until the matter ends up in court. While each one loves the dog, both old men refuse to buy a license for him, arguing that Bobby is still the dog of the man whose grave he sleeps on at night.

Edinburgh law makes it illegal for stray or unlicensed dogs to roam the city, which means if Bobby has no owner or license, he must be destroyed. Bobby is saved when the children of Edinburgh interrupt the proceedings and offer to pool their pennies to pay for Bobby's license. The judge declares Bobby a free dog of the city. Each day he makes the rounds of Edinburgh feeling the love and acceptance of the town's residents. Each night he returns to the cemetery. As the movie fades out, we hear the voices of Edinburgh's residents calling out, "Good night, Bobby," as he goes to sleep on his master's grave.

Greyfriars Bobby is a charming little film due largely to the wonderful performance of the dog playing Bobby. He is greatly aided by wonderful old character actors Crisp and Naismith whose efforts to take care of Bobby slowly and believably build into a feud between two old men with long-standing resentments. Both men do what they do out of love, but they wear their crusty anger like a shield against the world. Like other Disney males, they are wary of showing their emotional sides. Only when they talk to Bobby do they open up.

What lingers in my mind after the film is over is the devotion of Bobby to his lost owner—the pure and simple love that stays long after most of us have passed on. Is there anything more devoted to humans than a dog? It seems unlikely, unless it is a horse.

Horses

Before trains and automobiles were invented, riding a horse was the fastest way for a human to travel. Horse racing was the premiere sport. The Pony Express was the fastest way to deliver mail. And fox hunting was the pinnacle activity of high society.

Horses figured in Walt Disney's films from the very beginning. Horace Horsecollar was an early supporting character in Mickey Mouse cartoons. Horses had their own personality whether it be the Prince's horse in *Snow White* or Gunpowder in *Sleepy Hollow* or Samson in *Sleeping Beauty*. As the decades went by, Walt returned to the subject again and again. Maybe his connection with horses dated back to his childhood years on the family farm outside Marceline, Missouri. Maybe it was a holdover from his polo playing days in Hollywood during the 1930s before a bad fall sidelined him. For whatever reason, horses starred in a number of Disney movies and *World of Disney* episodes.

The Horse with the Flying Tail (1960)

TV Premiere: March 10, 1963

This Oscar-winning documentary tells the unusual story of a golden Palomino horse who took an odd route to finding his calling as an award-winning member of the U.S. Equestrian Team. As a colt on the South Springs Ranch in New Mexico, the colt ran free during his first year with the other ranch horses. His distinctive yellow coat made him stand out from the herd, and his frequent visits to the local Pueblo Indian village earned him the name of Injun Joe. The ranchers intended Joe to be a cow horse. but he proved too lively for cowboys to ride. Disappointed, his owners turned him over to a neighbor who trained jumping horses. The rancher's daughter realized Joe's potential and taught him the jumping skills necessary to perform in equestrian competitions. Every time Joe completed a successful jump, his tail would fly high in the air. Hence, his nickname "the horse with the flying tail." Unfortunately, subsequent owners failed to see Joe's potential. They seemed more intent on turning Joe into the kind of horse they wanted him to be rather than letting him be the horse he clearly aspired to be. Fox hunting horse, show horse, member of a small riding school where members rode him for a dollar, Joe never fit in wherever he went. His unbounded enthusiasm put riders and owners off every time. Eventually, he caught the eye of professional rider Hugh Wiley. He convinced the U.S. Equestrian Team to purchase Joe and bring him to their training facilities in Connecticut. There, Wiley reawakened Joe's love of jumping. He taught him that a good rider rides a horse smoothly and with great tact. They ask the horse to give only what he needs to get over the next jump.

After medalling in American competitions, Joe (now named Nautical) travels overseas to compete in Europe. Good showings in Paris and Germany prepare him for the big competition: the Royal International Horse Show in London. The winner gets the King George V Cup, "the most coveted international trophy of all" and Hugh Wiley is the defending champion. Wiley and Nautical win the cup without making an error, resulting in Wiley becoming the third-ever two-time winner of the event. The King George V Cup is presented by the king's widow Queen Elizabeth, accompanied by her daughter Princess Margaret.

The Horse with the Flying Tail captures the wonder of a horse in full flight while helping the viewer see the precision required to excel on the equestrian circuit. Horses are among the most beautiful creatures in the world and the sight of horse and rider together is magic on screen. The story also reinforces the point that even a horse (or person) who starts with nothing can still rise through adversity to win at the top of their chosen profession.

The Horse in the Gray Flannel Suit (1968)

TV Premiere: November 14, 21, 1971

The Horse in the Grey Flannel Suit is one of the first Disney movies I remember seeing in a theater (at the Grand Theater in Steubenville, Ohio) and truth be told the animated short before it, *Winnie the Pooh and the Blustery Day*, made a greater impression on me. The somewhat far-out plot involves an advertising man (Dean Jones) who convinces an antacid pill client seeking to raise his sales among the rich and elite to buy a horse for his daughter to ride in equestrian shows. It is not a bad story idea, but it gets jettisoned about two thirds of the way through the movie. In its place comes less-than-hilarious comedy scenes made more interminable by Dean Jones's mugging and outsized double takes. For most of the movie, it seems like Dean's daughter and her riding school instructor Susie Clemens (Diane Baker) are the only sane cast members. Only when the movie reaches its climax at the Washington D.C. horse show, where Baker takes over riding the horse and Jones is relegated to watching from the grandstands, does the movie right itself.

In many ways, it is a transitional movie between the films made by Walt and the long decade of the 1970s when the studio tried making movies the way Walt would and largely failing. I am sure that Walt approved the movie—Walt greenlit films all the way up to *The Love Bug* (1969) and *The Aristocats* (1970)—but the picture is already showing signs of the post-Walt years. The comedy is broad and goes on far too long. Dean Jones' guffaws and forced outrage gets old really fast. One cherishes the moments when he is off screen.

The beauty of the horses jumping and the closeness of the final competition provide a gripping climax regardless of the goofy premise (it is difficult to see how winning a major horse show will really help boost the sales of antacid pills). The characters accept the trophy and pose for victory photographs. Jones and Baker decided to marry even though they have demonstrated little romantic interest toward each other. It is the last Disney film to exalt the equestrian world.

The Love Bug (1969)

TV Premiere: September 23, 1979

While not strictly a pets-and-horses movie, this enchanting story of Herbie, the Volkswagon with a heart, fits all the other criteria for a Disney pet movie. *The Love Bug* was the number one box-office hit of 1969 and the last big live-action hit the studio would enjoy until *Splash* (1984). Herbie became Disney's gold standard through the creative drought of the 1970s. He generated sequels like *Herbie Rides Again* (1974), *Herbie Goes to Monte Carlo* (1977) and *Herbie Goes Bananas* (1980); a short-lived TV series, *Herbie The Love Bug* (1982); and two movie reboots, *The Love Bug* (1997) and *Herbie Fully Loaded* (2005).

The Love Bug remains a sentimental charmer about Jim Douglas (Dean Jones), a washed-up race car driver with a reputation for going fast but also for crashing. He seem to be going nowhere until one day when a Volkswagon Beetle literally rolls out of a showroom and into his life. After a few futile attempts to deny the car is his, Jim buys the used car and, more for a lark, takes it to a local sports car race and wins. That catches the eye of his former rival Peter Thorndyke (David Tomlinson). Their rivalry renews on sports car circuits around California and comes to a head on the El Dorado road race through the Sierra Nevada Mountains.

I first saw *The Love Bug* at the movies at the Grand Theater in Steubenville. Like millions of other kids, I found the little VW Beetle irresistible. He was cute and full of love. The scene where Jim takes credit for all of Herbie's wins, thus breaking Herbie's heart and causing Jim to finally recognize that the car has a personality, is heartbreaking. Jim's pursuit of the runaway Herbie through fog-shrouded San Francisco followed by his discovery of Herbie trying to drive off the Golden Gate Bridge gets me every time.

Herbie is the perfect pet, better than a dog because you can ride him, better than a horse because you can go faster and not have to feed him beyond a tank of gas. He is the perfect pet for car-crazy America at its peak before skyrocketing gas prices, emissions, catalytic converters, and fuel economy came to be preferred options in our cars.

After seeing the movie, I remember buying a VW Beetle toy car then drawing and taping Herbie's red, white, and blue stripes on the hood and the number "53" on its side. Years later, when Disney put out an official model of Herbie, I convinced my aunt to buy it for me. I put it together as perfectly as possible then played with it as gently as possible. I believe I still have it wrapped up in a box with the other models down in my basement. My sisters bought the novelization and I borrowed it from them and read it as often as I could.

I loved Herbie's personality, his never-say-die attitude that pulls him through to win. In retrospect, the absurdity of a VW Beetle winning races against Alfa Romeos, Maseratis, Cobras, Lamborghinis, and Jaguars is clear to see up on the screen, but I didn't care. The sight of the little car beating all the super cars appealed to the underdog in me and showed that victory was always possible as long as you had heart.

The spectacle of the self-driving Herbie just may have planted the idea in all those future auto engineers of trying to make the self-driving car a reality. It's a chance for all of us to have our own personal love bug, even if it won't have the heart of a Herbie.

My affection for Herbie became the measuring stick for my overall enthusiasm for Disney as the 1970s progressed. I thoroughly dug *The Love Bug* in 1969 even while thinking that Buddy Hackett's hippie mysticism was already feeling dated as the 1960s came to an end. I was grateful for another adventure when *Herbie Rides Again* appeared five years later, even though I thought Helen Hayes was a poor substitute for Dean Jones. I was a teenager by the time *Herbie Goes to Monte Carlo* came along. I was happy to have Dean Jones back, but the antics both on and off the race track seemed more than a little absurd. This was a movie for small children with none of the sophistication of the original. By the time *Herbie Goes Bananas* came along, I had turned eighteen and I was like, "Are you kidding me?" Put a fork in it. Herbie was done.

And yet when they finally got around to showing the original on *World of Disney* in the fall of 1979, I was there watching it again and realizing that the movies and the adventures of Herbie had not changed as much as I had. And if I just found my inner child again that had made me fall in love with Herbie and Disney and the show in the first place, I would be able to keep my love of Disney alive.

Hall of Fame Pets and Horses Episode

The Horsemasters (1961)

TV Premiere: October 1, 8, 1961

For me, the ultimate horse and pet episode, even the ultimate *World of Disney* episode, is this original made-for-TV drama that aired right after the show's NBC color premiere. *The Horsemasters* has everything that made a Disney drama a classic for me. It has horses. It is set in England. It features one of my favorite Disney stars Tommy Kirk. It stars two of my favorite Disney girls, Janet Munro and Annette Funicello. And it contains life lessons that have stuck with me for fifty years.

Teenagers from around the world travelled to England's prestigious Valley Wood riding school with dreams of becoming international equestrian competitors like those in the real-life *Horse with the Flying Tail*. Naturally, the characters have arrived carrying their own personal baggage. The students are Danny Grant (Tommy Kirk), a poor American who works at the school to pay his way through; David Lawford (John Fraser), who can become a champion if he could ditch the entitled attitude and outsized ego too large for any horse to jump over; and Dinah Wilcox (Annette Funicello), the daughter of a former riding champion who still carries the memories of the jumping accident that ended her mother's career. She feels compelled to follow in her mother's footsteps, but afraid she'll get hurt. Their instructor is hard-nosed Janet Hale (Janet Munro) whose teaching methods are exemplified by the school's owner, "People are like horses. If you don't ride them, they will ride you."

Over the course of a summer, the students learn not only the requirements to be a championship rider but also the essential elements to make them (and us) winners in life. I remember loving to learn the training methods of the school, but more important to me were the life lessons:

- "How you treat your horses reflects how you treat people."
- "Whenever you do well in anything, never be proud for yourself. Only be proud for the horse who makes it all possible."
- "If it is not in your blood, I cannot put it there. And if it is in your blood, then I cannot stop you."

Two of them have stuck with me and informed my life.

Early in the story, Captain Pinski (Donald Pleasance), a former champion, visits to check on the students' progress. He ends up yelling and berating the students to the point that the egotistic Lawson stomps off and threatens to quit the school. Pinski apologies by telling a story about how Pinski himself used to be like Lawson. One day an instructor berated Pinski in the same way he critiqued Lawson. When the young Pinski threatened to quit, the instructor told him, "It is possible that you do not have hands like a gorilla. But you are an insolent young man. And if you do not get back on your horse, in two years' time you will not be champion of Poland."

From that vignette, I discovered that the key to learning, to becoming a master at anything, is understanding the concept that I may have done the best I can do at the moment, but that may not be the best I can ever do. To move to the next level, I need to put my ego in my back pocket and focus on what I must learn to move to the next level.

Dinah's fear of jumping eventually threatens her standing at the school. Even private tutoring doesn't work. Finally, Pinski tells her he too was afraid to jump until one of his fellow competitors told him her secret for overcoming her fears: "Throw your heart over first and then jump after it." Of course the competitor turns out to be Dinah's mother. And, of course, Dinah uses that advice to defeat her fears. Pinski's moral has become one of my mantras. Whenever I fear doing something (like writing this book), I follow that advice. I toss my heart over first and then jump after it.

Naturally, everyone ends up graduating. Janet ends up with David. The students come to appreciate that Janet's harsh methods have made them championship riders. And there are hints that Danny might just end up with Dinah. *The Horsemasters* proved so popular in its time that it inspired a book series and I happily read any installment I could find.

So much of my adult viewpoint has its genesis in *The Horsemasters*. I dreamed of attending Valley Wood school. I pretended to ride a horse around our yard. In my mind, I was galloping across the English countryside with Annette at my side, although, in reality, I probably looked and sounded more like the coconut-clacking knights in *Monty Python and the Holy Grail*. It marked the beginning of my love affair with England. It marked the beginning of my love for horses.

Lastly, it marked the beginning of my juvenile crush on Annette (it would be a few years before I came to appreciate Janet's more mature qualities). I mean, come on, just watching her twirling around the school parlor singing "The Strumming Song"? What's not to fall in love with? (See chapter 12)

I wanted to go to England more than anything. I wanted to travel around the world when I grew up. But, until then, that was something I could do any week on *The Wonderful World of Disney*.

A Carousel of Fabulous, Faraway Places

Shows about South American, Asia, and Europe

Foreign lands have always fascinated me. Perhaps because I grew up in a secluded river valley on a remote bend of the Ohio River, it seemed the rest of the world lay far away, or because of my love of history and the stories that other lands can teach us. Perhaps it has to do with my never-ending fascination with other people and other cultures and their different ways of doing things. Perhaps in the case of Europe, it was a chance to learn about our ancestors prior to our revolution. Whether it be the sceptered island of Britain, the Emerald Isle of Ireland, the Alps of Switzerland or Austria, the wine country of France, or the Teutonic beauty of Germany, Europe loomed large in my imagination. It became my primer for better understanding the American way.

South America

A Present for Donald / The Three Caballeros (1945)

TV Premiere: December 22, 1954

For two decades, *A Present for Donald* became the alternate Christmas show to *From All of Us to All of You*. It had the same format, a series of clips and short subjects built around Donald Duck opening a series of Christmas boxes. The only difference was that *A Present for Donald* was a repackaged and trimmed-down version of *The Three Caballeros* (1945), Disney's animated omnibus salute to South American music and culture. The movie was re-edited to make it appear Donald was receiving presents for Christmas. Instead of a card declaring "Happy Birthday," he found a card saying "Feliz Navidad"—my first exposure to the Spanish phrase for "Merry Christmas." (Jose Feliciano's classic holiday song of the same name would not come along until 1970).

My familiarity with things south of the border was limited in the 1960s and 1970s. It mostly consisted of Mexican stereotypes like the Frito Bandito or the bandit chief from *The Treasure of the Sierra Madre* (1948) who sneered, "Badges? We don't need no stinking badges." *A Present for Donald* did away with that. It introduced me to a new world of music and a different way of life that was colorful and fun and worth checking out.

Donald's first opened box contained two short films. The first introduced us to Pablo the Penguin who was always too cold in Antarctica so he set out across the ocean to find the warmth of the South Seas. The second film, "Little Gauchito," concerned a boy who discovered a flying burro whom he befriends and then enters in a race.

The second box contains Donald's friend Joe Carioca, a parrot who takes him on a whirlwind tour of Brazil. In quick succession, we meet the landscapes and music in that lovely land devoted to the samba. Joe introduces Donald to the real-life singer Aurora Miranda who sings a flashy rendition of "Bahia" while leading the smitten duck on a kaleidoscopic tour of Brazilian music and culture. The sequence reminds me of the "Pink Elephants" scene in *Dumbo* (1941) or the Heffalumps and Woozles scene in *Winnie the Pooh and the Blustery Day* (1968). The energy of the dances, the loveliness of the Brazilian landscapes, and the beat of the music pulled me in.

Donald's last present contains his other Latino friend, Panchito, a Mexican rooster dressed like a cowboy. He takes Donald and Joe on a flying carpet tour of Mexico. They see how children celebrate Christmas there. They hang out on the beach at Acapulco where Donald fruitlessly tries to impress the gorgeous human bathing beauties. The special comes to an end with Donald, Joe, and Panchito coming together to sing a rousing version of "The Three Caballeros" in one of the most frenetic and exhilarating scenes Disney ever animated. Fireworks shoot up into the sky and spell out "Merry Christmas."

The sequence in this show that has always stuck with me is Mexican singer Dora Luz serenading Donald and his pals with "You Belong to My Heart." The sultry romance of the lyrics, the way she sings them as Donald sashays among the stars—that alone was enough to get me excited to head south of the border.

Treasure Island (1950)

TV Premiere: January 5, 12, 1955

Probably no book fascinated me more as a child than Robert Louis Stevenson's classic 1883 novel about pirates and buried treasure. The tale of Jim Hawkins, a boy stuck running a failing English inn who suddenly finds himself in possession of a treasure map, was something I probably read five or six times before turning fifteen. It contained so many story elements I loved: 18th century England, a long sea voyage on the good sailing ship *Hispaniola*, pirates, and a treasure search on a deserted Caribbean island that Robinson Crusoe would be happy to be marooned on (if Ben Gunn hadn't gotten there first).

The whole story anchored around Jim's friendship with one of the great characters in world literature, the pirate Long John Silver who embodies everything we dislike but never fully dislike. We continue to root for Long John even as he switches allegiances from scene to scene.

My familiarity with the book gave me worries about seeing the Disney adaptation. Its reputation preceded itself. The movie was considered the definitive movie version of the tale. Robert Newton's performance as Long John Silver was considered the definitive portrayal. The star of the film was Bobby Driscoll, Disney's top child star of the late 1940s. I had previously seen him in Disney's 1970 re-release of *Song of the South* (1946). He had also done *So Dear to My Heart* (1948) and been the voice of Peter Pan in the movie of the same name. *Treasure Island*'s cast was rounded out with some of the best British character actors of their generation, including Finlay Currie, Ralph Truman, Basil Sydney, Walter Fitzgerald, Francis de Wolff, Denis O'Dea, and Geoffrey Keen.

I needn't have worried. *Treasure Island* turned out to be a rip-roaring adventure movie that perfectly captures the book. The amazing thing for me was that it captured the book as I saw it in my head. Bobby Driscoll is perfect as Jim Hawkins—just the right combination of pluck and intelligence. He is "smart as paint" as Silver keeps describing him, while still being the boy he is. Without a doubt the movie belongs to Robert Newton as Long John Silver. He captures the complexity of the role (he is required to be a father figure, a friend, and a believable threat to Jim all while never losing the audience's sympathy). When Silver bellows out in a fit of anger, "Them that dies will be the lucky ones!" we believe him. How Newton did not end up with an Oscar nomination I do not know, though it probably had to do with the fact that he was acting in a "children's movie."

Why are pirates so intriguing? Probably for the way they develop their own society and codes of conduct (though they be more guide-lines than rules). Maybe it is just the notion of living outside the norm. As the opening card to the movie tells us:

> If sailor tales and sailor tunes,
> Storm and adventure, heat and cold,
> If schooners, islands, and maroons
> And Buccaneers and buried Gold

And all the old romance, retold,
Exactly in the ancient way,
Can please, as me they pleased of old,
The wiser youngsters of to-day:
So be it!

Treasure Island captures the wonder and fun of the story. It remains an adventure I would still happily go on and it still speaks to children. You can see elements of Stevenson's story in Pirates of the Caribbean, both the amusement park ride and the movies. Who is Captain Jack Sparrow but Long John Silver updated for a younger generation. *Treasure Island* remains an important part of my childhood, the first steps along the road toward growth and adulthood. And I was so happy that when I saw it toward the end of my childhood in the heart of my adolescent years that Walt and company had gotten it right. It would be a touchstone I could use to revisit a treasured part of my childhood.

Asia, Africa, Australia, the Arctic, and the Middle East

While at the time I enjoyed *World of Disney* episodes set in these various locales, none of them stuck with or influenced me.

Asia remained largely untouched. Communist China was off limits to the rest of the world. The same was true for the Soviet Union. The Indian subcontinent, specifically Sri Lanka, was featured in *Chandar, the Black Leopard of Ceylon* (1973). The aboriginal people of Australia were chronicled in *The Journey to the Valley of the Emu* (1978). Africa featured only in the TV premiere of the True Life Adventure feature documentary *The African Lion* (1955).

The Arctic came to life not only in the True Life Adventure documentary *White Wilderness* (1958), but in the drama *Two Against the Artic* (1974). The episode I most wish I could have located for this book was *A Salute to Alaska* (1967), not only for its history of our northern state but to see Walt Disney's final introduction recorded before his death.

Probably the most prescient episode was *Hamad and the Pirates* (1971). Set in the Middle East in modern Bahrain, the title would seem to hint at an old-fashioned *Arabian Nights* kind of story. Up to that point, my only knowledge of the Middle East was colored by exotic fantasy stories like Aladdin, *Kismet*, and *Jason and the Argonauts*; Saturday morning cartoons like *Shazzan*; and the occasional Bugs Bunny cartoon set there like "A Lad in His Lamp" and "Ali Baba Bunny."

Hamad was a Disney co-production with the government of Bahrain. Narrated by actor Michael Ansara, it feels almost like a documentary. It tells the story of Hamad (Khalik Marshad), an orphan living in Bahrain's capital city of Manama. His late father was a sailor on a pearl diving boat. Hamad still goes to sea with the boat and watches the divers ply their trade. Using weights to help them reach the bottom in the extra salt of the Arabian Sea, we see them descend and scoop up as many clams and oysters that they can before they must rise to the surface to breathe.

The trip feels comfortable and Hamad feels at home. But overnight, a storm surprises them and washes Hamad overboard. Because this happens in the early morning, no one is awake to see the boy swept over. He floats in the sea for quite awhile before he is picked up by another boat. Unfortunately, he discovers his rescuers are pirates stealing ancient artifacts and selling them on the black market. Hamad manages to escape and make his way to shore. He then treks across Dubai and Saudi Arabia to return to Manama. As he travels, we get to see how modern sections of the Middle East have little to do with harems and flying carpets and mythical genies in a bottle. Once he returns to Manama, Hamad alerts the police who locate and arrest the pirates when they come ashore with their ill-gotten loot.

This is not the Middle East I was raised on. Its Muslim faith is clearly on display. The pirates' stealing of the artifacts foreshadows battles to recover ancient archaeological finds taken in the 19th and 20th centuries to museums in Europe and America. *Hamad and the Pirates* showcases the modern, oil-rich Middle East, ready to assert itself on the world stage and change the balance of international politics.

Continental Europe

Bon Voyage! (1962)

TV Premiere: January 11, 18, 25, 1970

As a kid, I always wanted to sail on a transatlantic ocean liner to Europe, despite the fact that I grew up reading about the *Titanic*, seeing the *Queen Mary* and *Queen Elizabeth* in the newspapers, and watching and reading *The Poseidon Adventure* (1972). Perhaps I was born thirty years too late, but five days on a luxury liner seems infinitely better than five hours on a plane. My father, for all his plusses, never saw the point of vacationing in Europe when there was still so much of the United States to see. It seemed the only way I was going to enjoy a trans-Atlantic trip would be by watching this movie.

Partially filmed aboard the S.S. *United States*, the fastest ocean liner ever built, I have to admit that the ship held my interest much more than the movie did. It tells the story of the Willards, an American family on their first trip to Europe. Unfortunately, none of the Willards come across as real-life people. Even as a kid, I recognized they were types, not individuals. Well-meaning but bumbling Dad (Fred MacMurray), patient yet understanding Mom (Jane Wyman), boy-crazy daughter (Deborah Walley) whose hormone-driven moods change from hour to hour even as she is convinced each mood is how she will feel forever and ever, moody adolescent son (Tommy Kirk) still trying on different personas that will get him a girl while somehow forgetting he just needs to be himself, and mischievous baby brother (Kevin Corcoran) always running off and getting into trouble.

All I could do was sit back and enjoy whatever glimpses of the ocean liner I could. Once the ship reaches Europe at the end of the first act, the Willards push on to Paris and, once again, I prefer the tourist sites they visit (Eiffel Tower, Champs Elysees, Notre Dame) over the soap opera developments in the love lives as Walley, Kirk, and MacMurray's Midwest values run smack dab into sophisticated, amoral Europe.

For the third act, the family finishes their dream vacation on the French Riviera. I had stopped caring about the Willards. I just wanted to hop in a rental car and drive down the coast to Monaco and see if the Grand Prix was on. Now that I am an adult, I still haven't made an ocean crossing. I still haven't been to Paris. I still haven't gone to Monaco. But I haven't given up on my dream to do so.

Hans Brinker or the Silver Skates (1962)

TV Premiere: January 7, 14, 1962

Hans Brinker is probably the oldest *World of Disney* show I have a memory of watching. For most of my childhood, I thought the title was *Hans Brinker AND the Silver Skates* but it turns out to be *Hans Brinker OR the Silver Skates*, a distinction made obvious at the climax. I did not remember the story in its entirety, but there were several moments that stuck with me in my childhood and helped color my outlook.

The story is based on Mary Mapes Dodge's classic 1865 children's novel adapted and directed by Norman Foster of Davy Crockett fame. I certainly didn't understand at the time that the lovely seasonal photography of the Dutch landscape was captured by award-winning cinematographers Gunnar Fischer and Sven Nykvist, regular collaborators of the great Swedish filmmaker Ingmar Bergman.

Hans Brinker follows the trials of a young boy named Hans Brinker (Rony Zeaner) as he tries to make his way in the world in late 19th century Holland. The book is credited with popularizing the story of the little boy sticking his finger in the dike and thus saving his town (though it is not Hans Brinker who does this) and also the sport of speed skating.

Hans lives with his family. His father makes a good living as a fisherman, although he is not as well off as many others in the village. Hans wishes to become an artist and spends his spare time drawing local people and locales. He has his eyes on the attractive daughter of the town mayor, a man who looks down his nose at the poor Brinker family. It doesn't help that Hilda has also caught the eye of Hans' skating rival Ludwig Schimmel (Lennart Klefbom).

The first thing I remember was the camaraderie and love of the Brinker family. I remember the friendly rivalry between father and son as they raced around the windmills and back, probably because it stood in stark contrast to the more serious rivalry between Hans and Ludwig.

I remember the class distinctions in the town and how the prominent citizens used it as a weapon to keep the poor in their place, and how pursuing the life of an artist in a small town was viewed less favorably than that of pursuing a trade. I remember that when love is at stake, anything goes as far as your romantic rivals are concerned. And by anything, I mean cheating, making you look bad in the eyes of her father, you name it.

The scariest thing I remember from the episode is that of Hans' father, Raff Brinker (Erik Strandmark), getting hit over the head while helping the villagers fight a flood. I felt the horror of how a life could be turned upside down in an instant, and for years to come, through an accident that was no one's fault.

And I remember the speed skating race itself, with Hans Brinker racing to win so that he could pay for his father's operation (even then the cost of health care was something just out of reach of the average family), charging across the frozen ice of the Zuiderzee, the huge inland bay adjacent to the North Sea. I *thought* I remembered Hans winning the race and claiming those silver skates—a memory that turned out to be bogus. But the result of the race did introduce me to the concept of a "moral victory" and how someone could still win by losing.

The Waltz King (1963)

TV Premiere: October 27, November 3, 1963

By the time I was a child in the 1960s, classical music and the composers who wrote them were no longer hip and cool. The symphonies, waltzes, and operas were now considered boring and their composers who used to be at the center of 18th and 19th century pop culture were just a bunch of boring guys wearing funny wigs. *The Waltz King* changed my perspective and opened the door on the world of classical music.

The movie tells the story of Johann Strauss II (Kerwin Mathews). As the film begins, he is a young musician trying to make ends meet in

19th century Vienna. Unfortunately, he lives in the shadow of his father, Johann Strauss Sr. (Brian Aherne) who is Vienna's current "waltz king." Strauss Sr. wants his son to give up this crazy idea of music and settle down to a more acceptable livelihood like business. Strauss Jr. refuses. He has music in his heart and he cannot stop trying to express it.

He tries to step out of his father's shadow with the aid and romantic interest of opera singer Henriette Treffz (Senta Berger). His father uses his leverage and reputation to stall and intimidate any concert hall owners or music publishers from supporting his son's ambitions. What he hasn't counted on is Henriette's determination to give young Johann his chance. Eventually, Johann Jr. is able to find a concert hall for his debut. And despite his father planting hecklers in the premiere's audience to ruin the concert, Johann's debut is a stirring success. Even his father is forced to admit that his son's got talent.

In part two, Johann is now the "waltz king" of Europe. He has written such popular waltzes as "The Blue Danube" (1867) and "Tales from the Vienna Woods" (1868). He is the toast of Europe and the most popular guy in Vienna. He ought to be happy, but he finds himself tired, burned out, and cynical—exactly where his father was at the beginning of the movie. Looking to reignite his creative spark, Strauss decides to try writing an operetta called *Die Fledermaus*. The move threatens to alienate his audience, his supporters, and even, based on the subject matter, royalty and political leaders. It is his debut concert all over again, but the brilliance of the music wins everyone over. Strauss is king once again.

The Waltz King opened me up to the world of classical music. I am sure it is not a coincidence that the movie came out in the same year that Beatlemania was unleashed on the world. Prior to rock and roll, prior to big band, prior to ragtime, composers like Strauss, Wagner, and others like them were the rock stars. People flocked to their concerts. Fans followed them around town. They had groupies. They had to wear disguises in order to go out in public or leave their concerts ("Johann has left the building").

Other than the social commentary, the movie made me appreciate the complexity and exhilarating beauty of classical music, its ability to sweep me off my feet and bring me closer to what it means to be human, and to feel like I could touch the divine even if only through the sounds. I have always found the sight of a waltzing couple, the circling swirl of a ball gown, and men in tie and tails to be gorgeous and beautiful and stirring. I could watch them dance all night.

Third Man on the Mountain / Banner in the Sky (1959)
TV Premiere: February 17, 24, 1963

I have come to love few Disney movies the way I love this adaptation of the James Ramsey Ullman book. It tells the story of Rudi Matt (James MacArthur), the son of Joseph Matt. Rudi's father used to be the top mountain guide in their small Swiss village until he died trying to scale the nearby unconquered mountain called the Citadel ("played" in the movie by the distinctively recognizable Matterhorn). Since his father's death, Rudi's mother (Nora Swinbourne) and uncle (James Donald) have forced Rudi to give up his dream of following in his father's footholds by forcing him to work as a dishwasher in the local hotel, but their efforts prove futile. Rudi steals away every chance he gets and dreams of getting the opportunity to prove his father had found a way to get to the top of the Citadel at the time of his death. He is aided in his ambitions by the hotel owner's pretty daughter, Lizbeth (Janet Munro), who has her eyes set on marrying Rudi, but only after he has fulfilled his ambition to reach the top of the Citadel and plant his father's banner there. That chance comes when he saves the life of famed mountain climber Colonel John Winter (Michael Rennie). Winter then invites Rudi to join his climbing party to the top of the Citadel.

I had no trouble as a child identifying with what Rudi was going through. He and I were both boys who didn't quite fit in with their peers and who had their eyes fixed elsewhere. I did not want to become a mountain climber, but I did want to become a writer (which has its own "mountains" to climb). I was already being told to give up my dreams and find a practical trade like dishwasher that paid the bills and had less danger. Unlike Rudi, I had no Colonel Winter who believed in me nor a pretty girl like Lizbeth to wish me on. And yet the more people urged me to give up my dreams and focus on the practical, the more like Rudi I became—stubborn and determined to steal away and work on my craft and prove everyone wrong. But I was also motivated to learn the correct lessons along the way.

"A guide doesn't climb alone. What does the word guide mean? It means to lead others." Writers may write alone, but they too do not write alone. They have their fans and their readers.

When Rudi pays the price for showing off on an early climb, Colonel Winter rebukes him. "You did a thing to be ashamed of. You were looking for praise and for gain, two things your father never sought. He was the greatest climber of them all. He could go places other men could only dream of. He didn't die because a mountain was too high or for conquest or for glory. He gave his life because he thought only of the man in his charge." I decided that I would never be caught showboating or bragging or calling attention to myself—even as it became a central expectation of our society.

One of the ironic things about this movie is that it opened my eyes to the world of mountain climbing—an odd development since I have such an overwhelming fear of heights. But for a while there, I indulged in the fantasy of scaling the world's peaks: the Matterhorn, Mount Everest in the Himalayas, or a smaller American peak—all done in the safety of my backyard. Our home had a hillside, probably not as steep as I remember, so it was easy to lie down and pretend it was a mountain cliff requiring rope and careful toeholds in order to climb.

Like I did with any topic that intrigued me, I went to the library to learn more about it. I found the book *Mountain Conquest* (1966) by Eric Earle Shipton and published by Horizon Caravel, sort of the world history division of the American Heritage Junior Library. (Fun side note: this movie was the inspiration for Disney building the Matterhorn Bobsleds in Disneyland, a ride that straddles the border between Fantasyland and Tomorrowland much as the real Matterhorn straddles the border between Switzerland and France.)

The movie was also my introduction to the loveliness of Janet Munro. Her portrayal of Lizbeth was everything my young teenaged self wanted in a woman: spunky and resourceful, not interested in being a lady, not interested in boundaries and social conventions. She is interested in what she is interested in and will do what she can to pursue it. You must accept her as she is and she expects you to be who you are, not to conform to what she and others expect you to be. Rudi was the person I wanted to be and Lizbeth was the person I wanted to be with.

Besides a temporary infatuation with mountain climbing, *Third Man* taught me the skills I would need to achieve my dreams. It turns out that being a successful writer is not too different from being a successful mountain climber who lives to climb another day. Don't be afraid to try something new. When trying to do something that you have not done before, you must prepare. You must have the best equipment. You must know your route. You must not pay any attention to the naysayers. The more they say you cannot do something, the more you must try to do it. Often they are motivated by jealousy on their own part or fear that you might get hurt trying to reach your dreams. You must push all that aside and do what you can to reach the summit of your ambitions. And no amount of work can change a person into something they were not meant to be.

"Would you want to be the wife of a guide?" Rudi's mother asks Lizbeth.

"Yes." Lizbeth replies with a defiant tilt of her chin. "Or of a dishwasher, or a hotel proprietor. But never the wife of a hotel proprietor who wanted to climb mountains! Because a man must do what he feels he must do; or he isn't a man. And no one, wife, mother or sweetheart, has the right to make him into something that he wasn't meant to be."

I decided to never let anyone do that to me. I was going to climb the mountain of my ambitions and no one would talk me out of it.

Flight of the White Stallions / Miracle of the White Stallions (1963)

TV Premiere: October 17, 24, 1965

The dying days of World War II. Germany is on the verge of losing the war, but the Nazi officials in Vienna, Austria, refuse to accept it and refuse to allow anything that the general public could construe as admitting defeat. One of the things they insist on is maintaining the presence of the Spanish Riding School in Vienna, home of the world famous Lipizzaner horses. A holdover from the lost Hapsburg dynasty that ruled Austria for centuries, the Lipizzaners are world famous for their equestrian skills and admired the world over. The leader of the school, Colonel Podhajsky (Robert Taylor), longs to move them out of the city before another Allied bombing raid accidentally strikes the school and destroys both horses and facilities. And yet how does one sneak dozens of white horses out of town?

Aided by his wife Vedena (Lilli Palmer) and the rest of the riding school instructors, Podhajsky engineers a mass escape worthy of Oskar Schindler. They find refuge on a country estate where horses and humans are able to relax. The only problem remains that early in the war, the Germans had separated the mares from the stallions and sent them to Czechoslovakia. Now, in the final days of the war and with the Soviet Russians threatening to occupy Czechoslovakia, Podhajsky fears the mares will never be reunited with the rest of the horses. The Lipizzaner breed might die out. Fortunately, General George S. Patton (John Larch) passes through. Podhajsky and the others stage an impromptu horse show for the general, a known horse lover. The plan works. Podhajsky tells Patton of the need to rescue the mares. Patton throws "Operation Cowboy" together. His soldiers briefly invade Czechoslovakia and steal the horses out from under the noses of the Germans. They then manage to avoid the Russians in their rush back in what can only be described as a 20th century horse drive with the soldiers as cowboys and tanks as their protection. The mission is a success. The horses are reunited and saved. And the movie ends with a performance by the Lipizzaners as they return to perform at the riding school in Vienna.

White Stallions continues Walt Disney's infatuation with horses and equestrian shows, but the movie is not a popular one with many

Disney enthusiasts. Many cite Robert Taylor's cold performance as Podhajsky. While he may not be the warm individual we would like to follow through a movie, it is an accurate characterization of the real-life man. He is no-nonsense because that is his military character. He is also obsessed with saving the horses. His zeal borders on obsession and the obsession borders on fanaticism that threatens to alienate the very people he needs to save the stallions. Over the course of the movie, his wife and his friend Otto (Eddie Albert) convince him that he must temper his zeal with patience and emotional appeals. Don't tell them why they should save the Lipizzaners. Show them why! That was the beginning of my key lesson as a writer: show, don't tell.

I also had two personal reasons for liking this movie. First, this was one of the few Disney movies my mother would take the time to sit down and watch in its entirety. I think she did so because she enjoyed Robert Taylor, always one of her favorite movie stars from Hollywood's golden age. I also think she found a lot of similarities between herself and Podhajsky's wife (whom she physically resembled). She and I also shared a love of the Lipizzaner horses. In the years since the true events portrayed in the movie, an American branch of the Lipizzaners had been set up on a farm in West Virginia. Mom and I would regularly go see them perform at the civic center in Charleston and it was just like watching them perform at the Spanish Riding School. It made me appreciate the beauty, size, grace, and strength of these horses.

While in the process of writing this book, I was depressed to learn that the American Lipizzaner show had filed for bankruptcy and their West Virginia farm was up for sale. For a brief moment, I fantasized about becoming Dean Jones, buying the farm in some odd combination of *The Horse in the Gray Flannel Suit*, *Snowball Express*, and *Miracle of the White Stallions* (call it "We Bought a Horse Farm"), and bringing them back to success. I hope in this fast-paced 21st century there is still a place for the simple beauty of a horse and a rider working together.

Escapade in Florence (1962)

TV Premiere: September 30, October 7, 1962

My memory of this delightful thriller was my childhood introduction to romance amid the backdrop of Italian art and intrigue. Tom Carpenter (Tommy Kirk) is an American art student studying in Florence for a year. In the opening scene of the movie, Tom rides around the city, renowned for being one of the most beautiful in Europe. Riding on his motor scooter, he gives us a chance to see why so many people (including my own father when he toured Europe in his retirement years) fell in love with Florence.

His reverie comes to an abrupt end when he literally runs into Annette Funicello, knocking her down. (Maybe an early example of a rom com's "meet cute" moment?) She plays Annette Allotto, another American who came to Florence to study. She splits her time between working as a painter and singing at her Italian relatives' restaurant. This was an Annette we Disney fans had never seen before. This is not the radiant adolescent Annette of *The Mickey Mouse Club* years. This is not the fairy tale Annette from *Babes in Toyland* or the shy teen from *The Horsemasters*. This is not the girlfriend Annette playing second banana to Tommy Kirk yet again in the upcoming *Merlin Jones* movies or even opposite Frankie Avalon in the American International Pictures beach movies to follow. This is the only time we got to view the adult Annette on screen. Ironically, this episode is also the only time when Annette is listed by her full name in the opening credits. In all her other Disney movies she is credited simply as "Annette."

This Annette is nobody's girlfriend. She is her own woman and committed to stay that way. In the film's early scenes, I almost feel Annette is channelling her real-life world weariness at having the unwanted mantle of "America's girlfriend" foisted upon her. Of having hundreds of unknown boys mailing her engagement rings. I imagine the song "Dream Boy," which she sings in the restaurant, perfectly encapsulates how she feels as both an actress and a woman. She wants to do her own thing in her own way and she feels no need to become any guy's girl, least of all Tom, the man who just knocked her down.

Like any good red-blooded American male, Tom takes Annette's rejection as mere encouragement to pursue. He tracks her down to the restaurant. Of course, Annette sings (she was one of the top pop singers in the country at the time), but it is there that Tom encounters his main romantic rival, Bruno (Nino Castelnuovo). I find it interesting that Annette encourages neither of them (she just wants to be friends with both), but the two boys immediately start one upping each other for the chance to be beside her and make the other look bad. All Annette can do is roll her eyes and hope they get over this needless rivalry as soon as possible.

Fortunately, the thriller plot surges in to interrupt any romantic hopes. It turns out that Annette has unwittingly gotten herself involved in an art forgery ring. They are using her paintings as covers to smuggle the real masterpieces out of the city museum and replace them with forgeries. Tom realizes what is up and enlists Annette and Bruno to get to the bottom of it. Yes, in exotic Europe, mystery comes before romance.

The primary villain is Count Roberto (Ivan Desny), a rich playboy who has gone through all his money and is trying to come up with a way to refill his coffers. When Tom tries to convince him that what he is up to is a crime, Roberto laughs it off. "You Americans always see things in black and white." Some will put that off as European amorality, but I think it more accurate to call it the entitled mentality of upper-class people regardless of country.

The whole thing reaches a climax amid the legendary Palio di Siena horse race through the streets of nearby Siena. That was my first encounter with this almost 400-year-old event, though it would turn up again in future books and movies. As for *Escapade In Florence*, all turns out well. The villains are arrested. The paintings are returned. And Tom, Annette, and Bruno share a final celebratory meal at the restaurant with hints of a possible romance to come.

For both Annette and Tommy Kirk, it is the peak of their Disney involvement. Within the year, Annette would be off to make the beach pictures with Frankie Avalon. She made two more Disney films, both with Tommy as her romantic partner, before she married and retired from the screen. After leaving Disney, Tommy made some B movies before his career petered out. But here they are in exotic Florence as young, vibrant adults. They made me want to be there. They made me want to be them. Is there anything else a performer needs to do?

England

Out of all the countries in Europe, Great Britain had more Disney episodes set there than anywhere else. It may be because the company had substantial war-time profits trapped there by government regulation. It may be that Walt was naturally drawn to stories set there. Perhaps it was his Irish heritage. But I found myself equally drawn to such stories. Of all the stories presented, these stood out the most.

The Sword and the Rose (1963)

TV Premiere: January 4, 11, 1956

Set in the court of King Henry VIII (James Robertson Justice), this period drama is a loose telling of the true story of Princess Mary Tudor (Glynis Johns), the sister of Henry, and her love for Charles Brandon (Richard Todd), a commoner who is also captain of the guards. Impulsive and vivacious, Mary finds herself falling for the handsome Brandon mostly because he stands up to her—unlike everyone else at court. Mary, in turn, is the only person able to stand up to her kingly brother and his volcanic temper. Henry has royal plans for his sister. He wishes to marry her off to the king of France in exchange for money and a royal alliance. Mary refuses to allow herself to be married off for anything but love. Waiting patiently on the sidelines is the Duke of Buckingham (Michael Gough). He is a descendant of the former Plantagenet dynasty that Henry and Mary's father dethroned fifty years earlier in the War of the Roses. Mary agrees to marry France's old King Louis XII so long as she can pick her next husband, with her eyes clearly on Brandon. Buckingham supports her plan because he schemes to be that man after eliminating Brandon.

The Sword and the Rose, based on the novel *When Knighthood Was In Flower* (1898), was a surprising departure for Disney. When I first saw it, I remember being enchanted by the look of the film. The sumptuous nature of the sets and the costumes drew me in. The cast was equally enjoyable. Richard Todd was a wonderful leading man and a Disney favorite in the early 1950s. He never seemed to get the fame his talent deserved. Prior to this, I had only seen Glynis Johns as Mrs. Banks in *Mary Poppins* (1964). It was fun to see her as the flirtatious Mary. And James Robertson Justice's performance as Henry VIII is still one of the best Henry interpretations, right up there with Charles Laughton in *The Private Life of Henry VIII* (1933) and Keith Mitchell in *The Six Wives of Henry VIII* (1969).

I also enjoyed the swordplay and action scenes. Their derring-do reminded me of similar action scenes in other childhood favorites of mine: *The Adventures of Robin Hood* (1938), *Camelot* (1967), and *Knights of the Round Table* (1954).

But the movie taught me a few other things that would prove useful for the future. The first was the verbal sophistication of the court dialogue where characters appear to be in agreement when what they are actually saying to each other is an insult. And the subtext of what they are trying to say is not lost on the other. Mary, on the surface, appears to be complying with court decorum while the meaning in her words and her actions speaks something else entirely.

The other thing it taught me was that the things we most want may take longer to achieve than we originally hoped, and that sometimes we must lose the early rounds in order to win in the end. Patience and constant vigilance orchestrating the details are the keys to victory, especially long-term ambitions.

The Prince and the Pauper (1962)

TV Premiere: March 11, 18, 25, 1962

The Prince and the Pauper continued the story of Henry VIII, toward the end of his reign. The king is in poor health, but his son, Prince Edward (Sean Scully), is less concerned with learning how to be a king and more interested in running and playing like the boys he sees out his palace windows. Across the London Bridge on the poor side of the Thames River, young Tom Candy (Sean Scully again) lives a wretched life begging in the streets and suffering under an abusive father who beats him each night. Tom manages to survive by dreaming of becoming rich and living in the palace he sees on the other side of the river. Neither Tom nor Edward realize that they look exactly alike. One day, Tom goes to visit the palace. The prince sees him from the window and beckons him inside.

Once they realize their physical likeness, Edward proposes they switch clothes for a few hours. Tom will stay in the palace and pretend he is the prince while Edward spends a few hours playing out of sight of the royal advisors. They agree and it all seems to be going to plan until Henry unexpectedly dies and Tom is proclaimed the new king. When Edward tries to return, no one can see past his beggar clothes and he is rudely tossed back out into the street. Only a soldier of the court, Miles Herndon (Guy Williams), takes pity on the boy and that is only because he thinks Edward is touched in the head. Gradually, though, Edward convinces him that he is, in fact, the new king and they set out to restore him to the throne. All ends well. Edward as Tom learns that the life of the poor is not so great while Tom as Edward attempts to inject a little more humanity into the laws of the land.

This was my first exposure to the classic Mark Twain story. It was the first time I had seen Sean Scully (though not the last), but I took to him right away, identifying with him on several fronts. I did not come from a poor family with an abusive father and a neglectful mother, but I did long to be able to live like a rich aristocrat. And, no, I was not a royal prince, but who doesn't react to the responsibilities of adulthood by wishing they could steal away and play all day.

Of course, I recognized Guy Williams right away. He had previously been Zorro and I also knew him as Prof. John Robinson on *Lost in Space*. Who wouldn't want him by your side in a difficult circumstance? Although I didn't know who she was at the time, I was taken by the fetching Jane Asher as Lady Jane Gray. It would be years before I learned that she was the 1960s girlfriend of Beatle Paul McCartney.

The biggest lesson I took away from this telling of the Mark Twain tale was to learn to treat others with kindness, to be wary of draconian laws that unnecessarily burden the poor, and to be wary of anyone who proposes such a law. The humanity of the circumstances were to be considered above all else. In short: to do uonto others the way you would want them to do unto you. I vowed to remember that no matter how far or how high my life's ambitions took me.

Kidnapped (1960)

TV Premiere: March 17, 24, 1963

Kidnapped was my first exposure to the works of Robert Louis Stevenson. It predated my reading of *Treasure Island* by two or three years. It also left a fear in my psyche that remains to this day. *Kidnapped* is the story of young David Balfour (James MacArthur). When his father dies, David travels to see his Uncle Ebenezer (his first name a virtual tip off for anyone familiar with *A Christmas Carol*) to receive his share of his inheritance. Uncle Ebenezer lives in a large, unfinished house. When David is sent by his uncle to fetch a box from the attic, David is shocked to find that the staircase is unfinished and only a flash of well-timed lightning prevents him from falling to his death.

Later, his uncle has David shanghaied by a local ship's captain and sent to America as an indentured servant. His life takes a turn for the good when he befriends Alan Breck (Peter Finch) aboard ship. When David overhears plans to take Alan hostage, he tells Breck. The two take a stand in the ship's cabin and defeat the villainous crew who attack them. Once back on shore, the two friends first settle Alan's problems (he is a Scottish chieftain on the outs with his clan) then confront David's uncle to win David's inheritance. David and Alan part as friends.

Kidnapped, at least in its early scenes, scared the heck out of me as a child. I understood the excitement of traveling to a new town. But David's arrival at the creepy House of Shaws seemed like something out of a horror movie. His Uncle Ebenezer was appropriately named as his personality matched that of the more famous Mr. Scrooge. And then the unexpected terror of climbing the stairs only to have them end in mid-step. Yikes! It was enough to convince me that where money is concerned family goes by the boards.

The rest of the movie never quite lives up to the early part. The scenes on the ship are fine, but the stand-off in the cabin goes on too long. The end has always struck me as unsatisfying. The two friends just bid farewell and go their separate ways. It was the closest thing to a "to be continued" in movies or literature, only it was not continued.

Once again, James MacArthur is first class in the starring role. He is zealous and certain and the setbacks he suffers on his way to final success convinced me to go with the flow during my own setbacks in life. Victory would be just around the bend.

Hall of Fame Faraway Places Episode

The Scarecrow of Romney Marsh (1964)

TV Premiere: February 9, 16, 23, 1964

If there is one *Wonderful World of Disney* episode I would declare the best, it is this grand three-part adventure epic. Patrick McGoohan stars as Dr. Syn, the local vicar/parson of the village of Dymchurch in southeast England. He lives during the reign of King George III, the same time the American Revolution breaks out across the ocean. Dymchurch is a poor parish and Dr. Syn recognizes that the poor farmers and merchants often fail to pay the king's high taxes. So by night Dr. Syn transforms himself into the Scarecrow, a scary mask and costume that makes him look as frightening as anything I might encounter on Halloween night (except a devil kid).

With the help of his church sexton Mipps (George Cole), disguised as Hellspite, and John Banks (Sean Scully) disguised as Curlew but really the teenaged son of the local squire (Michael Hordern), Dr. Syn operates a smuggling ring. He takes advantage of the coastline to import contraband goods through the parish from overseas to raise the locals' tax money.

Naturally, the crown takes a dim view of this Robin Hood-type operation and dispatches their hardest army officer, General Pugh (Geoffrey Keen), to stamp out the ring, identify the Scarecrow's true identity, and make him and his associates hang. The result is a cat-and-mouse duel between Syn and Pugh over the course of the three episodes. In part one, Dr. Syn deals with a naval press gang who has invaded the parish to gather up unwilling males to serve in the navy and possibly spill the beans on the Scarecrow's identity. Part two finds Syn confronting a turncoat in his own gang, a moody farmer named Ransley (Patrick Wymark), and part three finds Squire Banks' press-ganged son Harry (David Buck) deserting the navy and returning to Dymchurch only to be arrested and imprisoned in Dover Castle. Pugh believes he can torture the boy and a few other comrades to finger the Scarecrow. To prevent it, Dr. Syn leads a raiding party into the castle and rescues the men right out from under General Pugh's nose. Pugh's career is destroyed and the Scarecrow is left to fight another day.

Whenever the next week's preview appeared at the end of each episode, my family would fervently pray that it would be time to show *Scarecrow* again (we usually got *Yellowstone Cubs*). As the decades went by, no DVD release was more requested than this one. I am not alone in that sentiment. So what is it about this story that makes it my perfect *World of Disney* episode?

I suspect I am drawn to its three-part structure. Having it play out over three episodes gives it the feel of a novel come to life. (*Scarecrow* was shortened by almost a third and released as a feature film overseas.) Having it play out in three parts allows time for more small character moments that help us better identify with the characters. One moment I particularly like and which always gets a laugh comes early on when Mipps comes down during a church service to warn Dr. Syn that the naval press gang is on its way to the church. Rather than stating so, he joins the congregation singing the final hymn only he skips the lyrics and sings, "The press gang is on the road." He then rejoins the townspeople on "Amen."

Making the Scarecrow Dr. Syn's secret identity gives the character both a superhero and a Robin Hood quality. The fact that he runs a smuggling operation also gives him the allure of a pirate. Patrick McGoohan gives a masterful performance. His Dr. Syn is a modicum of virtue and calm rectitude. We can see why members of his parish flock to his side in times of trouble. The Scarecrow is the flipside and McGoohan plays that side of Syn's personality to the hilt. There is a dark side to Dr. Syn that unsettles us, kind of like the dark side of Long John Silver in *Treasure Island*. The horrible laugh McGoohan gives the Scarecrow used to send shivers up my young spine. He looks and acts like a character who stepped out of a horror film and wandered into a Disney episode. There are moments of genuine terror with the Scarecrow when we are not sure how far he will go in his search for justice. Knowing that it is the local minister under the costume actually made it scarier and kept us on the edge of our childhood seats.

The late-night barn trial of Ransley before the Scarecrow's hooded gang remains a highlight of the show. Its twists and turns and an unexpected conclusion plays out in a ghoulish way—necessary for the Scarecrow to keep his men from turning informant—and yet it all ends on a humane note known only to Scarecrow, Hellspite, Curlew, and us.

I also enjoy the slow transformation of Philip Brackenbury (Eric Flynn), General Pugh's lieutenant, from loyal second in command to the general to Scarecrow sympathizer. This happens gradually and believably due to his growing revulsion of Pugh's "the ends justify the means" methods and his growing love for the squire's daughter Kate (Jill Corzon). The final way he gets back at Pugh at the end of the show always gets a deserving laugh.

Among the Scarecrow's men are Ben Davis (Gordon Gostelow) and Sam Farley (Robert Brown). Sam sees the benefits of what Scarecrow is doing for the parish and follows his orders without question. Ben is a bit more circumspect but still goes along. His expressed doubts also create some of the show's laughs.

"You've blackmailed the vicar?" he exclaims when Scarecrow (really Dr. Syn) informs them that Dr. Syn will be leading them into Dover castle.

The whole thing is tied together by the infectious theme song composed by Terry Gilkyson. It opens and closes each episode and is rousing enough and simple enough to have us all singing it by the end of the show. We would continue to sing it for years after as we impatiently waited for the show to air again.

Despite the near misses, everything ends well with the Scarecrow's smuggling outfit still in operation and no one the wiser about his real identity. There are a few who suspect, but their admiration for what Dr. Syn is up to keeps them from talking. *The Scarecrow of Romney Marsh* is the lone Disney show that I wish they had made further installments of like they did with Texas John Slaughter and the Swamp Fox.

In a bit of historic irony, *Scarecrow* premiered on *World of Disney* the same night and at the same time that The Beatles made their American debut on *The Ed Sullivan Show*. VCRs hadn't been invented yet. Our family had to choose one or the other to watch. Guess which one we watched?

CHAPTER SEVEN

Walt and His Park

Shows about Disneyland

The episodes that I most looked forward to were the ones involving Disneyland. It is hard to convey how miraculous, how amazing, how futuristic, how totally out of this world Walt's Magic Kingdom appeared to us through the screen of our color TVs. Disneyland contained vistas that could not be found anywhere outside the movies. We could walk down the streets of a turn-of-the-century town on Main Street, U.S.A., take a boat down tropical rivers in Adventureland, journey back to the days of the Wild West in Frontierland, and ride a canoe or a keelboat or Mississippi stern-wheeler. We could explore Nature's Wonderland aboard pack mules, a stagecoach, or a mine train. It was like all those True-Life Adventure movies come to life.

In the time before VCRs, we could go to Fantasyland and step into our favorite Disney movies aboard attractions like Snow White's Adventures, Peter Plan's Flight, Mr. Toad's Wild Ride, and Alice In Wonderland. We could spin on a Mad Tea Party, fly with Dumbo, or climb aboard Casey Jr.'s Circus Train. In Tomorrowland, we could scale the Matterhorn, drive our own car on the Autopia, steer our boat on the Motor Boat Cruise, or ride a monorail. We could blast into outer space on Flight to the Moon or board an atomic sub for a submarine voyage through liquid space. In an era when our television screens were only eleven inches wide, we could see America the Beautiful in Circle Vision 360 or catch a glimpse of future everyday life in the House of the Future. How amazing was all that?

For children living east of the Mississippi River, Disneyland might as well be on the far side of the Earth rather than California. The Golden State was a long way to drive in a time when the interstate highway system was still being finished and commercial aviation was out of the price range of the average American family.

So all we could do was wait for the episodes devoted to Disneyland and the amazing new attractions Walt kept adding every year, each more ingenious and futuristic than what had come before—which of course made us want to go there even more.

The Disneyland Story (1954)

TV Premiere: October 27, 1954

I was not alive for the premiere episode of the show that would become *The Wonderful World of Disney*. It starts out with the camera roving around the Walt Disney Studios on a "typical day." On one soundstage Kirk Douglas gets ready for his scenes in *20,000 Leagues under the Sea*. On another stage, James Mason battles the giant squid for the same film. In a studio, artists draw movement sketches for the next animated feature *Sleeping Beauty*. Finally, the camera ends up in Walt's office where he outlined his plans and dreams for *Disneyland* the show as well as Disneyland the park. "We want you to see and share the experience of building Disneyland."

The two projects had been tied together for maximum impact: generate excitement for the show and excitement for the park. Walt encouraged this connection right in the first episode.

"Disneyland the place," he said, "and *Disneyland* the TV show are all part of the same."

Both were initially called "Disneyland." Both were divided into different lands for us to travel in: Adventureland, Frontierland, Fantasyland, and Tomorrowland.

"We hope," Walt continued, "that it will be unlike anything on this earth. A fair, an amusement park, an exhibition, a city from the Arabian nights, a metropolis of the future; in fact, a place of hopes and dreams, facts and fancy all in one."

Frontierland represented "the treasure of our native folklore," as well as "true stories about real people who became legends, like Davy Crockett." Adventureland would star nature's animals in "remote adventure stories from the far corners of the earth." Tomorrowland would continue man's forward march of science. His hope was that both the park and the show would prove "a place of knowledge and happiness."

In both respects, he proved to be correct.

Disneyland after Dark (1962)

TV Premiere: April 15, 1962

One of my favorite episodes about the park, it starts with guests boarding the monorail at the Disneyland Hotel stop and riding the "highway of the future" into the park for an evening of fun. We get fleeting glimpses of some of the top thrill rides in Tomorrowland before docking at the station. The camera switches to Walt standing in the plaza at the end of Main Street, U.S.A., even though it was clearly filmed in the studio using back projection. Still, Walt's comedy bit of wanting to show the audience around the park only to have autograph seekers prevent him from going anywhere is funny and Walt plays it well.

The rest of the episode is very musical and it does a great job of showing off Disneyland as a hip, happening, and cool place to spend the night. The segments are wisely geared to present an act for each age group. Down on Main Street, U.S.A., a barbershop quartet performs to the delight of its older crowd who probably remember when barbershop crooning was the bee's knees.

At the Tomorrowland Terrace, teenagers and college students dance to rock-and-roll and pop songs. Former Mouseketeers Bobby Burgess and Annette Funicello are among the dancers. Annette gets coaxed on stage and entertains the audience with "I Like To Dance." She then brings up pop star Bobby Rydell. I love the contrast in audience expressions while each artist performs. While Annette sings, the guys gawk with rapt expressions and amorous smiles while the girls frown. When Bobby Rydell takes the stage, the expressions switch. The girls bob their heads and grin with amorous glee while the boys frown. It is a fun segment and leaves us with the feeling that you never know who might turn up when you visit Disneyland.

The episode moves to Adventureland for the nightly luau at the Tahitian Terrace restaurant. The audience is made up largely of middle-aged parents who have let their children loose in the Magic Kingdom so that they can enjoy a leisurely dinner. Polynesian dancers and musicians entertain the packed tables. The men gape at the female belly dancers with the same expression the guys gave Annette back in Tomorrowland. The only difference is that they are at the same time stuffing their faces from plates of spare ribs. The wives' expressions vary from the same stony gaze their younger female counterparts gave Annette to bemused wonder at the rapt, near-drooling expressions of their men.

Off we go again. This time we board the *Mark Twain* Riverboat in Frontierland, sailing the Rivers of America while being entertained by some great Dixieland jazz. Louis Armstrong is there and for twenty minutes he serenades us as only Satchmo could—singing songs, sharing the spotlight with the other members of the band, and even acknowledging when he is singing a composition by one of the musicians. Together, they reminisce about the early days of their careers and how far they have come from the real Dixieland. The feeling is one of a convivial party hosted by one of America's consummate entertainers. I could literally have spent all night riding the river and listening to them play.

For the final part of the show, we congregate at the Plaza Gardens, an entertainment pavilion that used to be located just off the central plaza in the shadow of Sleeping Beauty Castle. The musical stylings of this band are more Lawrence Welk than rock and roll, closer to Perry Como than Elvis Presley. But since I grew up listening to these kinds of records playing almost every day on my parents' stereo, I learned to enjoy it. Making the evening even better we see the debut of the Osmond Brothers. They look quite young yet are already complete professionals as they serenade and charm the crowd. It is the perfect way to cap off the episode and the night. And just like every other Disneyland episode, it made me want to travel there all the more.

Holiday Time at Disneyland (1962)

TV Premiere: December 23, 1962

We open with a group of carolers singing Christmas carols as it snows in front of Sleeping Beauty Castle. And darn if one of the carolers doesn't turn out to be Walt. The one and only Santa Claus makes a quick appearance before zooming back to the North Pole for his final holiday preparations. The funny thing about the segment is how much it works to establish that, in that time and place, Uncle Walt was just as revered by children as was good old Saint Nick. Walt can even do magic like Santa as when he commands Tinker Bell to stop the snow.

We then get a quick overview of people having fun at Disneyland. Frontierland finds families traveling the Rivers of America on the many forms of transportation, from riverboat to raft to canoe to keelboat. We see them enjoying Nature's Wonderland by mine train or pack mules. Fantasyland shows people enjoying the Mad Tea Party, Carousel, Dumbo the Flying Elephant, Casey Jr. Circus Train, and Storybook Land Canal Boats. We take the Jungle Cruise in Adventureland before the tour wraps up in Tomorrowland with glimpses of the Autopia, Rocket Jets, and Flying Saucers rides.

A turn-of-the-century Easter parade marches down Main Street, U.S.A. and we are treated to a lovely collection of old cars and fine ladies wearing Easter bonnets. The climax is a launch of the same hot air balloon that flew in *Around the World in Eighty Days* (1956).

Walt steps in to remind us of the many new attractions that have opened recently at the park. We get flashbacks to the dedications of the Matterhorn Bobsleds, monorail, and Submarine Voyage. Vice President Richard Nixon and his family open the monorail while actors Fred MacMurray and Robert Cummings look on. Mountain climbers scale the Matterhorn, the world's first steel roller coaster. Mermaids swim and perform water ballet as the atomic sub *Nautilus* sets out on its first voyage. The dedication of the Sailing Ship *Columbia* in Frontierland is capped by a mock robbery and shootout on the roof of the Golden Horseshoe Revue—something that would never happen these days.

For Disney fans, it is fun to see appearances by Disney stars of that era. The monorail dedication parade features Annette Funicello and Roberta Shore promoting *The Shaggy Dog* (1959). For ragtime fans there is an appearance by the Firehouse Five Plus Two, the Disney Studios' in-house band made up of animators. Texas John Slaughter, Elfego Baca, and Zorro ride by. We even get a glimpse of Roy Williams, the big Mooseketeer (as he was called) from *The Mickey Mouse Club*.

The overall feeling left in my heart was I WANT TO GET THERE. I wanted to stay at the Disneyland Hotel. I wanted to ride the monorail. I wanted to pilot a bobsled down the side of the Matterhorn. I wanted to take a submarine ride. I wanted to do it all. I needed to get to Disneyland.

Disneyland Goes to the World's Fair (1964)

TV Premiere: May 17, 1964

Walt spent this episode previewing the rides and attractions Walt Disney Productions had in the works for the 1964–65 New York World's Fair, what he termed "the greatest show on earth next to Disneyland." It begins with another humorous Ward Kimball animated segment profiling the history of world fairs and how many great inventions made their debuts at those fairs in the past. For example, McCormick's reaper, the Colt revolver, and false teeth appeared at the 1851 Crystal Palace exhibition in Britain (considered the first world's fair). Other notable inventions were the telephone at the 1876 Philadelphia Centennial Exposition, the Kodak camera and Eiffel Tower at the 1889 Paris World's Fair, and the Ferris wheel, Edison phonograph, and Henry Ford's horseless carriage at the 1893 Columbian Exhibition in Chicago.

Having laid the groundwork for past world fair innovations, Walt explains what his company has been working on. The core technology in their exhibits is what Walt calls "three- dimensional animated figures" or audio-animatronics. He explains how it all began with the giant squid in *20,000 Leagues under the Sea* (1954), then progressed to the mechanical birds singing and starring in the Enchanted Tiki Room which opened in Adventureland in 1961. Now they are ready to take it to another level. In the episode's entertaining opening, Walt addresses us flanked by three baby brontosauruses (as they were called then).

"How would you like to have one of these little dinosaurs as a pet?" he asks showing off his new audio-animatronic dinosaurs. Well, of course, we would. What flesh-and-blood boy would not?

The dinos are bound for the Magic Skyway ride at the Ford Motor Company's pavilion. Magic Skyway will take its riders through a time tunnel into a history of the ancient world, with sections for "The Dawn of Time" featuring the dinosaurs, "The Advent of Man," and "The City of Tomorrow."

The Illinois Pavilion featured Great Moments with Mr. Lincoln. The audience listened to an audio-animatronic figure of Abraham Lincoln come to life and reciting several of his most inspiring real-life speeches. Voiced by actor Royal Dano, Mr. Lincoln looks stunning, almost like having our 16th president himself standing in front of us and sharing his words of wisdom.

The UNICEF pavilion presented It's a Small World, a celebration of the children of the world. Riders boarded a boat that took them past each of the seven continents where children from each country, dressed in their traditional cultural outfits, sang and danced to arguably the most infectious song the Sherman Brothers ever composed.

Lastly, the General Electric Pavilion showcased Progressland and the Carousel of Progress, a history of how one American family's home life has improved with the help of electricity, from the 1890s to the near future.

It made me want to go to the World's Fair even though I knew the chances of our family traveling there from the Midwest were about as likely as journeying out to Disneyland itself: nil. Walt did mention that all these new attractions would eventually find a home at Disneyland, so there was a chance I might still see them some day.

This episode has always hung in my mind because it seemed like it was the moment when the future had arrived. Walt appeared to be opening the door for us and it looked pretty wondrous to behold. Life-like robots, dinosaurs brought back to life. It was the beginnings of *Westworld* and *Jurassic Park*. Could the life of *The Jetsons* be far behind? The travel vehicles for the Magic Skyway became the PeopleMover in Tomorrowland and the Omnimover vehicles taking riders through the Haunted Mansion and other rides. The boats for It's a Small World became the bayou boats in Pirates of the Caribbean.

Unbeknowst to us, Walt was using the World's Fair as a test for much grander plans. If Disney shows could succeed on the "sophisticated" East Coast, then maybe they were ready for an "East Coast Disneyland." The Carousel of Progress, Progressland, and the City of Tomorrow would lead to something beyond imagining: our first glimpse of EPCOT and the future Walt hoped for us all, done to the tunes of the Sherman Brothers' "It's a Small World" and "There's a Great Big Beautiful Tomorrow."

I could not wait.

Disneyland 10th Anniversary Show (1965)

TV Premiere: January 3, 1965

This episode remains a favorite for a good many reasons. For most of us, it was our first glimpse behind the scenes at WED Enterprises, the division of Disney that thought up and designed those amazing rides at the park. It was also our first chance to see how they did it. Here we are at the concept stage of some of Disney's classic rides.

The premise of the show was that, as part of celebrating Disneyland's tenth anniversary, Walt would preview some of the new attractions to Julie Riehm, the park tour guide chosen as "Miss Tencentennial." She would spend the year travelling the country as part of the celebration.

Watching it today, Walt spends a little too much time complimenting Julie on just how pretty she is, but that was standard for the time. Even Jose the audio-animatronic bird from the Enchanted Tiki Room wolf whistles Julie at one point and she takes it with the good humor of a woman not wishing to offend her boss. Speaking as a small boy, I was much more interested in the ride models and concept art that Walt had to show us. Girls were still icky. Today, the episode is doubly interesting because of the legendary Imagineers we see working on the rides.

Artist Mary Blair shows how she is designing the façade for It's a Small World as they prepare to move it from the World's Fair to Fantasyland. She walks us through how she uses various lights on a test model to decide the best colors to paint it in so as to show the ride off "like a piece of jewelry" regardless of the time of day.

Marc Davis displays concept art for the Haunted Mansion including the stretching portraits that would eventually grace the walls of the mansion's entrance hall. Rolly Crump shares his models for the Museum of the Weird. It would ultimately not be built, but parts would be incorporated into the Haunted Mansion. Walt even shows some of the tricks they will use to show off the ghosts while mentioning to Julie that Disney representatives are already traveling the world collecting ghosts to take up residence.

The future ride most interesting to Walt was Pirates of the Caribbean. After showing Julie the diorama for New Orleans Square and concept art for the Blue Bayou restaurant, he leads us into the centerpiece of the episode: the models and early character sculptures for Pirates. It blew my mind that they had built a scale model of the ride so they could literally walk through it and test it to see it from the perspective of future riders. I tried building small-scale models for my own Pirates ride but had no talent to do so. It surprises me that Walt gives away the entire ride and yet it looks so amazing that I (and millions of children like me) still could not wait to experience the actual attraction.

The episode concludes with a quick tour of the park itself. Highlights include the John Mills family—including Disney star Hayley Mills—touring the Swiss Family Treehouse in Adventureland. These days, my interest lies in the defunct rides like Frontierland's Mine Ride and Pack Mules through Nature's Wonderland and the Flying Saucers (bumper cars of the future!) in Tomorrowland. The extended clip of the Enchanted Tiki Room is doubly entertaining since it has always been one of my favorite Disney shows.

It made me want to see the park even more. It made me wish to be a tour guide (did they hire boys for that job?) and work at the park, maybe even work alongside Walt himself. This episode was probably the beginning of my wanting to work at an amusement park (something I would do during the summers of my college years).

Disneyland around the Seasons (1966)

TV Premiere: December 18, 1966

By 1966, it had almost become a tradition to do a Christmas show at Disneyland. It was an easy way for Walt to promote the latest stuff at the park and a great way for us children to stare wide-eyed at the TV screen and make another silent wish: "next year in Disneyland." For this episode, Walt decided to highlight what a year spent at Disneyland was like. We open at the park ringing in the new year at midnight, January 1, 1966, with fireworks over Sleeping Beauty Castle and sparklers everywhere.

Walt primarily wants to show us the new rides, most moved from the New York World's Fair to the park. So we relive the dedication of and take an extended ride on It's a Small World in Fantasyland. We catch the opening of Great Moments with Mr. Lincoln at Main Street opera house. I recognized tour guide Julie Riehm from the Disneyland 10th Anniversary episode as she helped Walt cut the ribbon. We once again hear extended excerpts from Lincoln's speeches while the audience sits mesmerized. Both of these rides were made possible by audio-animatronics, Walt's ground-breaking advancement in robotics. This was the first time I had seen it in full motion. The effect was uncanny.

After a commercial, we travelled over for the opening of New Orleans Square, the latest themed land located adjacent to Frontierland on the Rivers of America. With its 1850s architecture, the narrow courtyards and streets, the dozens of small shops, and the Dixieland jazz bands playing throughout, New Orleans Square felt just like being in the Big Easy. Only the dancing African-American shoeshine boys feel out of step with the times. Could the promised Pirates of the Caribbean ride from last year not be far away?

A trip aboard the Disneyland Railroad sweeps us into a new tunnel and the Primeval World dinosaurs (from the Magic Skyway) lurk within. Just like Lincoln, the audio-animatronic dinosaurs look, feel, and sound alive; they were the closest thing to real "terrible lizards" until *Jurassic Park* (1993) came along. The climax is like a scene out of *Fantasia* (1940) come to life as we witness a battle between a Tyrannosaurus and a Stegosaurus.

As usual with the Disneyland shows, the episode closes with a parade down Main Street and I always find it intriguing what Disney characters they choose to include or not include in the parade. For the first time we see Winnie the Pooh and his friends since they have just made their Disney debut in *Winnie the Pooh and the Honey Tree* (1966). Mary Poppins is prominently featured. We get to see characters from *Fantasia* because that classic film that critics derided and audiences largely stayed away from back in 1940 was finally starting to find an appreciative audience in the 1960s. Probably the oddest cartoon character included in the parade is the Reluctant Dragon from Disney's first, nearly-forgotten live action film made in 1941. The holiday festivities and episode end with a candlelight procession and the forming of a living Christmas tree on the steps of the Main Street Station while choirs and the crowd sing an a cappella rendition of "Silent Night." It is a beautiful moment on which to close out the year and set the stage for the holiday.

I remember coming away from that episode blown away and amazed by all the new rides and how futuristic those audio-animatronic figures appeared. It seemed there was nothing that Walt Disney could not do.

But I also watched this episode on that Sunday night in 1966 with a broken and heavy heart for I knew, despite the fact that he was up there on the screen as smiling and welcoming as ever, that—unbelievably, unimaginably—Walt Disney had died just three days before.

"Next year in Disneyland, Walt," I whispered to myself. "Next year."

CHAPTER EIGHT

The Show after Walt

To this day I can recall the shock of Walt Disney's sudden death on December 15, 1966. I found out about it the same way I found out about the assassinations of Martin Luther King Jr. and Robert Kennedy two years later: by watching the evening news. My family would usually finish eating dinner together around the dining room table just in time for the start of the newscast at 6:30pm EST. My mother would turn on the TV and listen as she cleared the dirty dishes from the table and carried them back to the kitchen. My sisters would usually run off to parts unknown in our house, but I would stick around to learn what was happening in the world. And that is how I learned that Walt had died that day from lung cancer.

For a moment, I thought I must have heard wrong. I remember Mom stopping in her task (still wearing the apron she wore when cooking), setting the stack of dirty plates back on the table, and strolling over to sit down and listen. It was the kind of news where everyone stopped what they were doing and gathered around the TV set as we collectively shared the first stage of another national mourning. Even as a young child, I knew what it meant to die. But the fact that Walt Disney had seemed so darn healthy on TV right up to the very last episode made his loss even more shocking. There had been no news that he was ill, no news that he had even been ailing.

Walt Disney's death was the first significant loss I felt in my life, the first time I experienced grief, the first time I felt the world had changed forever and not for the good. I would never see it in quite the same way again.

What made it extra troubling was that Walt continued to "host" the show for months after his death (since he had filmed the introductions in advance), all the way up to "A Salute to Alaska" which aired on April 2, 1967. The effect was comforting and confusing. It was comforting to have more time with Uncle Walt, like having a beloved come back from the dead to talk. But it was also confusing because, well, he was dead. How was he continuing to do the show? Was he sending these segments down from heaven? The concept of filming things way in advance did not occur to my young mind. Still, I valued those remaining introductions that aired in the months following his death.

When the show kicked off its next season in the autumn of 1967, the host introductions were eliminated. I learned years later that the company agonized whether to bring in a new host or not, but decided against it. And speaking as a child of that time, it was the right call to make. I would not have enjoyed having anyone else filling in for Walt. Twenty years later, when Disney CEO Michael Eisner appointed himself the host of ABC's *Disney Sunday Nights*, it still felt awkward and wrong.

The company made one more change beginning with the 1968–1969 season, adopting the new title *The Wonderful World of Disney*. The previous title had outworn its relevance anyway. Walt Disney was no longer with us and there was no longer a need to emphasize color, since color TVs were now prevalent in most living rooms across America (we hung onto our own RCA Victor TV well into the mid-1970s until the channel changer acted up and the picture tube started to go bad).

To make up for the absent host, a new opening credit sequence took its place and the choice of clips says a lot about how the company wanted the public to remember Walt Disney's legacy. The opening began the same way as before, with Tinker Bell setting off the animated fireworks over Sleeping Beauty Castle. It then launched into a montage of clips: Cinderella dancing with her prince from *Cinderella* (1950), the Dumbo ride at Disneyland, the opening dance number from *Babes in Toyland* (1961), a dapper Mickey Mouse in a clip from a 1940s short, the It's a Small World ride, shots of a smiling Walt in a parade at Disneyland, the EPCOT model from Carousel of Progress, Great Moments with Mr. Lincoln, the marching cards from *Alice in Wonderland* (1951), the Russian dance segment from *Fantasia* (1940), the dancing chimney sweeps from *Mary Poppins* (1964), the Disneyland monorail speeding along its tracks, the Seven Dwarfs on parade, the Mad Tea Party ride, Davy Crockett's profile, clips from the True-Life Adventures documentaries, and the march of the wooden soldiers from *Babes in Toyland*. Underscoring it all was the theme song made up of stanzas from "Some Day My Prince Will Come," "Whistle While You Work," "When You Wish upon a Star" (underscoring the clips of Walt and EPCOT), "Chim Chim Cheree," "Ballad of Davy Crockett," and "March of the Wooden Soldiers."

The effect produced a combination of hopefulness and nostalgia, but also a feeling, intentional or not, that the best days of the show and the company were in the past. Whatever else happened, it was always going to be a pale imitation of what Walt would have done. The show was now making us look forward to what lay ahead while at the same time having us look backward at what was and what could have been.

It conjured up a dual expectation within us children watching that we did not really understand at the time, but learned as we got older, that they were the first pangs of adulthood growing inside of us.

Ironically, the unexpected death of Walt Disney set up an expectation in both the company he left behind and the viewing audience that would play out over the next several years. John F. Kennedy's shocking assassination in 1963 galvanized our country to fulfill his wish that we land a man on the moon before the end of the decade. Walt's shocking death had a similar effect, the expectation that his company would honor his passing by seeing his final dreams to completion:

- Complete Pirates of the Caribbean in Disneyland's New Orleans Square while also updating Tomorrowland to include rides like the PeopleMover, Carousel of Progress (with its EPCOT model), Adventures in Inner Space, and the Rocket Jets.
- Finish the Haunted Mansion perched on the hill between New Orleans Square and Frontierland.
- Build Disney World in Florida.
- Bring Walt's final dream to life—Phase 2 of Disney World, the Experimental Prototype Community of Tomorrow (EPCOT).

I first heard of EPCOT the same way most of us did, through newspaper articles covering Roy Disney's February 2, 1967, announcement about the plans for Disney World. I could not read yet, but I remember the concept art very well, especially that shimmering view of the EPCOT skyline off in the distance like some futuristic city on a hill. Even as a small boy, I knew this was borderline utopia stuff, the kind of idealistic vision that usually did not match reality. But, frankly, I didn't care. Walt wanted to build a city of the future? Yes, I was in.

The World of Disney would take us along for the ride over the next few years as we watched three of the four dreams triumphantly achieved. None of it surprised us since, as Walt proclaimed many times, "anything is possible at Disneyland," and I still believed anything was possible at The Walt Disney Company and at WED Enterprises.

Disneyland: From Pirates of the Caribbean to the World of Tomorrow (1968)

TV Premiere: January 21, 1968

The next step forward came with this episode. The occasion was the opening of Pirates of the Caribbean in New Orleans Square and the debut of the new Tomorrowland, a major renovation designed to bring that future world forward from the now outdated future of the 1950s to the more contemporary looking future of the 1960s.

Seeing Pirates of the Caribbean was especially enjoyable. We'd been following it over the previous three or four years, from concept to completion. The episode even featured clips from the *Disneyland 10th Anniversary Show* where Walt proudly showed off the ride models at WED to tour guide Julie Riehm. Now we got to see it come to life.

Just the fact that we were back in Disneyland was enough to put me in ecstasy. Looking back at the episode, I am surprised by how much of the ride they highlighted on the show, practically the entire thing. It still made me antsy to get to the Blue Bayou and crawl aboard the ride itself—something I would not do until 1980.

But the part I found more intriguing was the new Tomorrowland. Here we were taking a tour on the new PeopleMover going from building to building and previewing each attraction—in particular, the Carousel of Progress, just arrived from the New York World's Fair, and its model for EPCOT intrigued me. As the narration promised:

> There's a great big beautiful tomorrow and you can get a view of tomorrow: a model city of the future. It's based on a concept developed by Walt Disney for a community he called EPCOT (Experimental Prototype Community of Tomorrow). Realistic to the smallest detail, this animated model is a living blueprint of new ideas and systems for future cities. The concept for EPCOT is one part of Walt Disney's master plan for the future Disney World in Florida, the city of tomorrow possible today with the technology and imagination of American industry.

No, the future had not yet arrived, but I could sense it getting closer.

Disneyland Showtime (1970)

TV Premiere: March 22, 1970

This was the last of the great *World of Disney* episodes set at the park. This time, celebrities gathered to share the opening of the Haunted Mansion. For me, this was even more fascinating than the opening of Pirates of the Caribbean, since I have always had a love for ghosts and spooky stuff.

On hand for the fun was Disney star Kurt Russell. The Osmond Brothers were back, older and now with their young brother (and teen idol) Donny. Rounding out the episode cast was actress E.J. Peaker from *Hello, Dolly!* (1969).

The episode proved another fun tour of Disneyland at arguably its height, teetering on the edge between what Walt designed and what the Imagineers would do with it without his guidance. The premise is that Kurt, E.J. Peaker, and the Osmonds all have shows to do, but all of them, and Donny in particular, keep stealing away. They just want to have fun and ride the rides, with Haunted Mansion number one on the list.

Remembering back to 1970, it was the musical numbers that hung in my memory. The Osmond Brothers singing "Down on the Corner" (a contemporary hit for Creedence Clearwater Revival) as they rode the omnibus up Main Street, U.S.A., E.J. Peaker singing "It Must Be Him," Tomorrowland Terrace's Kids of the Kingdom belting out "This Land Is Your Land" on that rising stage that came out of the floor, Kurt Russell singing "Sugar Sugar" (the number one hit of 1969) while wearing the same double-breasted jacket and turtleneck sweater he wore in *The Computer Wore Tennis Shoes* (1969), and finally the Osmonds closing out the concert with "Aquarius" from *Hair*. Popular music had come a long way since the performances of Annette Funicello and Bobby Rydell, or even the Osmonds from earlier in the decade.

Finally, everyone went in the Haunted Mansion—the thing I had been waiting the entire episode to see. It looked as scary and innovative and wonderful as Walt had promised it would be five years before.

At the time, my sisters were more excited about seeing the Osmond Brothers. The park and the ride mostly excited me. I even liked the twist at the end of the episode when Donny goes missing. Maybe the ghosts in the mansion had grabbed him? Maybe he just doesn't want to leave the park ever ever ever? I could relate to that, even though I had not been there yet.

Disneyland Showtime marked the last major episode centered around Walt's original Magic Kingdom. As the 1970s progressed, *World of Disney* would have fewer and fewer episodes set at the parks, and when it did, the episode would invariably be set in that newer kingdom to the east, in Florida. Disneyland receded as a focus for the show just as Walt himself slowly receded as the center of both the show and the company he founded.

And yet his influence and his hopes and dreams never truly faded away. As journalist Eric Sevareid said back in 1966 in a special introduction that aired before *Disneyland around the Seasons*:

> It would take more time than anybody has...to think of the right thing to say about Walt Disney. He was an original; not just an American original but an original, period. He was a happy accident; one of the happiest this century has experienced; and judging by the way it's been behaving in spite of all Disney tried to tell it about laughter, love, children, puppies, and sunrises, the century hardly deserved him.
>
> He probably did more to heal or at least to soothe troubled human spirits than all the psychiatrists in the world. But what

Walt Disney seemed to know was that while there is very little grown-up in a child, there is a lot of child in every grown-up. To a child this weary world is brand new, gift wrapped. Disney tried to keep it that way for adults. By the conventional wisdom, mighty mice, flying elephants, Snow White and Happy, Grumpy, Sneezy, and Dopey, all these were fantasy, escapism from reality. It's a question of whether they are any less real, any more fantastic than intercontinental missiles, poisoned air, defoliated forests, and scraps from the moon. This is the age of fantasy, however you look at it, but Disney's fantasy wasn't lethal. People are saying we'll never see his like again.

And we haven't. But even then I knew I had to do what the rest of the world was doing: move on and grow up. Close the door on childhood, but keep Walt's memories and lessons locked securely inside my heart and mind while still believing in the great big beautiful tomorrow.

Fads and Evolutions

One family doesn't spend a decade and a half sharing the same meal with the same menu every Sunday night without a few fads, variations, and evolutions intruding. As mentioned during the previous commercial break, the making of pizza remained the same, but the ingredients evolved through the years. The only distinctive fad or variation I can recall was our flirtation with pizza burgers in the early 1970s.

I don't recall how pizza burgers got started other than probably a desire to change up the menu a bit. The idea might have come from us children as I remember pizza burgers being on the hot lunch menu at school. Mom decided to make only one pizza each week and the other would be a tray of pizza burgers. As I recall, pizza burgers were nothing more than your basic pizza ingredients, only instead of a crust she spread them on half of a hamburger bun or a hot dog bun. Mom may even have used a hoagie bun which I guess would have made them pizza bread instead of pizza burgers. We did that for a year, then went back to two pizzas.

Evolution of Popcorn

The popcorn we made didn't change so much through the years as how we popped it. Dad started with a basic bag of popcorn kernels. He poured some vegetable oil into our Mirro Rocket Ship Electric Popcorn Popper, then poured the kernels in on top. While the popcorn popped, Dad melted a half stick of butter on the stove. When the popcorn was ready, he poured it into the family popcorn bowl (used for no other purpose), poured the butter on top, and then mixed it all together. Yum! Better than any synthetic popcorn butter you can get these days at a movie theater.

Occasionally, we kids convinced our parents to try another kind of popcorn, like those popular stovetop popcorns that pop in a jiffy (hint, hint), but they never tasted as good and burned way more often. Soon enough we would return to Dad's way of making it.

I vividly recall the day in the mid-1970s when the Mirro popcorn maker started going bad. It felt like one of our favorite pets was dying. Dad tried fixing the fraying electrical cord as best as he could, but it never really worked as well after that and was a fire just waiting to happen. When the heating element in the lower half started acting up as well, we knew it was time to let it go. We did not bury it in our backyard, but it felt like one of our dogs or cats had left the family when we tossed it in the garbage.

Our replacement was a West Bend Stir Crazy Automatic Popcorn Popper. It was great because it actually had a little rod that rotated around to mix the popcorn and the oil as it popped. Dad then loaded the butter in a compartment in the lid. The heat of the oil caused the butter to melt and drip down on the popcorn as it popped. It made more than the Mirro did.

For a while, we flirted with the Wearever Popcorn Pumper because air popcorn was supposedly healthier, or so they told us in the 1970s. Eventually, we went back to the West Bend popper. We used it until it went bad sometime in the 1980s. We have used microwave popcorn ever since.

Soda-ology, or Pop Goes the Choices

Probably no area of Pizza Night evolved more than the soda we used to drink. This seemed to be the one area where each of us could express our individual preferences. Of course, we had the basic caramel sodas and we had to have one of each because one sister preferred Coca-Cola while the other preferred Pepsi-Cola. I liked either, but if I had to decide which to have on a deserted island, I would ask you to hand me a Coke. I grew to like Dr. Pepper, partly because I liked the taste and partly because of that catchy commercial tune they had in the 1970s: "I'm a pepper... you're a pepper...she's a pepper." You get the idea. Tab also had a taste that I liked. Dad liked to have RC Cola around, but not all the time.

Mom was not a huge soda drinker, but when she did drink it, she would have Sprite or Fresca. We all enjoyed 7 Up—"the Un-cola" as actor Geoffrey Holder called it in the commercials. For a few years in the 1970s, Pepsi made a Pepsi Light that added a taste of lemon to their cola. Mom loved it. I loved it. But not enough other people did and it was discontinued after a few years.

We experimented with all kinds of root beer, from Shasta to A&W. In the mid- to late 1960s, we all drank Mountain Dew because it had just arrived on the market and we thought the hillbilly logo was funny. When we found out we were moving to West Virginia in 1968, we joked that we were finally going to find out where Mountain Dew was made.

I dabbled sometimes with fruity sodas like Orange Crush or all the flavors of Nehi not to mention Fanta sodas like grape and orange. My favorite was Fanta red cream soda. Its brilliancy of taste was only eclipsed by the difficulty in finding it. But I do believe it is the only drink they serve in Heaven.

Desserts

We always had something sweet for dessert, but it was not always candy bars. Sometimes, Mom would make a pan of fudge. Other times she would make blonde brownies or chocolate chip cookies or "on top of the stove" cookies. She would also occasionally make those peanut butter cookies with a Hershey kiss on top.

After Halloween or Easter, we would have the candy in our baskets to dip into.

But our favorite Sunday night dessert was S'mores. Mom made them upstairs in the oven. I think she tended to not make them often because they were very messy and very gooey and Mom hated messes of any sort. So we did the best we could with them and cherished the lucky times we got to eat them.

All this while watching *The Wonderful World of Disney* play out on our TV screen each Sunday night.

CHAPTER NINE

Solving a Mystery

What kid doesn't want to solve a mystery? What is it that children find intriguing about mysteries anyway? I suspect they like them because solving a mystery is one of our first chances to show adults we can do something on our own, demonstrate ourselves as resourceful and contributing members of society, and prove that something is there that adults are too preoccupied to see and get a bit of a thrill off the danger. Plus, it adds a little color to our otherwise ordinary lives. Growing up, nothing was as intriguing as a Disney mystery.

Emil and the Detectives (1964)

TV Premiere: September 11, 18, 1966

Based on the classic children's book of the same name, this movie tells the story of Emil, a young German boy taking a solo bus trip for the first time to visit his grandparents in Berlin. While riding on the bus, his envelope of money meant for his grandmother gets stolen by a thief. Rather than facing the wrath of his elders, Emil gets off the bus and sets off to get his money back. Along the way, he stumbles onto a group of child detectives willing to help him. He also discovers that his thief is part of a larger criminal enterprise plotting to rob a major Berlin bank. Emil and the boys set out to spoil their plan.

There was a lot about this two-parter that engaged me from the beginning. The first thing was how much Emil (Bryan Russell) reminded me of me: a solitary boy without a lot of friends alone in a big city. If you want to see me as I was, look no further than Emil. A bit fussy, a bit of a stick in the mud, with a clear sense of what is right or wrong, he is also a tad defensive, wary of strangers, and always operating with his guard up. He wants to fit in with the boys, but knows letting his guard down usually leads to embarrassment and humiliation. I was (and in some ways still am) Emil.

I may have been Emil, but I wanted to be Gustav Fleishmann, the Artful Dodger of this story. It was the performance of Roger Mobley as Gustav that made me (and thousands of other boys) feel the same way. Maybe it says something about Mobley's performance that I failed to notice when he became Disney's Gallegher, cub reporter, the following year.

Gustav is a jack-of-all-trades. What do you need him to be? A tour guide? A private detective? If there is money in it, Gustave can do it. Or at least convince us that he can. Gustav's pint-sized detectives take Emil's case and they solve it despite the lack of interest from the "brass buttons," i.e., police and patronizing grown ups, or the biggest problem of all, the interference of big sisters who delay the investigation by spending hours chatting on the phone with boyfriends and then with their girlfriends talking about their boyfriends.

I loved the exotic location of Berlin in the 1960s, the experience of being in a foreign land and noting the differences in restaurants, police comportment, and apartments. It surprised me that Berlin still had wreckage, collapsed buildings and other rubble left over from World War II which had ended twenty years before.

I liked the one kid detective passing the time by reading the Classics Illustrated version of *Jane Eyre*. That would be me, too. I also liked how the criminals were threatening but not too dangerous.

Though I could not put my finger on it at the time, I now appreciate how director Peter Tewkesbury gave the film the look and feel of a Roald Dahl story. The villains, the adults, and the industrial town setting remind me of similar elements in other Dahl movies like *Willy Wonka & the Chocolate Factory* (1971) and *Chitty, Chitty, Bang, Bang* (1968)—two of the best non-Disney children's films ever made which are often mistaken by the public to be Disney films.

I liked how, when things turn against them and are looking bad, the kid detectives realize they are in over their heads and must involve the police, even over Gustav's objections. "You're still playing detective," Emil's teenaged cousin (and cub reporter) Penny admonishes him, "and acting like you're on television or in the movies or something."

Last of all, I liked how the kid detectives could rally the children of Berlin to defeat the bank robbers at the end. It was another example that if we worked together, there was nothing we could not do, even kids, even in a world full of "shrinks" (adults).

Emil and the Detectives began my love affair with kid detectives solving crimes that adults could not or would not, and taking on the cases that adults felt were beneath them. Years later, when I first started writing, my initial short stories were about a group of kid detectives working to solve crimes in their small West Virginia city. There was more than a little bit of *Emil* in those stories.

Gallegher (1965)
TV Premiere: July 25; August 1, 8, 1965

The Further Adventures of Gallegher (1966)
TV Premiere: June 19, 26; July 3, 1966

Gallegher Goes West (1966)
TV Premiere: October 23, 30, 1966

Gallegher: Tragedy On the Trail (1967)
TV Premiere: January 29; February 5, 1967

Gallegher: The Mystery of Edward Sims (1968)
TV Premiere: March 31; April 7, 1968

In the world of teenage Disney sleuths, there were few more popular than Gallegher, a boy in his early teens who worked as a copy boy for *The Daily Press* newspaper in an unnamed big city (possibly Philadelphia) in the final decade of the 19th century, but who dreams of being a star reporter. His refusal to wait till he grows up and his persistence in solving big stories that make headlines draws the ire (and quiet admiration) of his boss, city editor Mr. Crowley (Edmund O'Brien). Gallegher manages to find support among the newspaper's real reporters including Brownie (Harvey Korman before *The Carol Burnett Show*) and Adeline Jones (Anne Francis), another person in the same career situation as Gallegher. She also dreams of becoming a big city reporter, but, in her case, Crowley only assigns her the stories women are supposed to handle—society stories, gossip columns, and advice to the lovelorn.

Based on the 1891 book by Richard Harding Davis, the first three-part adventure finds Gallegher trying to prove he has the skills of a reporter by solving a bank robbery. Along the way, he clears the police chief of bribery charges, and proves that a famous western bandit, Zip Wyatt (Dean Fredericks), is behind another bank robbery.

The story affirms that children make great detectives because they see things that adults don't. Adults are too caught up in their day-to-day concerns (a metaphor for the hands-off style of parenting back then) to notice what should be obvious and it takes a child to bring these things to their attention. Crowley is less a big-city editor and more a typical father of the time who wished children would be seen and not heard.

The Further Adventures of Gallegher finds Gallegher in familiar straits. Still trying to prove to Crowley that he is more than a copy boy, he sniffs out more cases to solve. The first story lands in his lap when fellow reporter Brownie gives a bad review to visiting actor Richard Westby's (Peter Wyngarde) performance in a new production of Shakespeare's *Hamlet*. Westby challenges Brownie to a duel. When

Westby is found dead before the showdown, Brownie becomes the main suspect. Gallegher must clear his friend. For the second case, he teams up with Adeline Jones to solve the mystery of a con man going around town breaking widows' hearts and stealing their money. In the last mystery, a series of gas line explosions around town hint at graft and corruption at city hall. When Crowley gets arrested for libel for publishing such a story, Gallegher sets out to clear his name.

Gallegher Goes West follows the familiar 1960s TV trend when westerns were all the rage: it sends our favorite kid sleuth out west. Frustrated that, after such a successful track record, Crowley still refuses to make him a full reporter, Gallegher travels to Brimstone, Arizona, where he has convinced the editor of the *Brimstone Blast* to make him one. Unfortunately, once the editor (John McIntire) gets a look at the age (or lack thereof) of his new reporter, Gallegher finds himself on the street once more and having to prove himself once again. Fortunately, an old colleague from back east, Detective Snead (Ray Teal), is in town. He and Gallegher team up to bring the Sundown Kid (Dennis Weaver) to justice. Later episodes find Gallegher battling city corruption (again) and fraudulent land claims. He even finds time for a bit of romance with local girl Laurie Carlson (Darleen Carr).

The last installment of the series, *The Mystery of Edward Sims*, finds Gallegher coming to the aid of an immigrant family newly arrived in Brimstone with a land claim that turns out to be fraudulent, signed by a fictional land agent named Edward Sims. When the family refuses to leave town till the mystery is solved, Gallegher pledges to find out who the real culprit is.

Gallegher is just plain fun. Perhaps it was the bouncy barbershop quartet theme song written by the Sherman brothers that makes it that way or maybe it was just the style in Gallegher's walk. Roger Mobley returns from *Emil and the Detectives* and his take on Gallegher is not too different from the way he played Gustave in the previous film. This time around, though, Gallegher is less cocky than Gustave. There is less of an aura of the used car salesman, jack-of-all-trades, and con man. He is just as stubbornly sure of himself as Gustave, but this time around Mobley combines his force of personality with a bit of Irish charm. It also didn't hurt that Roger Mobley became a bit of a teen idol at the time with lots of teenaged girls falling for that charm.

Like many a resourceful Disney child, Gallegher is practically an orphan—all he says is that he comes from a family of twelve so he has experience in getting himself noticed. Later, when out west, he confides to Laurie Carlson that he has no first name. His name is just "Gallegher" because that is the only name anyone ever called him. It seems Walt Disney saw a lot of himself in the character—a boy with big dreams unwilling to settle for the role his parents, adults, or big business wanted to force on him. When he couldn't achieve his dream in the big cities of Chicago or Kansas City, Walt (like Gallegher) headed west to achieve those dreams.

Maybe *Gallegher* remains popular because he became the symbol for us Baby Boomers (both male and female) of how we wished to be seen: determined, resourceful, and valued by our community. And maybe end up with a girl at the end. Cue that theme song!

The Secret of Boyne Castle (1969)

TV Premiere: February 9, 16, 23, 1969

This mystery is just a good old-fashioned chase movie filled with all the dramatic elements young boys like me loved. Rich Evans (Kurt Russell)—he even has the right first name!—is an American student attending a private school in Ireland. One day, a wounded man stumbles out of the heather while Rich is practicing with the school's lacrosse team. The man urges Rich to search his room at nearby Boyne Castle and then contact Rich's brother, Tom. Rich finds this very confusing because his brother Tom Evans (Glenn Corbett) is just a salesman for an American steel company.

Of course, it turns out that Rich's brother is really a secret agent for the U.S. government and he is in Ireland to help a Russian scientist defect to the west, a common event during the Cold War. And, naturally, there are enemy agents involved to prevent such a thing from happening. Rich and his friend Sean O'Connor (Patrick Dawson) are unlucky pawns caught in the middle. Soon enough, they team up with Tom in a race across the Emerald Isle to reach Boyne Castle before the bad guys, with turncoats a-plenty to bar their way.

Boyne Castle was another three-part episode on *World of Disney* like *Scarecrow of Romney Marsh*. What I liked about this story is its secret agent feel. This is as close to a James Bond thriller that Disney ever made, with the stakes for world peace appropriately high. The Irish locations were appealingly exotic while still including enough touches of real people leading real lives to make it believable. The perils Rich and Sean found themselves in seemed a bit more threatening than in the average Disney film. The arch villain Kersner (Alfred Burke) seemed more ruthless and psychopathic than the usual Disney bad guy. There were even a few glamorous girls along the way to help Rich and Sean, like Kathleen, the waitress at a local pub.

The scene I most remember is the climax where Rich and Sean defeat the enemy spies by dropping cannonballs from a helicopter on their escaping speedboat. The falling metal projectiles smash right through

the hull and the bad guys are soon scrambling for their lives. I particularly remember Kersner the senior spy clinging to the shattered hull
and screaming like a scared little boy, "I can't swim!" as the wreck goes
under. Oh, how the mighty fall!

In the end, Rich proves to his older brother that he has the stuff to
be an agent and that he is not a little boy anymore. Tom accepts him as
an equal (which is really the point of mysteries: to prove we have the
brains and guts to take our place among the adults) and there are hints
of more adventures for the brothers in the future.

Secrets of the Pirate's Inn (1969)

TV Premiere: November 23, 30, 1969

My favorite pair of mystery episodes on *World of Disney* is two shows
set on the bayou, possibly Louisiana, near the small town of Calio Bay.
This time, our intrepid detectives were twelve-year-old Scott Durden
(Jimmy Bracken), his best friend Wilbur "Catfish" Jones (Patrick
Creamer), and Scott's younger sister Tippy (Annie McEveety).

Scott is their natural leader able to catch the inconsistencies
between what people are saying and what they are doing. Catfish is the
comic relief. He is the guy who is not quite as brave as the others and
yet gets shoved forward by his friends to investigate a strange dark
room or to strike up a conversation with a stranger. Catfish also has
an artistic side. Many times in both episodes he claims he must run
off for a violin lesson. In one scene, we see him recite a poem he has
written. Catfish works as the audience surrogate on screen.

Tippy has an air of no-nonsense around her. Especially in the first
mystery, she knows she is only part of the team because the two boys
can't run fast enough to ditch her. She is also the level-headed member
of the trio. When the other two get carried away with their impossible
solutions to a mystery, Tippy brings them back to earth with com-
mon-sense insights about how what they are proposing is not possible.
She also has a greater faith in adults and human nature than the other
two. She tends to see beneath the hard surface adults project and per-
ceives their true sentiment. We can tell that the three children like
each other and have each other's backs. Rounding out the team is Scott
and Tippy's dog, Tramp, a typical Disney mutt.

Secrets of the Pirate's Inn is set during summer vacation. Adults forget
that summer used to be spent trying to figure out how to fill long, hot,
empty days. Scott and Catfish have decided to spend the time checking
out the new resident at the abandoned inn on the shore of the bayou. The
resident turns out to be Captain McCarthy (Ed Begley), a retired sailor
who has inherited the place from his late brother. For years, McCarthy's

brother searched the grounds and rooms of the inn, convinced that the treasure of pirate Jean Lafitte lay buried there. The children strike up a friendship with the old man and the four of them are soon enough following the clues and searching the house for the treasure.

Complicating things are a series of unsolved break ins and the disappearance of valuable clues. Carl Buchanan (Charles Aidman), a reporter from out of town, offers his help. And then there is Mr. Padgett (Paul Fix), the crusty curmudgeon who rents the shack behind the inn. Both men seem to have more on their minds than helping. The treasure is found, and that is when the other characters begin to show their true colors.

What I found intriguing about *Pirate's Inn* upon its premiere was the basic mystery, and how the children systemically solved the clues along the way. I enjoyed the enormous number of secret passages in this small inn, from the hidden sliding door that led to a passage within the walls to the fake wine barrel in the basement that led to a hidden staircase and an underground cave to the sea. The twists and turns were just so fascinating. Scenes remained vivid in my imagination, like the ambush under the covered bridge and the shot of the abandoned speedboat carrying the treasure out to sea.

The episode taught me to beware of adults who are just a little too eager to smile and make friends with you, especially when they also ask too many questions about what you are up to. Authority figures like Sheriff Wiley (Bill Zuckert) are again too busy to give much credence to what children have to say. They assume children are just playing and intent on distracting them from adult things that need to get done. But it also taught me that children should believe in themselves and follow the clues even if it meant taking risks and standing up for what they believe to be right.

Soon enough, I was hanging out in my imagination with Catfish and Tippy, though not with Scott. I had somehow replaced him as leader of the group. In my mind, we ran around the confines of Calio Bay, finding treasure everywhere.

More importantly, I began writing down the adventures I had with Catfish and Tippy, the mysteries we were solving. It was the beginning of my writing career.

The Strange Monster of Strawberry Cove (1971)

TV Premiere: October 31; November 7, 1971

I still remember the joy I felt when at the end of one week's episode, the teaser for next week promised more adventures for Scott, Catfish, and Tippy. It didn't hurt that it was dealing with a strange sea creature.

By then I was already intrigued by the mystery of the Loch Ness Monster. Here were my favorite pint-sized detectives (and imaginary best friends) taking on one of my favorite crypto-creature mysteries. Sorry, Bigfoot!. It didn't hurt that part one of the episode was aired on Halloween. Sorry, Sleepy Hollow!

Summer was over and the kids are back in school. Being a small town, Calio Bay has a one-room schoolhouse presided over by the town's popular teacher, Mr. Mead (Burgess Meredith). The students are abuzz because that weekend is the annual overnight class trip to nearby Strawberry Cove. Less exciting is that their class will be accompanied by the local female bird watchers headed by stuffy old Miss Pringle (Agnes Moorehead). One night after everyone has gone to bed, Mr. Mead wanders down to the shore for a nighttime smoke. Standing there, he (and we viewers) appear to see a sea monster shaped like Nessie swim by.

When news gets around Calio Bay of what Mr. Mead saw, he is labeled as a quack. A citizen's group led by Miss Pringle urges the mayor (Parley Bauer) to declare him unfit and remove him from his teaching post. Scott, Catfish, and Tippy come to Mead's defense by creating a fake monster built around a rowboat and employing a twin bike to steer and power it through the water. Soon enough, the kids' fake monster is making news, but the only person who sees it is the already under suspicion Mr. Mead.

What no one realizes is that the "monster" Mead first saw was a loaded swamp boat that appeared to have the shape of a monster due to the fog. The swamp boat is operated by a pair of criminals intent on smuggling stolen Mexican antiquities into the U.S. News of the monster threatens their operation and they are eager to keep it all quiet.

Once again, Sheriff Wiley labels the children as "just a bunch of kids letting their imaginations run wild." But the trio soon convince him that something odd is going on down at the cove. For some reason, I found their tape recording done in a slowed-down voice and played over the pay phone when they call the sheriff to be endlessly hilarious as only a nine year old can: "Sheriff Wiley, this is a friend. Come to Strawberry Cove tonight if you want to see the monster." For weeks afterward, I would walk around and muttered that message to myself either under my breath or out loud when I was alone and laugh myself silly.

Of course, everything works out in the end. The criminals are caught. The real boss behind the operation is revealed. Mr. Mead is reinstated as the kids' teacher. Miss Pringle is shown up as the thoughtless busybody she is. There is nothing for Mr. Mead to do but dance a jig down the street. The whole thing was a fitting sequel to *Pirates' Inn*. I hoped there would be more adventures with Scott, Catfish, and Tippy, but there were not.

The Mystery in Dracula's Castle (1973)

TV Premiere: January 7, 14, 1973

This mystery also hooked me from the moment it premiered on the show, maybe because it starred Johnny Whittaker. I had first seen him on TV in the sitcom *Family Affair* before he starred in several Disney movies including *Napoleon and Samantha* (1972). It might also have been that this was the period in my life when I first discovered Dracula and this story came along at just the right time.

Dracula's Castle tells the tale of two brothers who have arrived in a small coastal town for the summer and need to find something to fill their time while their single mom author (Mariette Hartley) finishes her latest mystery novel. Alfie Booth (Johnny Whittaker) is an aspiring filmmaker with dreams of taking his Super 8 camera and making the scariest Dracula movie of all. He has drafted his younger brother Leonard (Scott Kolden) to play the part of Dracula. To keep the boys out of trouble, their mom has hired the sheriff's daughter Jean (Maggie Wellman) to watch over them. Alfie quickly co-opts Jean by casting her as the object of Dracula's romantic intentions.

The only problem is that Leonard is not too interested in playing the famous vampire. He would rather be another major literary figure, Sherlock Holmes. Leonard loves mysteries and sees them everywhere, usually around the town jewelry store owned by grumpy Bill Wasdahl (John Fiedler) who doesn't seem to like children. Leonard adopts a local stray dog to be his sidekick and appropriately names him Watson. One day while shooting on the beach, the brothers discover an old lighthouse that Alfie is convinced will make the perfect Dracula's castle for his film.

Unfortunately, the lighthouse is the headquarters for a pair of art thieves and forgers named Keith (Clu Gulager) and Noah (Mills Watson). When the boys' movie-making crosses paths with their criminal enterprise, the thieves pretend to help the brothers make their movie, even as they prepare to meet evil Mr. Big to fence their latest stolen goods. Jean even falls for Keith's laidback good looks while Alfie is just thrilled to have this major location and someone to hold the lights while they film.

In the end, Leonard's fledgling detective skills reveal their supposed friends for who they really are. Mr. Big gets exposed as well, and Alfie gets his movie which comes to an explosive climax atop Dracula's castle. It all adds up to an exciting summer that will make a great essay on "What I Did Last Summer" when they return to school in the fall.

I remember being especially intrigued by the lighthouse. Alfie is right; it *is* a creepy setting. Perhaps it is the loner in me, but I have always found the privacy of lighthouses comforting—being cut off from the world, left to do my own thing with the only responsibility being to turn on the light at night so as to provide a beacon to keep ships off the rocks below. It still sounds like a cool job to me.

Michael O'Hara the Fourth (1972)

TV Premiere: March 26; April 2, 1972

A contemporary stand for feminism and equality, this unusual detective story followed the exploits of Mike O'Hara IV, a fourth-generation descendent of a long line of distinguished police officers. Mike IV would desperately love to join the illustrious ranks of their family's predecessors. The only problem is, yep, Mike O'Hara IV (Jo Ann Harris) is a woman and so her police detective father, Michael O'Hara III (Dan Dailey), will not allow her to become a cop.

That was the state of male-female relationships back in the early 1970s. Fortunately, Mike IV has all the personality traits that made the previous O'Hara's successful: stubbornness and determination. With the help of her friend Norman (Michael McGreevey), who would like to be more than just friends, Mike goes around town trying to solve crimes as an unofficial private detective. Unfortunately, most of her "cases" turn out to be not genuine crimes but misunderstandings that leave Mike apologizing to her father who in turn looks bad to his fellow cops.

In the first episode, "To Trap a Thief," Mike tries to expose a counterfeiting ring only to have her plan go embarrassingly awry. The second episode, "The Deceptive Detective," finds Mike and Norman trying to solve a murder. When she attempts to blackmail her suspect, her bungling only succeeds in framing her father then having to clear his name.

This was another *World of Disney* episode I remember but could not locate a copy to watch for the book. What I recall about this show, besides its fun hijinks, are the winning performances of Jo Ann Harris as the resourceful, well-meaning, but prone to jump the gun Michael the IV; the exasperated yet still loving performance of veteran Dan Dailey as her police captain father; and Disney vet Michael McGreevey as Norman, the ever-hopeful best friend who never seems to get around to saying what he feels.

The other thing I remember is the novelty of having a female lead as the detective and not just the tagalong sister of the male lead. For ten-year-old me, this was a sign of progress in society, that women were just as capable as men of solving crimes. The smiling face of Jo Ann Harris was a harbinger that women were going to make tremendous strides in the 1970s and I was looking forward to seeing equality become the norm in society.

The Whiz Kid and the Mystery of Riverton (1974)

TV Premiere: January 6, 13, 1974

In the mid-1970s, the biggest child actors were Eric Shea and Kim Richards. Eric was a member of the Shea family of acting brothers. Both his older brother Chris and his younger brother Stephen had provided the voice of Linus in the *Peanuts* TV specials. Eric had appeared in popular movies like *Yours, Mine and Ours* (1968) and the box office blockbuster *The Poseidon Adventure* (1972) alongside Gene Hackman and Ernest Borgnine. He had also made dozens of guest appearances on TV shows, from *Batman* to *Little House on the Prairie.*

Kim Richards had broken through in the early 1970s sitcom *Nanny and the Professor*, guest starred on hit TV shows, and would go on to star in the Disney movie *Escape to Witch Mountain* (1975). She too came from an acting family with her younger sister Kyle Richards already acting in films and TV.

In *Whiz Kid*, Shea plays Alvin Fernald the local brainiac in the town of Riverton. Like so many other juvenile fiction boys, he has a basement laboratory where he invents things to make life easier, like a bicycle-mounted newspaper launcher and other things to help him solve crimes. Of course, his inventions tend to break or get out of hand. Alvin the Whiz Kid is a prototype for future cartoon shows like *Dexter's Laboratory* and *Jimmy Neutron, Boy Genius*. In all these shows, creative boys without any discernible athletic talent fantasize about using their brain power to earn them fame and recognition.

Alvin works with his sidekick Shoie (Clay O'Brien) while Richards plays his younger sister Daphne "Daffy" Fernald. Daffy is another younger sister looking to tag along, but the boys view her as more of an irritant. Attempts to keep her out of his basement lab are thwarted when she simply slides down the coal chute (shades of another pesky blonde-haired sister in *Dexter's Laboratory*). While I shared Alvin's love for solving crimes and puzzles, I most identified with Daffy. Being the youngest in my circle of siblings and cousins, I was constantly tagging along and trying to be a part of their older group, while constantly being told I was too young and too much of a pain.

For *Mystery of Riverton*, Alvin finds himself knee deep in government corruption. While doing research for an essay contest on how to improve city government, Alvin overhears the treasurer planning to defraud city hall of $150,000. Naturally, he can't prove it nor do Mayor Massey (Edward Andrews) or any other city officials believe him.

When Alvin wins the essay contest and becomes mayor for a day, he enlists his fellow classmates to use the forces of government to track down and arrest the wrong-doers. There are a number of twists and turns. Daphne gets temporarily kidnapped, but cleverly turns the tables on the bad guys and uses her plight to signal Alvin and Shoie about her location. When the city treasurer and his henchmen are forced to flee on bicycles, the students roll tires down on them until they surrender. Alvin earns a large reward that he then shares with his teacher and fellow classmates. He also welcomes his sister into their "inner circle" as a valued (and equal) partner.

What strikes me looking back at the show are the small details that I shared with Alvin and his bunch. They ride around town on their bikes. Alvin's is the popular banana bike of its time (named after the shape of its seat)—a bike myself and dozens of my friends rode down our streets and around our towns. Shoie's bike is modeled after Peter Fonda's chopper in *Easy Rider* (1969).

The fact that they are even taking a civics class in school on how government works dates the show since civics is no longer a part of most public school curriculums. That the subject of the essay contest is "How to Improve City Government" seems appropriate in an era when the Watergate scandal had cast doubt on the ethics of all government at both the state and federal levels.

I laughed at the teen chauvinism of Alvin and Shoie refusing to let Daffy tag along. "I don't think we should tell her," Alvin advises as they start off to investigate a lead, "this is a man's job!" Fortunately, he proves that the younger males can still be educated when he invites his sister to join them for celebratory ice cream at the end.

Popular character and voice actor John Fiedler turns up again as the villain. This time, he plays the corrupt treasurer trying to scam the city. He kidnaps children. He bosses inept underlings around. This is a scary dude!

Of course, Alvin and his kid allies win the day. The bad guys are caught and faith in Riverton government is restored. Once again, it is the children saving the day, and isn't that how it is supposed to be: the young saving the old?

The Whiz Kid and the Carnival Caper (1976)

TV Premiere: January 11, 18, 1976

Whiz Kid and the Mystery of Riverton proved popular enough to warrant a sequel two years later. What a difference two years makes! Eric Shea's voice has changed. He is no longer a geeky, know-it-all kid but a gangly, know-it-all on the verge of teen-dom. Alvin and Shoie have traded in their previous bicycles for trendier mid-1970s models. Alvin's banana bike has been replaced by a ten-speed. Shoie's *Easy Rider* chopper is now a mountain bike.

Alvin is still interested in mysteries and inventions, but he is also now interested in girls, particularly the lovely and newly moved-in neighbor Cathy (played by Jaclyn Smith just before she gained stardom in *Charlie's Angels*). Shoie and Daphne find his infatuation more humorous than troublesome.

But when a carnival comes to town and the magician (John Calicos) and his assistant (Richard Bakalyan) take an unnatural interest in the local bank, Alvin and Shoie take an interest in them. As the investigation continues, Shoie and Daphne begin to suspect that lovely Cathy (the new bank teller) may not be as innocent as she appears. That only redoubles Alvin's efforts to solve the crime and prove Cathy's innocence.

Once again, I enjoyed the easy camaraderie between Alvin, Shoie, and Daphne. I remember the early scenes at the carnival when a scary Frankenstein's monster robot goes out of control and scares the carnival audience. I hate to say it, but that scene became a recurring nightmare for me in the years to come. I would be trapped in our basement and the monster would emerge from our furnace room and come after me while my feet remained anchored to the linoleum floor.

Alvin's initial assumptions of how they are robbing the bank turn out to be wrong and earn him the renewed ire of the police. But his second theory proves to be right. Some of our heroes get kidnapped and it all comes to a climax on the carnival midway. Alvin learns his first hard lesson in love, that his infatuation with Cathy and belief in her innocence were truly misplaced, and that this whole dating thing and male-female relations were a lot more complicated than he thought.

Like the other mysteries in this chapter, *Whiz Kid* taught me that if something looks suspicious, it probably is. It taught me to not accept surface explanations of grownups (politicians), especially if their rationale sounds too simple and is missing some important pieces, and to not stop figuring something out until I've gotten to the bottom of it. Lastly, it taught me that investigating mysteries is something you can't do entirely on your own. Rely on your friends, even if one of them is your kid brother or kid sister. The more brains and eyes you have solving a problem, the more likely you are to get to the real solution. And, most of the time, those magnificent monsters that haunt our imaginations live only there, in our imaginations, and not in the real world.

While knowing they are all fictional characters, I often wonder what Emil, Gallegher, Alfie and Leonard, the Whiz Kids, and Scott, Tippy, and Catfish did once they grew up. Their enthusiasms in these shows are what kids aspire to be when they are around ten years old: filmmaker, detective, investigative reporter—occupations all designed to make a name for yourself, get yourself in the papers, and let the world know who you are.

Maybe solving mysteries is just a necessary stage we children go through while standing on that threshold of the teenage years. We are no longer children, exactly, but then again not quite adults. Whether solving mysteries in real life or in our imaginations, it gives us the skill set and sharpens the instincts to prepare us for what lies ahead. It gets us ready to solve the greatest mystery of all—growing up.

CHAPTER TEN

Growing Up

Adventures with Runaways, Teenagers,
and Absent-Minded Professors

I first noticed things were starting to change in both myself and my family around the fall of 1970. I had turned eight that summer and it was the first time I felt like I was starting to look at the world through older eyes. *The Wonderful World of Disney* was still the highlight of my week, but this was the first time when I recall the primacy of watching the show threatened, or at least questioned.

My two older sisters were fifteen and thirteen that year, and like most girls their age, they had fallen under the spell of teen idols and pretty boys promoted by teen magazines such as *16 Magazine* and *Tiger Beat*. Teen idols they sighed over were already driving much of our television watching. We watched *Here Come the Brides* (1968–1970) because it starred Bobby Sherman and David Soul (did men really wear hip-hugger jeans in the Old West?). We watched *The Partridge Family* (1970–1974) so they could gaze at the beauty of David Cassidy. We even watched the short-lived TV series *Maya* (1970) about an elephant so they could drink in the Indian countenence of brief teen idol Sajid Khan. But in the fall of 1970, my sisters proposed out-and-out blasphemy.

They proclaimed to our parents that they had outgrown *World of Disney* and wanted to watch a new TV show debuting opposite *Disney* on ABC called *The Young Rebels* (1970–1971). Why? Because it starred two teen idols: Rick Ely and a French discovery named Philippe Forquet. Ely played the leader of a group of underground spies during the American Revolution who answered to the Marquis de Lafayette (Forquet) who answered directly to General George Washington. Personally, I found myself more interested in the lone female in the group played by a starlet named Hilary Thompson. Their secret organization was called the Yankee Doodle Society.

In order to understand why this was a problem, you have to understand a bit more on how things were in the time before we all had our own personal handheld device or even VHS cassette recorders. In our house, there were only two television sets. Everyone could watch shows on the RCA Victor in the basement family room. The other set was a Zenith portable color TV located in our parents' bedroom. None of us could just walk in and start watching something on that set. We needed permission, advanced permission, to watch anything on that set. It had to be cleared with both parents. The other rule was that we were not allowed to eat or drink anything in there. We might get something on the bedspread. So if my sisters wanted to start watching *The Young Rebels* on the downstairs set at the same time as *World of Disney*, then I would be banished to the upstairs set and not be able to eat the pizza or drink the soda that came along with watching the show.

It was a horrible turn of events and a major unhappy development, as all these things appear to be from our limited childhood perspective. In the end, my mother negotiated a compromise (as she always did). We would continue to watch *World of Disney* on the set in the family room, and my sisters could watch *Young Rebels* on the bedroom set upstairs, but only if they finished eating their pizza during *Wild Kingdom* which aired from 7:00pm to 7:30pm, and they dutifully did. Once Marlin Perkins gave his closing speech for each episode that always ended with the words "wild kingdom," my sisters raced upstairs to watch Ron Ely and a young Louis Gossett Jr. as those cute Revolutionary War spies.

In the end, *The Young Rebels* rebellion turned out to be a flash in the pan. The show was a ratings dud (like pretty much every other ABC show that aired opposite *Disney* and *Ed Sullivan*) and the network cancelled it after half a season. My sisters then resumed hanging out in the family room and watching *World of Disney* with the rest of us.

But the incident taught me that our family was growing up and a future lay ahead that might not include *World of Disney*. It was my first indication that Disney was something I could grow out of, and I fervently hoped that would be a day that never came.

Still, my own perspective was changing. I found myself getting older. I was thinking new thoughts and learning to adapt to new situations. I was watching more news and becoming more aware of what was happening out there in the wider world. Words like Vietnam, Kent State, and Watergate would come to dominate those events.

I was starting to grow up, and as I had so far in this life, I turned to the *World of Disney* to offer suggestions on how I was supposed to do that. As usual, they offered me the perfect examples for growing up through the performances of Kevin Corcoran, Tommy Kirk, Kurt Russell, and Ron Howard.

Toby Tyler (1960)

TV Premiere: November 22 & 29, 1964

What kid doesn't want to run away to the circus? I suppose those words are heretical to many people these days as circuses are generally condemned for inhumane treatment of animals. I grew up in the era when circuses were still among the greatest shows on earth. For people living in small towns in the late 19th and early 20th centuries, only when the circus came to town were they able to see exotic animals like elephants, tigers, lions, and bears. It was the only way to see high-wire acts like the Great Wallendas or experience great clowns like Emmett Kelly Jr. and Lou Jacobs, all presented in a dazzling three-ring show. It is a form of entertainment that is sadly dying in the 21st century, but I am happy to say I grew up at the tail end of that era where I could still appreciate the artistry and the glamor when the circus came to town. *Toby Tyler* captures that excitement well.

Toby (Kevin Corcoran) is an orphan sent to live with his aunt and uncle. He feels unloved and unneeded, so when Colonel Castle's Circus comes through town he jumps on board. Of course, no one in the circus is sure what to do with a ten-year-old boy. Toby is assigned to be a concession boy selling food to the spectators in the stands under the supervision of the less-than-honest, less-than-nice Mr. Tupper (Bob Sweeney). Toby starts up an unlikely friendship with a chimpanzee named Mr. Stubbs. And he can't seem to keep his eye off the prancing horse act performed by Ajax (Dennis Joel) and Jeanette (Barbara Beard), children not much older than he.

When Ajax grows jealous of the friendship between Toby and Jeanette, he tries to show off by performing a dangerous horse trick without a harness. He only succeeds in breaking his ankle. Toby ends up as Jeannette's new partner, which leads to circus stardom. His aunt and uncle come to see the show and they are reconciled.

Based on the classic 1881 children's novel, *Toby Tyler* taught me a number of things. First, that show-biz life like the circus may appear to be glamorous on the outside, but there is hard work and unsavory people behind the glitz. Ajax's boastfulness and showing off which leads to the end of his career became a cautionary tale of how not to behave. And Mr. Tupper taught me to be wary of adults who appear to have your best interests at heart.

Almost Angels (1962)

TV Premiere: February 28; March 7, 1965

What kid doesn't want to run away and join the Vienna Boys Choir? Okay, wait a minute, forget that. Most probably don't. And yet young

Toni (Vincent Winter) wants to do just that. He convinces his parents to let him audition for the prestigious choir and he is stunned when they accept him. As the new member of the all-boy group, Toni finds himself on the end of many jokes and much taunting by the choir's oldest member Peter (Sean Scully). Peter has the best voice in the group, so he can do pretty much anything he wants. Undeterred by the bullying, Toni forges a friendship with another new boy named Ferdy (Henny Scott) and soon enough Toni and Peter bridge their differences and become friends, too.

Just as the choir is about to go out on tour, Peter's voice begins to crack—he is approaching adolescence after all. As he starts to lose his singing voice, Peter fears being kicked out of the group. Being a member of the choir is the only thing he has. The boys try covering up Peter's voice issue by having someone sing for him while Peter lip-syncs the words, but the scheme fails. In the end, the managers of the choir decide to honor Peter for his years of service by promoting him to assistant conductor. At the story's climax, Peter conducts his first concert featuring Toni and Ferdy as the new soloists.

What captured my imagination about this movie was the boarding school. As someone with no brothers and two older sisters, the chance to hang out and have fun with a bunch of boys seemed like a lot of fun, and then to do it far away from your parents, well, that felt like a fantasy.

The part of the story that terrified me when I first saw it was the shock of Peter losing his voice. I learned that all good things do not last, and that at some point we are likely to be faced with the loss of the thing we value most and which gave us our standing. Our whole world will come crashing down, but there will be friends to see us through, and new opportunities better than the ones before.

For the Love of Willadean (1964)

TV Premiere: March 8, 15, 1964

For those who don't remember what childhood was like before the invention of video games and computers, or what kids used to do to fill those long, interminable days of summer vacation, *For the Love of Willadean* (1964) reminds us how the rituals of childhood, especially male childhood, used to go.

J.D. Gray (Michael McGreevey) is a boy on the edge of puberty with multiple problems. He has a cool tree house and is president of his own boys club (as in "no girls allowed"), but only his little brother Freddie (Billy Mumy) will be a member and even he is constantly challenging J.D.'s leadership. Even worse, J.D. is infatuated with the cute girl next door, Willadean Wills (Terry Burnham), but he is too insecure to admit to anyone that he has fallen for an icky girl. It also doesn't help that she is the daughter of Farmer Wills (John Anderson), the grumpiest man in their area of the country. That changes when young Harley Mason (Roger Mobley) and his family arrive from Detroit and move in next door.

At first, the brothers Gray are excited to have a new boy to play with, but they also fear he might be weak like they know all city boys to be. This turns out to be an unfounded concern when Harley shows be can hold his own in a rock fight. The boys are even more determined to have him in the club when they learn Harley's father has given him a horse named Prince. After all, club members must share equally what they own. A possible friendship is there for the making until J.D. realizes that Harley has caught the eye of Willadean and become a romantic rival. His games and pranks on Harley take a nastier edge.

The film does a wonderful job of conveying what those empty summer days of youth were like and how American childhood used to be about conjuring up make-believe adventures to fill the time. We built treehouses and created private clubs mostly so we could establish our own superiority by excluding specific people who threatened us. We held sleepovers and pretended that our neighbors were up to no good. We staged mock battles with slingshots and rocks to prove we were tough. We used telescopes to spy on cute girls and we snitched things from their yards for no other reason than to prove we were old enough to be worthy to be spoken to, even as we were too shy to just walk up and speak to them ourselves. And all of this was done to get a girl's attention.

"I can't understand any of this," young Freddie mutters at one point, and he is right.

Neither J.D. nor Harley know they are doing this stuff to get Willadean's attention (though she does). The movie captures all the things boys used to do to impress a girl while still going out of their way to avoid talking to her, and how the lazy boredom of summer days leads boys to do stupid things on dares without first thinking through the consequences of those actions, like when J.D. tricks Harley into stealing Farmer Wills' prize watermelon. It also demonstrates how growing up involves realizing and facing up to the consequences of our acts by taking responsibility and making amends.

In the second half of the story, J.D. decides that Willadean can join the club (over Freddie's objections). "I can see it now," he moans, "the women are taking over." The only way she can join is by spending time in the abandoned McTeague house which is rumored to be haunted. As usual, J.D. has an alternate agenda. He rigs up things in the house that he hopes will scare Harley and make him look bad to Willadean. They don't know that a traveling hobo named Alfred (Ed Wynn) is passing through and hiding in the house. It is fun noticing that the McTeague place is the same façade used for the British mansion in *The Swamp Fox* and will be the town hotel in *A Tiger Walks* and the future inn in *Secrets of the Pirates' Inn*.

J.D.—maybe short for "juvenile delinquent"—is a real piece of work.

He is rather mean and definitely passive-aggressive. He tries to make himself look good by tricking people into doing things to make them look bad. When those people turn out to be smarter, he covers his embarrassment by getting back at them for making him look bad when his loss of face is really just a result of his plans backfiring on him.

I knew several J.D.s in our neighborhood growing up and I had little patience for them. I was usually Harley in those situations, the new kid who had just moved to town. I grew tired of the ever-changing requirements neighborhood boys put on me to prove myself, especially when they were really excuses to exclude me. I also grew tired of the undependability of those boyhood friendships—one day you were friends, the next day they would turn on you.

Of course, in the end J.D. and Harley become friends since childhood friendships are based more on who you are against rather than traits you share. By the end of the summer, Willadean has outgrown both boys and started dating a high school athlete with his own car. The boys have in common their mutual unspoken disappointment that Willadean has moved on and left them behind.

The Legend of the Boy and the Eagle (1968)

TV Premiere: September 15, 1968

Set in the American West some time in the past, a Hopi Indian boy lives as an outcast in his village, taunted and victimized by the other boys. The only creature he connects with is the village's sacred eagle that they plan to sacrifice. Unable to accept the impending loss of his only friend, the boy sets the eagle free. For doing so, the tribal leaders banish him from the village. The boy struggles to survive alone in the desert until the eagle drops out of the sky and teaches him how to hunt. With the help of the eagle, the boy grows up.

When he returns to the village as a seasoned hunter, the villagers cannot see the fine warrior he has become. They only see what he was. The same boys who taunted him earlier chase him out of the village and up on a cliff. Trapped with nowhere to go, the boy chooses to jump to his death. Instead of falling, though, the boy transforms into an eagle and the two birds fly off together as the shocked villagers watch. The story became a Hopi myth told from village to village down through the centuries.

I have not seen this episode in almost fifty years, but still remember bonding with the plight of the boy. As mentioned before, I too found myself a frequent outcast taunted by boys my age. I never understood why, as I had never done anything to them. The movie helped me to understand there are just some boys who get "chosen" to be the community scapegoat for reasons unknown. But it also taught me that even outcast boys have an inner worth that no one can see. The moment when the boy becomes an eagle remains a liberating moment for me. I remember the thrill I felt not just because he had become a bird, but also that he had found his true calling—a greatness far beyond what anyone had suspected, even he.

Take care, the movie taught me, times may be hard now, but there is fulfillment in your future.

Call It Courage (1973)

TV Premiere: April 1, 1973

Mafatu is a Polynesian boy living in the South Seas. He fears the ocean because he saw his mother drown when he was little and for that his tribe has labeled him a coward. Making things worse, Mafatu is the son of the chief and future leader of the tribe. Even his father believes him to be a coward. Eager to prove them wrong, Mafatu steals a canoe and sets off across the ocean to conquer his fears. A storm blows up and destroys the canoe. Mafatu finds himself stranded on a deserted island. There he teaches himself to hunt and fish. He battles a shark then an octopus and defeats them both. When cannibals come to the island, he manages to hide from them. He comes to understand that he no longer fears the things he used to fear. He feels something else instead and calls it courage. He builds a new canoe and sails back to his home island. When he arrives, his tribe, even his own father, do not recognize him. But soon enough they do, and realize that Mafatu has become a man and a worthy future leader.

When I first saw it, *Call It Courage* was major inspiration for me, maybe because it brought out my latent *Robinson Crusoe* streak still present to this day—a desire to leave the world behind and spend my days alone on a deserted island with nothing but animals and books to pass my time.

The episode made me run out and borrow Armstrong Sperry's original 1940 novel from the library. I devoured it and loved it. Soon enough, I checked out James Michener's classic novel *Hawaii* (1959) and became a Michener fan for life. I watched the 1966 movie adaptation of *Hawaii* with Max Von Sydow and Julie Andrews. It marked the beginning of my interest in the South Seas and Polynesian culture that remains to this day. I checked out the book *Mutiny on the Bounty* (1932) by Charles Nordhoff and James Norman Hall and its two sequels, *Men Against the Sea* (1934) and *Pitcairn's Island* (1934), and watched all the movie adaptations of that story as well, which led to my love of sailing ship stories which ultimately resulted in my reading Herman Melville's *Moby Dick* (1851). I read Thor Heyerdahl's *Kon-Tiki* (1950) and loved his tale about journeying across the Pacific in a bamboo raft to prove ancient South Seas mariners could have traveled the distances they did, which led me to his 1971 book *The Ra Expeditions* about ancient Egyptian mariners. It is amazing how far one can sail and how much one can learn once you set out on the ocean of the imagination and let your mind guide the way.

I also started fantasizing about traveling the South Seas on a raft. I would build one out of Tinker Toys complete with rudder and oars and a modest shelter made out of two dining room chairs with a bedspread hung between them and pretend I was sailing the South Seas just like Mafatu and Captain Bligh and Heyerdahl and Fletcher Christian and Crusoe. Crazy, huh? All because of one episode of *World of Disney*.

But more than that, I took from *Call It Courage* that succeeding in life meant facing your fears and conquering them, whether an ocean (like Mafatu, I had a fear of the water when I was a child) or anything else. Grab a canoe and set out on the ocean of your imagination to conquer it. Only then will you be able to hold your head up and become a man.

Those Calloways (1965)

TV Premiere: January 12, 19, 26, 1969

Set in rural Vermont during the 1920s, *Those Calloways* tells the story of the Calloway family, an eccentric brood living on the outskirts of the village of Stillwater. But, as they say, still waters run deep. The main character is young Bucky Calloway (Brandon De Wilde). He has to put up with the catcalls of the local bullies who view him as a weakling and see his father Cam Calloway (Brian Keith) as a loon. Cam wants to set up a bird sanctuary on the shores of the local lake to protect the Canadian geese who migrate through the area every year. The fact that Cam was raised by Indians makes him even more of an outsider.

The local business leaders have different ideas. They want to use the geese to attract hunters and boost the small town's economy. It is a traditional battle between nature and big business and you can guess what side the movie comes down on. When a big businessman lends Cam the money to plant corn along the lakeshore to attract the birds, Cam thinks his bird sanctuary is finally getting started. But the businessman is really a hunter and when the birds return he shows up with his buddies to shoot them out of the sky. A fight ensues and Cam gets shot.

Those Calloways helped form my views of life and what to value as an adult. Even as a youngster, I could identify with young Bucky. Like him, I had to put up with daily razzing and bullying. Some of it was directed at my father who, while not an eccentric nature lover, was a high-ranking school official of the local school system. I would get taunted for school not being cancelled due to weather or for an unpopular new policy ,and even by some of the teachers (usually the bad ones) who disliked those new policies. It all made me feel like Bucky.

The movie also contributed to my love of nature in general and Canadian geese in particular. It sealed my life-long dislike of hunting. The businessmen and hunters in the movie don't see the beauty of the birds. They think of them only as "nasty dirty birds" to shoot and kill, or to exploit for monetary gain.

I have never felt the joy found in killing a living thing. Nor have I understood anyone who claimed they had the right to kill something, like the businessmen in the film who claim that right because they provided the money that paid for the corn to attract the birds. In their minds, they "own" the birds and can do with them what they wish. Whenever I hear about the joys of hunting, I think back to the dead birds falling out of the sky in *Those Calloways* and shake my head.

For most of my adult life, my wife and I have lived on rural property with a pond at its center. Like in *Calloways*, twice a year flocks of geese come to land on our pond and take a break from their north-south migration. And just like Bucky, I still enjoy watching them come in to land, and hearing their happy honks as they communicate to each other across the water. It is not unusual to have twenty to fifty of them spend the night. A few through the years have even stayed through spring and summer to nest and raise families. I totally understand the beauty that the Calloways saw in those birds.

Beyond the film's ecological message, it also has a number of other life lessons I took to heart. My father was a good man, but also a quiet man when it came to teaching a boy the lessons of life. The words of many a Disney father figure helped fill that gap and Cam Calloway (Brian Keith) was one of the best. When Bucky gets beat up by the town bully (Tom Skerritt), his father is philosophical about it. "As long as you don't stay licked. That's what counts." He then helps his son learn how to fight. Just like Bucky, I too got a book that taught me how to fight and how to stand up to my bullies.

I also find myself appreciating the unheralded saint of the movie, Bucky's mother and Cam's wife, Liddy (Vera Miles). Liddy Calloway's personality is my mom on film. So many of her statements are things my mother could have said as she tried to make ends meet, sometimes through no help from her husband (as she saw it). But I think Liddy's assessment of Cam also captures how my mother probably felt about my father: "I knew immediately that you were a man who will never be able to give me what I want, but will give me everything I need."

I also learned a few things I have never needed to use, like how to set a broken leg when stranded out in the wild. Or how to track and kill a wolverine, "the only critter that will kill just for the sheer joy of killing," Bucky says, though he has forgotten that man does the same thing.

The gorgeous autumn photography in the movie (done by the under-rated Edward Coleman)—perfectly accented by Max Steiner's last film score—reconfirmed autumn as my favorite season, with its colors, the refreshing cold snap in the air that hints at the winter to come, the gatherings inside around the fire that bring family and friends closer together, the quiet Christmas celebrations of the past like reading *A Christmas Carol* aloud to the family on Christmas Eve, the old-fashioned notions of hospitality, the home-spun wisdom of the old village folks like Ed Wynn (in his last film) and Walter Brennan sitting around the fire at the general store and waxing nostalgic about life and times and the joy of not constantly striving to make a buck.

Those Calloways is a rambling beauty of a movie. It requires a viewer to be uninterested in plot and willing to just sit back and watch and listen and let its story play out at its own pace, like those old guys at the general store. You will not be disappointed.

Smoke (1970)

TV Premiere: February 1, 8, 1970

Whenever a list is compiled of the best *World of Disney* episodes, *Smoke* rarely appears but few episodes taught me more about the right way to grow up and how to handle the traumas of life.

Smoke is the story of a stray and injured German shepherd found by fourteen-year-old Chris Long (Ron Howard) who is himself going through a difficult time in his life. His beloved father (played by his real-life father Rance Howard) died less than a year earlier in a car accident that Chris somehow survived. His mother Fran (Jacqueline Scott) has remarried a stern but good-hearted man named Cal (Earl Holliman), but Chris is not ready to let go of the past and move on. He resents his younger sister Susan (Pamelyn Ferdin) accepting their new stepfather. Chris refuses to call Cal "dad." Life moves on, whether you want it to or not, but nobody fights change like a teenage boy.

"Chris," his mom scolds him, "don't be stubborn."

He has hopes of getting away, of spending the summer picking fruit so he can save enough money to buy a used car and pay for college, but his stepfather nixes his plans because he is too young.

"Kids are older these days than when you were kids," Chris argues without effect. Maybe next year his parents tell him, and Chris' retort perfectly echoes the impatience of teenaged boys who are in a hurry to grow up, "Anything I really want is next year."

Mostly, Chris is suffering from survivor's guilt: the fact that he was thrown clear of the accident and unable to rescue his dad.

I learned so many lessons from *Smoke*.

It taught how the trauma of one moment can change a whole life, even if you didn't do anything wrong.

I learned that sometimes bad things happen; bad things that we don't want to accept: the loss of a parent or loved one, even the ending of a marriage or relationship. We refuse to accept them so much that we dig in our heels and refuse to acknowledge that they even happened. We will not let life move on because we want to remain in that good time and hang onto those memories of when things were perfect and life untroubled. We want to stay there so much that we begin to shut out the world and anyone that might convince us to change our mind. And, like in *The Three Lives of Thomasina*, we do this mostly through the anger of unresolved grief.

Later on, Susan asks Chris what it is like to be too old to cry anymore, i.e., grown up. "You go on being a kid," he answers, "and when something happens that you can't handle, you bawl. And then a grownup comes along and tells you everything will be better. One day, something will happen and you'll all of a sudden know you can't cry about it. Because you know you have to handle things all by yourself from now on." We realize he is talking about the car accident. "Crying couldn't put out that fire. And it couldn't make him alive again either."

Smoke also taught me that grief is a dangerous thing because we usually take it out on the people who caused us the least offense. "If you start taking out your feelings on all the Herbies in the world," Cal cautions Chris after he punches his visiting cousin, "then soon you are hurting people who did nothing to you."

Things come to a head when Smoke's original owner (Andy Devine) comes to reclaim the dog. Chris is once again confronted with losing a thing he most loves.

"Chris, it isn't the end of everything," his mother tries to explain, but, to Chris' fourteen-year-old mind, it *is* the end of everything (again).

I well understand Chris' anguish in that moment. It is the same anguish I felt when my parents told us once again we were moving to a new town when I was in kindergarten and sixth grade and halfway through my senior year of high school. I was going to have to give up my friends and start over once more in a strange new school—only with each move it became harder and harder to make new friends.

When Cal and Fran offer to get another dog to take Smoke's place, Chris explodes, "Take his place? You think one dog is as good as another just like you think one husband is as good as another."

That night, Chris runs away and takes Smoke with him. While traveling cross-country, they spend the night in the barn of a farmer and his wife. Smoke wakes Chris in the middle of the night. The farmhouse is ablaze and the sight of the burning house triggers a flashback to the accident and the death of his father.

He and Smoke break into the house and save the couple like he couldn't rescue his dad.

"We're alright," Chris tells Smoke as he lies on the ground. "We're going to be alright."

"Any fool young or old can run away," their elderly handyman tells Chris before he leaves. "It takes a man to come back."

His grief and anger finally purged, Chris does return like the prodigal son, ready to accept the consequences of his actions, even though Smoke's original owner has already decided Chris can keep the dog. Chris and Cal reconcile and, in a moment that still brings tears to my eyes, Chris calls him "Dad" for the first time. They hug.

Smoke taught me that life goes on whether we want it to or not. People we love enter our lives. People we love leave our lives. And if we spend all our time mourning the people that leave, we will miss out on the new people wishing to love us just as much as our lost loved ones.

Dad, Can I Borrow the Car? (1970)

TV Premiere: April 9, 1972

Of course, growing up meant establishing my independence and establishing my independence meant learning how to drive a car. Few films capture the crazy, manic single-minded focus of mid-twentieth century teenaged American boys' love of cars better than Ward Kimball's follow up to *It's Tough to Be a Bird*. How obsessed were Baby Boomer boys with getting a car back then? In the 1960s and 1970s, the image of the American male was tied up in having a car. Narrated by Kurt Russell, this movie beautifully and humorously captured how ingrained it all used to be. Before cell phones and personal computers and gaming systems, men and boys obsessed over cars.

"I was born with wheels on the ground," proclaims our unnamed high school narrator. When he is born and the obstetrician slaps him on the butt, a car horn sounds. Rewatching it as an adult, it made me remember how much of the culture around us was geared toward cars.

As a baby, my car seat had the same features as the boy in the film: a steering wheel and a gearshift lever. I was learning to drive and handle a manual transmission before I could even walk. Seeing the nursery school and kindergarten classrooms in the film reminds me of things I took for granted back then. First, that the children even have recess time to play. And second, that the toys the boys are playing with are all cars, pushing them around the classroom, making the engine noises as they do. And they were all kinds of toy cars as well: sedans and sports cars for showing off, trucks and construction vehicles that could become the center of a future job, race cars that the lucky ones will get to put through their paces on tracks like those at Indianapolis, Daytona, Riverside, and Sebring. The large number of toy stop signs and traffic lights in the classroom unconsciously taught them traffic laws and the rules of the road before they had even entered first grade. I like how the girls want to play with the cars, too, but the boys fight to keep them for themselves.

The movie recalls how much of our childhood play was geared toward transportation: kiddie cars, peddle cars, tricycles, bicycles, skateboards. All our toys had wheels. As we grew up, our male hobbies included model cars. It reminded me of all the Saturday and Sunday afternoons my dad and I spent building model cars, ships, trucks, planes, and spaceships in the same family room where we watched *World of Disney*.

Once boys get older, they indulged that love of speed in machines like soapbox derby racers and go karts. I learned that victory on the track meant success with the girls—symbolized by that Victory Lane kiss.

As teenagers, the fun of going out with friends was tempered by the growing sense of humiliation that we were still dependent on our parents, usually our mothers, to drive us where we wanted to go. Driver Education could not get here soon enough. And becoming old enough to get our drivers license was as big a milestone as our first date or that first kiss. Having a car, being able to drive, was directly tied to a successful love life. No wonder we felt so much was riding on our passing Driver Ed.

I remember my disappointment on my first day of real Driver Ed that my high school did not have the cool car simulators shown in the film. All my fellow students and I had to learn from were books and watching movies about car crashes and the dangers of not focusing on the road.

The movie captures the tension of how passing Driver Ed gave way to the mortifying fear of going down to the Department of Motor Vehicles to pass the driving test and get our license with nothing less than our entrance to manhood riding on it.

My own driving test seemed to mirror the boy's in the film: full of mistakes and seeming errors committed under the scowling eye of the instructor, followed by the unexpected words, "Congratulations, you passed."

Then the struggle of working up the courage to ask my parents to, well, borrow the car, which resulted in that lecture from Dad, and then my first solo drive—done behind the wheel of a Chevy Bel Air two-door. In the episode, the solo drive ends in a lack of focus, a run of a red light, flashing police lights, and a traffic ticket.

Once a guy had a license then the whole rest of the car culture world opened up to him: car magazines, dune buggies, drag racing, sports car racing, even demolition derby (the earliest memories I have are watching this sport on TV with a babysitter).

"If a guy doesn't have a car, he is out of luck."

That was so very true then. And Kimball's film brilliantly captures the truth underlying the mania and obsession.

It is sad that our love of cars and driving has somehow gotten lost in the past forty years. So much of being a good driver is tied to being a responsible adult and a contributing member of society. But the love of cars has been replaced by the equally manic obsession with games and constant video watching. There is no time or interest in finding the joy of driving a car. In fact, the driving of the car takes away from the constant need to be watching, to be entertained. Thus the development of the self-driving car. Let computers do the driving so we can continue to entertain ourselves.

"Dad, can I borrow the car?" is a question we used to build our entire childhood toward. No more, and that makes me sad.

Once we learn to drive, we can go anywhere. Even to college.

Higher Learning

As a kid, the idea of going off to college felt like a dream. Yes, we were expected to attend classes and study and learn new things. Yes, we might experiment with new subjects before figuring out the major that will lead to our vocation. Yes, we might even experiment with a few more things than that. But let's not forget the most important part about college—we don't have to go home at night. We don't have to answer to anyone. In short, no parents! We don't have to ask anyone for permission. We can just do it. But some of us haven't learned that with great freedom comes great responsibility.

If you were a Disney teen character and you headed off to college, the only institution of higher learning you could apparently attend was Medfield College. Four sets of Disney college students made it to Medfield (Midvale as one set called it), though it certainly comes across as not always the best place to get an advanced degree. And yet, in its own way, Medfield taught its students (and us) everything we needed to know about dealing with academia.

The Absent-Minded Professor (1961)
TV Premiere: November 1, 1975

Son of Flubber (1963)
TV Premiere: March 16, 1980

The Absent-Minded Professor was our introduction to Medfield College, a pleasant enough campus, not quite Ivy League, not quite Midwestern. (The filmmakers took advantage of the Disney studio's collegiate architectural style for the Medfield campus.) And yet the leaders of Medfield usually do not have learning on their minds. All college president Rufus Daggett (Leon Ames) can think about is money, especially the large amount given by local businessman Alonzo Hawk (Keenan Wynn) who seems to think this allows his star athlete son Biff (Tommy Kirk) to play basketball despite failing grades. Even in 1961 some quarters of society viewed athletic ability as more important than learning.

Of course, the class Biff is failing is the science class of Prof. Ned Brainard (Fred MacMurray), the absent-minded professor of the title. Ned frequently gets so wrapped up in experiments conducted in his garage lab (I guess Medfield has no campus facilities) that he keeps forgetting to show up to marry his fiancé, Betsy Carlisle (Nancy Olson).

One night, Ned accidently invents a strange rubbery substance that makes everything around it weightless. He promptly puts it in his old Model T car and turns it into a flying machine. He dubs the invention "flubber"—short for flying rubber. To try and prove his invention to the jilted Betsy, he applies it to the soles of the Medfield basketball team and they easily win their big game by bouncing higher and farther than their rivals. The one person who believes Ned is Hawk, who wants to buy the invention and use it to cash in. Being the good patriot that he is, Ned prefers giving it to the government (which produces a funny rivalry between the three armed forces trying to get flubber for themselves). Through several clever twists and turns, it all ends well.

The sequel, *Son of Flubber* (1963), is one of those films that understands what scenes the audience enjoyed in the first movie and replicates them. The flying car is there. Instead of a basketball game, Medfield plays a flubberized football game. Once again, Ned follows romantic rival and English professor Shelby Ashton (Elliott Reid) home, but this time terrorizes him by making it rain inside his car. The military is still arguing amongst itself on how to best use flubber for national defense. Frustrated on all fronts, Ned has invented "flubber gas" to save Medfield College once more from the clutches of Alonzo Hawk. And of course everything turns out right in the end.

Son of Flubber was the first movie sequel Disney ever made and it is safe to say that it is more of the same. However, the movies manage to entertain while educating us on age-old stereotypes of academia: athletes who want to game the system and who feel their athletic abilities afford them special treatment, rich donors who think their money earns them special access, college presidents more interested in the bottom line than in furthering the cause of science or education. Somehow the educating of students never seems to be a factor in these movies, and that absence speaks volumes.

The Shaggy Dog (1959)
TV Premiere: January 29, 1978

The Shaggy Dog manages to combine almost all the elements celebrated in other Disney episodes: growing up, romance, solving a mystery, and pets. We can even throw in the European neighbors across the street. And while not set at Medfield College, *The Shaggy Dog* take place in the town of Medfield which in the meta world of Disney we can assume means the story takes place in the same college town.

I did see not *The Shaggy Dog* until late in my *World of Disney* watching, but I already felt intimately familiar with it because we owned a Gold Key comic book of the story (also containing *The Absent-Minded Professor*) for most of my childhood. I read the comic book more often than I have seen the movie. I was also familiar with the movie's youthful cast because of their time on *The Mickey Mouse Club* (no, I had not watched the show's original airing back in 1955–1959, but I had caught its re-airing in the mid-1970s). Tommy Kirk, Kevin Corcoran, Tim Considine, Roberta Shore, and Annette Funicello were all MMC alums.

Wilby Daniels (Tommy Kirk) is a misunderstood boy whom nobody seems to know what to do with. His rather stern father (Fred MacMurray) wonders why he wastes his time in his basement laboratory. Cool, handsome Steve (Tim Considine) finds Wilby amusing in a condescending way. The lovely Allison (Annette Funicello) looks down her nose at him and sees only a gawky boy rather than the smart man he can become. Only his younger brother (Kevin Corcoran) believes in him.

When a European professor and his sophisticated daughter Francheska (Roberta Shore) move in across the street—maybe he is a guest lecturer at the college?—the story is set in motion. Wilby finds an ancient ring. When he reads the inscription, it turns him into a big shaggy dog. Strangely enough he becomes the same breed of dog that Francheska owns. This allows Wilby to cuddle up with the latest girl of his dreams. Unfortunately, throughout the rest of the film, Wilby involuntarily switches back and forth between a boy and a dog. That is how he learns that Francheska's father is really the head of a spy ring. He then proceeds to defeat them.

The Shaggy Dog is a fine mystery comedy that features some of the best sight gags ever in a Disney film. Probably the classic one is Wilby as a dog chasing the crooks through town while driving Steve's jalopy. In the end, Wilby gets rid of the ring so he can stay a boy and Francheska's dog gets all the credit for saving her life and catching the criminals.

The movie serves as a fine transition for its youthful cast on the cusp of adulthood. Some like Tim Considine and Roberta Shore opted to retire and leave the movies. Other like Tommy Kirk, Annette Funicello, and Kevin Corcoran would continue on to be among Disney's biggest stars of the early 1960s. It was also Fred MacMurray's first Disney movie. He too would go on to star in many of the studios' best movies over the next ten years.

The film also made it clear that childish things can be fun, but they all have their time and place in our lives, and there inevitably comes a point when we have to box them up and put them away so that we can embrace the more adventurous things that age and expanded freedom allows, like a car or a girlfriend. And, of course, those pursuits are best done while in the sheltered setting of a college.

The Misadventures of Merlin Jones (1964) / The Monkey's Uncle (1965)

TV Premiere: November 26; December 3, 1967

The Misadventures of Merlin Jones is a bit unique in that it never aired as an episode of *World of Disney*. It was conceived and filmed as one, but, at the last minute, Walt changed his mind and released it as a theatrical feature instead. It then proved so unexpectedly popular that a sequel, *The Monkey's Uncle*, was rushed into production and that did receive multiple airings on the TV show. The two films also marked the final Disney appearances for its now grown up stars Tommy Kirk and Annette Funicello.

The Merlin Jones films also provide an interesting transition in the Medfield College saga from the *Shaggy Dog* and *Absent-Minded Professor* days to *The Computer Wore Tennis Shoes* trilogy. One odd thing is that the two Jones films are set not at Medfield but at Midvale College. This is especially odd since the look and feel of Midvale is incredibly similar to Medfield. Perhaps the college went broke and had to rename itself to escape Alonzo Hawk and its other creditors (who are nowhere in sight for these films).

Confusing things further is that we have several hold-over actors back in *Merlin Jones* who appeared in the previous *Professor* films. Tommy Kirk (previously Biff Hawk) plays Merlin Jones and it is easy to see how he could have been Wilby Daniels just a few years back.

Both love to experiment and invent things and both have their own home labs to indulge their creative thinking. And both characters tend to invent things with unintended side effects. Annette Funicello's Jennifer could just as easily be *The Shaggy Dog*'s Allison at college age—grown past her snootiness and "wait on me because I am beautiful" phase unable to see the virtues of brainiacs like Wilby or Merlin. Confusing things even further, former Medfield College president Leon Ames appears playing Judge Holmsby who has gotten himself elected to the Midvale Board of Regents. Yikes! And instead of a dog, we have Stanley, Merlin Jones' chimpanzee.

The sequel adds in more actors I recognize from other favorite TV shows of the mid-1960s. Mark Goddard (from *Lost In Space*) appears as athlete and rival Hayward while Cheryl Miller plays Jennifer's romantic rival Lisa. She would go on to co-star (along with Judy the Chimp who plays Stanley) in *Daktari*.

Midvale is short on cash and seeking a way for academically underperforming athletes to continue to play. Merlin Jones is the resident student genius that the administration comes to for help. *Merlin Jones* came out in the same year as the Disney animated feature *The Sword in the Stone* (1963), and not long after the popular Lerner and Loewe musical *Camelot*. In the first movie, Merlin mostly experiments on reading minds and then discovering the power (and unintentional consequences) of hypnotism. For *The Monkey's Uncle*, he is enlisted to save Midvale.

Merlin is asked to come up with a way for the college's star athletes to pass their tests. He decides to use a method he is already experimenting with on Stanley: sleep learning. It goes so well that the athletes are accused of cheating, but a simple explanation from Merlin makes the accusations go away. Then, we learn that Midvale can receive a million dollar donation, but only if they get rid of football. Judge Holmsby cannot imagine an institution of higher learning without football. He finds eccentric millionaire Darius Green (Arthur O'Connell) who agrees to give ten million to Midvale if the college can invent a human-powered airplane.

Naturally, they turn to Merlin and naturally he is able to create such a plane. And, naturally, it all goes awry with unexpected consequences.

One can view these films as the precursors to such 1990s children's shows like *Dexter's Laboratory* and *Jimmy Neutron, Boy Genius*, shows about pint-sized Merlin Joneses who invent marvelous things in their home laboratories only for them to be undone by a side effect they had not counted on.

Maybe the movies are too simplistic. Maybe their plots rely too much on coincidence to achieve their ends. All I know was that, as a child, they made me laugh. They made college appear to be a fun romp to look forward to, and that maybe college was a place where a nerd like me could end up with a girl like Jennifer. (I was more likely to end up with Stanley the chimp.) Most of all, they celebrated learning and the many benefits that knowledge can give you which will outlast any athletic ability.

And if all that turned out to be false, then call me a monkey's uncle.

The Computer Wore Tennis Shoes (1969)

TV Premiere: September 17, 24, 1972

The final set of Disney characters to head off to Medfield College revolved around Dexter Riley and his popular band of inventive underachievers. Unlike Merlin Jones, Dexter (Kurt Russell) is no brain. His grades are poor and his days are spent not making the dean's list and trying to stay off probation. Surrounding him are his good friends, many played by former child stars: Schuyler (Disney's own Michael McGreevey) and Bradley (*Lassie*'s Jon Provost). There is even a young Frank Welker on the cusp of providing the voices for *Scooby Doo, Where Are You*?

Times may have changed, but Medfield's predicaments have not. Once again, they are short on money and Dean Higgins (Joe Flynn) is feeling the pressure and cutting funding where he can. Alonzo Hawk is gone, but local crime boss A.J. Arno (Cesar Romero) has replaced him and he is still looking to exploit Medfield for his own greedy purposes. Rounding out the trilogy's cast is William Schallert as the popular science professor Quigley.

When I saw *The Computer Wore Tennis Shoes* back as a boy, I had no idea how prescient it would prove to be. At the time I knew about computers, but they were large boxy machines only needed to get men to the moon or run large corporations or even a school system (my father's school system had one). It would be another twenty years before I learned that computers had a place in everyday life, like writing this book you are reading right now.

But back then, computers seemed like an expensive luxury, a viewpoint shared by Dean Higgins. Dexter and his pals come to the rescue by going to A. J. Arno and asking if he would donate his computer to the school. Arno does, then uses it to get out of his pledge to give $20,000.

The part that made the biggest impression on me at the time was Quigley's demonstration of how a computer could be programmed to do household tasks for us when we were not home (shades of the future foreshadowed by the Carousel of Progress). And now we can literally do those things that Quigley demonstrates, by using our cell phones to issue those commands. What would Walt think of that?

Of course, the computer ends up malfunctioning and when Dexter tries to fix it himself, he gets zapped. The computer's data banks are transferred to his brain and Dexter becomes a walking, talking computer in tennis shoes. Improbable as it seems, I rather liked the idea of being the smartest guy in the room. It was already clear to my young self that I was not going to be the world's greatest athlete, or even a competitive one. Knowledge was going to be my ticket out, and just like other Disney films, *Computer* allowed me to experience the fantasy of being a national celebrity for my mind. Those were the days!

There are several topical moments in the movie that feel quaint now.

- The whole notion of leading a student delegation to talk with Arno, only they are not interested in protesting the Vietnam War or marching for civil rights or working to save the environment. They just want a computer for their school.

- When setting up the computer at school proves a big task, one of the students complains that they should try something simpler next time, "like hijacking a Cuban airliner." Another time, someone remarks that if Quigley had been in charge, "Russia would have made that five-year plan."

- After Dexter becomes a celebrity, one of the stops on his nation-wide tour is Cape Kennedy where he watches an Apollo rocket lifting off for the moon (a common occurrence back then).

- Dexter's encyclopedic knowledge (spelled using the Jiminy Cricket song) makes him the object of desire not only for women but also for State College which wants him to transfer there and Arno who wants to exploit Dexter for his own criminal pursuits.

I came away with a lot of things from this movie, mostly questions: Why are the popular teachers (Quigley) always the ones who are unpopular with the administration? Why are college presidents so obsessed with status and being bigger than their rivals? Why are they focused so much on cultivating relationships with corporations and big business and so little on education?

I resolved that, if I became a big-shot like Dexter, I would not lose touch with the people who are my real friends.

By the end of the movie, Dexter is able to use his knowledge to save Medfield by winning $100,000 on a college quiz bowl show (another quaint thing from the past). He then loses his knowledge and goes back to being normal Dexter, a state of mind he and his friends vastly prefer.

Now You See Him, Now You Don't (1972)
TV Premiere: November 26, 1975

The Strongest Man in The World (1975)
TV Premiere: February 27, 1977

The Computer Wore Tennis Shoes set up the template for two sequels that pretty much followed the same stories. Once again, Medfield faces financial hard times. Once again, Dexter accidentally invents some miracle process: a spray that makes people invisible in *Now You See Him* and a breakfast cereal that makes people stronger in *Strongest Man*. Once again, A.J. Arno wants to steal it and use it for a crime. Once again, Dean Higgins wants to use it to earn Medfield some much-needed cash. Once again, Higgins' rival from State College wants it for himself. And, once again, Dexter is able to avoid all of the above and use the invention to save Medfield, or at least stave off the creditors until the next large bill arrives.

The movies were formulaic—I would never argue they are great films—but they worked as fantasy films that taught me that even an average Joe like Dexter could make a difference; that higher education was not the bucolic place where a student learned from the greats, but a jungle of competing interests, from administration to athletics to donors to big business to the government; and that it all revolved around money. Faculty were close to the bottom unless they created some kind of fantastic moneymaking invention. Knowledge and students were at the bottom of the list, but a student could still turn things around with a little know-how and a little luck. Still, I couldn't wait to get there.

I was almost done with growing up. I was ready for the final phase, romance, and the Disney girls who were going to help me along. But, first, I had some final Disney discovering to do.

CHAPTER ELEVEN

Discovering the Classics

NBC All-Disney Saturday Night at the Movies

By the mid-1970s, it was no longer cool to like Disney. Of course, there were many of my classmates who had felt that way all along. But as the decade progressed and we began to approach the tenth anniversary of Walt's death, it became obvious to even a diehard fan like me that the company and the movies it turned out had seen better days.

Perhaps part of this was due to me getting older. I was twelve now, less interested in playing and pretending. My family had moved from the small West Virginia steel town in the northern panhandle to the state capital of Charleston in the center of the state. My oldest sister had graduated from high school and moved away. My other sister was beginning her senior year in high school. She would go to college within a year. In a funny kind of way, this just made me hang on to *The Wonderful World of Disney* even more. And I wasn't the only one confronting the future by hanging on to the past.

Without Walt to guide them and without a Disney at the helm for the first time since its founding, Walt Disney Productions was trying to get by on the maxim, "What Would Walt Do?" The problem was that no one knew exactly what that would have been because nobody in the company had thought the way he did. They did continue to turn out movies in the mold he established. The Nine Old Men, Walt's most talented animators, who really were old by this point, made *The Aristocats* (1970) and *Robin Hood* (1973), both fun movies, but I could not help noticing that *Aristocats* leaned heavily on story elements from *101 Dalmatians* (1961) and *Robin Hood* shared the look and feel and voice talents of *The Jungle Book* (1967).

They were still making zany comedies like *Snowball Express* (1972) and *The World's Greatest Athlete* (1973) and *One of Our Dinosaurs Is Missing* (1975). They were trying to recapture the magic of *Mary Poppins* with musicals like *Bedknobs and Broomsticks* (1971). They were trying to capture Jules Verne-ian adventure with sagas like *The Island at the Top of the World* (1974). But no matter how they tried, the movies always missed something: that spark, that indescribable source of inspiration that made the previous films feel cutting edge and trendy. Rather than breaking new ground, Disney felt rooted in the past and it was a past that predated even the progressive 1960s.

Even *World of Disney* looked a bit long in the tooth as the number of original episodes began to shrink. The schedule was filled more and more by re-running classic episodes from the 1960s. Not that I minded because I loved those shows, but even to twelve-year-old me there was no escaping that Disney's better days seemed behind them. Movie critics and academics published books like *The Disney Version* (1968) by Richard Schickel which focused on the negative sides of Walt Disney's personality, claiming how he had been a primary contributor to the downfall of American life and culture. It became trendy and an accepted trope of pop culture to bash Disney as being old-fashioned and sentimental and just about as square as something could get.

This perception started to change in two ways.

First, Christopher Finch published his massive coffee-table tome titled *The Art of Walt Disney: From Mickey Mouse to the Magic Kingdoms* (1973) which recounted in glorious detail and brilliant color illustrations what groundbreaking work Walt Disney had contributed to the movies and to our cultural heritage. It was a tonic to remind us what the man had done, in a time when it had started to be forgotten.

As a kid whose allowance was a mere five dollars a week, I could not afford to buy such a book even though I very much wanted to. It also didn't help that our local library had the book shelved in their reference section so I could not check it out. Consequently, it took many a trip to the library over several weeks and a few hours each time sitting at a library table for me to read the book cover to cover. God bless my mother who would drop me off at the library and go shopping for an hour or two so I could read the next chapter of the book. When she picked me up, we would walk across the street to an old-fashioned drug store. It looked like something from the 1950s. We would sit at their lunch counter and eat club sandwiches with fries and sip on chocolate sodas. This lasted until one of my sisters gave me the "concise edition" of the book for my thirteenth birthday. (I eventually bought a copy of the complete book from the Book of the Month Club in the 1980s.)

The second act that changed things was that Disney decided to open up its vaults and air some of its classic movies that had never been featured on the TV show and had not been re-released into theaters for over a decade. The films would not air on *The Wonderful World of Disney*, but would be broadcast the evening before as part of the new *NBC All-Disney Saturday Night at the Movies*. A classic Disney movie would be paired up with a classic Disney short to create a three-hour prime-time block of entertainment. The lead-off movie would be just the ratings hit the company was looking for and just the film to restore my faith in Disney at the moment it was starting to waver.

20,000 Leagues Under the Sea (1954)

TV Premiere: February 23, 1974

Even before sitting down to watch the movie, like *Treasure Island*, I was already familiar with Jules Verne's classic 1870 tale of Captain Nemo, his amazing submarine the *Nautilus*, and their fantastic journey around the world under the sea. My first exposure to the story was when Kenner Toy's *Famous Classic Tales* had shown an animated version on TV in 1973. It had interested me enough to buy the book from our Scholastic club at school and read it. I had also read the *Classics Illustrated* comic-book version and I had even ridden the 20,000 Leagues under the Sea ride at Walt Disney World when we vacationed there in 1972. I had seen photos of the movie in various Disney books (including the Finch book). Their ground-breaking blend of futuristic fantasy and 19th century décor gave it a steam-punk look decades before the term had been coined. I could not wait for it to air on *All-Disney Saturday Night at the Movies*.

The movie begins in 1868 and tells the "whale of a tale" (to borrow a phrase from Kirk Douglas' song in the film) about a mysterious monster that is sinking vessels across the Pacific Ocean. The U.S. government dispatches one of its top warships, the U.S.S. *Abraham Lincoln*, to investigate. On board is the world's leading ocean expert, Prof. Pierre Aronnax (Paul Lukas), his assistant Conseil (Peter Lorre), and Ned Land, the world's best harpooner (Kirk Douglas). After months of fruitless searching, the *Lincoln* is about to give up when it finally runs into the monster. The vessels collide and our heroes tumble into the sea. When they wake up, they find themselves on board the "monster" which turns out to be a futuristic submarine commanded by the enigmatic Captain Nemo (James Mason), a genius scientist and inventor who is obsessed with preserving the peaceful beauty of the oceans by enacting revenge against the world governments who have hounded him to reveal his brilliant secrets.

Aronnax sees the beauty and benefits of Nemo's discoveries and hopes to convince him to lay down his grudge against the world and use his secrets for the benefit of humankind. But underneath his gentlemanly exterior, Nemo is a man with a dark side. "I am not what is called a civilized man, Professor," he declares. "I have done with society for reasons that seem good to me. Therefore, I do not obey its laws."

Ned Land views the *Nautilus* as a prison and Nemo as a mad man. He thinks only of escape. Conseil finds himself stuck between the two sides. As Nemo shares the wonders of the ocean with his captives, he also shares the reasons for his all-consuming revenge. Along the way, they encounter various creatures of the deep including the classic fight with the giant squid, as well as humans on the different islands where they stop, from native tribes to island prison camps.

Aronnax fails to see how much Nemo's persecution has warped his mind and left him a bitter man.

"What you fail to understand," he tells the professor, "is the power of hate. It can fill the heart as surely as love can."

"I feel sorry for you," Aronnax replies. "It is a bitter substitute."

Only the ocean soothes his tortured soul. "See how peaceful it is here."

It all climaxes at Nemo's home base of Vulcania. A multi-national force waits there to seize Nemo's inventions for themselves. Nemo is killed. Vulcania erupts in a mighty mushroom cloud (clearly an atomic bomb to us Cold War kids) and the *Nautilus* is scuttled to keep it out of the hands of "that hated nation" (as Nemo calls it). Only Aronnax, Ned, and Conseil escaped in the *Nautilus'* skiff to tell the tale.

20,000 Leagues under the Sea blew my mind in a way no Disney film had up to that time. It took everything I had been feeling and discovering about life and combined it together into one film that I could obsess over and take to heart.

My Robinson Crusoe nature saw the appeal of turning my back on the world (with its hurts and pains) and living alone—though spending it on board a nuclear submarine with a band of faithful "My Man Friday" crew members who felt the same as I did was better than being on a deserted island (where I might become as crazy as Ben Gunn, says I).

It also connected with my love of the oceans at a time when they were perceived to be under threat. Ecology was on the rise and millions like me had spent a lot of the early 1970s watching the *Undersea World of Jacques Cousteau* (1968–1976) specials as he traveled the world and educated us on the beauty and plight of the oceans. Watching Cousteau, I had come to appreciate the fragile and delicate state they were in. How humans were putting its ecosystem in jeopardy through over-fishing and pollution. I liked the fact that Captain Nemo was taking a stand. He was a militant Jacques Cousteau with a much cooler vessel.

I became obsessed with the *Nautilus* itself. I drew blueprints of the ship in the pages of my school notebooks.

The movie continued my development as a writer because I started writing my own fan fiction (which I shared with no one) chronicling my own journeys with Captain Nemo. Sometimes, I wrote from Aronnax's point of view and sometimes I chose Nemo, using my own experiences with bullying at school as motivation for taking fictional acts of revenge against the world. Even as a twelve year old, I well understood the anger that motivated Nemo.

The movie also made me aware of some cold, hard facts about business and governments and how the two were intertwined. When Nemo shows the professor still-functioning slave labor camps, Aronnax is shocked. "I thought they had been abolished."

Nemo coldly replies, "Nothing is abolished that makes a profit."

I learned governments and industries would never miss a chance to weaponize and monetize any major scientific breakthrough. Nuclear armageddon comparisons could not be missed, nor could the realization that sometimes there are discoveries so ahead of their time that they must be buried or put aside until humans are ready for them. In Nemo's final words, spoken as a voiceover as the *Nautilus* goes down for the last time: "But there is hope for the future. When the world is ready for a new and better life, all this will someday come to pass, in God's good time."

The movie was an eye-opener: a live-action Disney classic at its best which my generation had never experienced before, a chance to see Disney in its prime. It was dazzling and incredible. *20,000 Leagues* was the last Disney show I can remember generating buzz amongst my fellow pre-teens. When we met in Mr. Albert's sixth grade science class on Monday morning, we were so full of questions about the movie and all the gadgetry aboard the *Nautilus* that we convinced him to scuttle his lesson plan for the day. We gathered our desks in a circle and spent the entire class discussing the movie and how the devices on the submarine worked. Mr. Albert patiently explained it all to us while smartly connecting the devices to the basic science principles we needed to learn. It remains one of my favorite classes.

Lastly, the movie made me a life-long lover of Jules Verne. I went on to read and treasure his other works, including *From the Earth to the Moon* (1865), *Journey to the Center of the Earth* (1864), and *Around the World in 80 Days* (1873). It reminded me that my admiration for the works of Walt Disney was not misplaced. I came away from the film more committed to Walt and his work than ever before.

The Parent Trap (1961)

TV Premiere: October 26, 1974

The night *The Parent Trap* aired, my parents were throwing a party at our house. My mother filled up a dinner plate with food and sent me down to the family room for the evening. Our RCA Victor TV had died by this point and we had a more modern Sony with a smaller screen.

This was the first movie I remember seeing Hayley Mills in, even though that turned out not to be true. I just didn't remember at the time. I had previously seen her in Disney films like *The Moon-Spinners* (1963) and *Summer Magic* (1963). But that had been about ten years ago and the memory had faded. So with this movie I was rediscovering Hayley Mills anew.

I was also not entirely unfamiliar with the movie. One of my sisters had the novelization on her bookshelf. I had borrowed it without asking and read it cover to cover at least three or four times. So I knew the basic plot line by heart. Two teens, Sharon and Susan (both played by Hayley Mills), meet at summer camp. At first they hate each other and play increasingly outrageous pranks on the other.

They soon come to realize that they are twin sisters (the different hairstyles confuse them for a bit) and that their parents divorced when they were very young. At the end of the summer, they agree to switch places (sort of a modern female *Prince and the Pauper*) so they can each meet the parent they have never known. Sharon goes west to her father Mitch (Brian Keith) who lives on a California ranch. Susan travels east to Boston to be with her mother Maggie (Maureen O'Hara). It doesn't take long for the switcheroo to be revealed. Mother and Susan travel to California where the twins waste no time trying to "trap" their divorced parents into getting back together.

The Parent Trap is a lot of fun, one of the best comedies Disney produced. Like all the projects at the time, its special effects were cutting edge. The traveling matte technique allowed Hayley Mills to play both twins and there are entire scenes where she is brilliantly acting and reacting to herself. Sharon and Susan may look alike, but Mills creates a different voice and a different character for each. It is an impressive performance and foreshadows the blue screen and CGI techniques actors will find themselves performing against in the future. It made me a Hayley Mills fan.

Brian Keith and Maureen O'Hara had been two of my favorite performers for years. Keith specialized in grouchy father characters who were soft-hearted underneath, and his Mitch in this movie is a variation on the same. He is the usual clueless dad who has no idea what he wants until it is shoved in his face. I knew Maureen O'Hara from several John Wayne movies, particularly *McLintock!* (1963). Her performance here was a sweet and subtle portrayal of a middle-aged woman rediscovering romance in her life.

Even though a comedy, the movie did treat seriously the issue of divorce at a time when it was not as common as it is now, and showed how the differing expectations of each partner, the contrast in upbringing as well as contrasting lifestyles and values, compound to create grudges and inevitable rifts. I laughed as I watched it, even as I could hear the laughter from my parents' dinner party overhead. In some ways my twelve-year-old self was whistling past the graveyard as I watched this light-hearted look at my (and any child's) own worst nightmare—parents divorcing. In retrospect, I guess my fear was justified since my parents did just that ten years later.

Pollyanna (1960)

TV Premiere: March 8, 1975

While I am sure I saw *Pollyanna* when it aired on *World of Disney* in the 1960s, it didn't have an impact on me until it re-aired on *NBC All-Disney Saturday Night at the Movies* a decade later. Going into it, I knew the film had the same creative team as the one behind *The Parent Trap* including writer/director David Swift, and that this was the role that made Hayley Mills a star.

It didn't take long for me to realize that this was an entirely different Hayley than the one in *The Parent Trap*. Susan and Sharon were spunky teens, but here in *Pollyanna* Hayley was playing a wide-eyed girl raised to see the good in everything and everyone, and can't understand why others cannot see this as well. Raised by missionary parents but now orphaned, Pollyanna has come to the small town of Harrington to live with her Aunt Polly (Jane Wyman). I am sure the similar names were no coincidence. Like Maureen O'Hara in *Parent Trap*, Aunt Polly is a woman who has let the duties of her life displace any love or romance. Since she is the wealthiest woman in town, she feels it is "her" town and that she can dictate what is to be done and who is allowed to see whom, even to the point of dictating the sermon topics for Sunday service, As a result, the entire town is uptight as if its social corset were strung too tight.

Eventually, Pollyanna's sunny disposition and optimistic outlook wins everyone over. First, Aunt Polly's grumpy servants, then the town's eccentric recluse Mr. Pendergast (Adolphe Menjou, in his last role), then Mrs. Snow (Agnes Moorehead), a hypochondriac convinced she will die any moment, and finally the town's minister Reverend Ford (Karl Malden). She does this largely by playing the Glad Game where a person tries to see the good in any situation they find themselves.

The hardest nut to crack is Aunt Polly herself. Her stubbornness and refusal to meet the town halfway when it plans a carnival to raise money for a new orphanage ends up costing her more than she expects. Pollyanna sneaks out without permission by climbing down a large tree outside her bedroom window. When she attempts to return, she falls out of the tree and is paralyzed from the waist down.

This twist devastates Pollyanna and sends her into a major depression. As Polly prepares to take Pollyanna to Baltimore for an operation to restore her legs, the townspeople gather to tell her how much she now means to them. It lifts her spirits again. As she and Aunt Polly board the train for Baltimore the town folk all come to see her off and someone hangs a sign that reads "Welcome to Harrington—The Glad Town."

Pollyanna is one of the loveliest films Walt Disney ever produced and a major achievement by writer/director David Swift. Skeptics like to knock its fundamentally optimistic message as "sentimental" and "saccharine," but that doesn't negate the fact that the film's message is dead on.

The first thing that struck me about the movie was its huge cast that included many of my favorite actors from the 1960s. It was like a reunion. Here were Agnes Moorehead (*Bewitched*), James Drury (*The Virginian*), Edward Platt (*Get Smart*), Mary Grace Canfield (*Green Acres*), and Karl Malden (*The Streets of San Francisco*). Reliable character actors like Donald Crisp, Adolphe Menjou, Rita Shaw, and Ian Wolfe rounded out the cast. There were even Disney regulars like Kevin Corcoran and Nancy Olsen.

Hayley Mills was a revelation as Pollyanna. It is easy to see why she received the final special Academy Award handed out for Best Juvenile Performance. Her Pollyanna refuses to accept the surface personas people give themselves. Instead, she wants to see the real person below that persona and she is not satisfied until she sees it.

Decades before Red (Morgan Freeman) proclaimed in *The Shawshank Redemption* (1994) that life had only two choices, "get busy living or get busy dying," Pollyanna offers up the same philosophy wrapped inside the Glad Game.

The film teaches that the way we look at things colors the world that we see. I came away determined to always find the good in life, and to remain skeptical toward those who always focus on the negative.

The movie also made it clear how stubbornness and pride and entrenched thinking can have unexpected consequences. Aunt Polly's refusal to change her patrician approach to "her" town and embrace the changing times sets up the circumstances that lead directly to Pollyanna's paralysis. Aunt Polly's denial of her loving side has led to a lonely and empty life, one she is just starting to toss aside at the movie's end. When Polly opens her mansion's doors to let the townsfolk in to wish Pollyanna well, she is symbolically opening her heart as well.

I even liked the way the movie left Pollyanna's recovery uncertain. The movie never tells us whether she walks again. But in dramatic terms, that question does not need to be answered. Pollyanna has already transformed Harrington and its people. As a result, they are able to reach out in her time of need and restore her spirit as well. I learned that when we suffer an injury impossible to recover from, it is up to each one of us to play the Glad Game: find the good in our new situation and then move on.

A major life-changing moment for me came when Pollyanna visits Reverend Ford and shares her father's favorite quote attributed to Abraham Lincoln: "When you look for the bad in mankind, expecting to find it, you surely will." That moment stunned me and gave me a reality check (before the term had been coined). I realized in that moment that it is always easy to find the bad side of life, to focus on the frustrating words and actions of others. But that doesn't contribute to our well-being in any productive way. And it doesn't make the people around us any happier or more content. One by one, Pollyanna's hopeful approach toward life changes everyone's perspective in town. Harrington becomes less stuffy, less rigid. It becomes a town with a community spirit and citizens willing to help one another.

As Reverend Ford tells Pollyanna at the end of the film, "We looked for the good in them, and we found it, didn't we?"

I resolved to do the same in my life from then on.

Old Yeller (1957)

TV Premiere: February 14, 1976

Is there anyone who doesn't know the plot for what I argue is the greatest "boy and his dog" movie ever made? Even back in 1976, I found it oddly appropriate that Disney chose to broadcast this on Valentine's Day because there is no greater love than the love we feel for a treasured pet when we are young.

For those not familiar with the story, *Old Yeller* tells the tale of the Coates family struggling to make a living on a Texas farm right after the Civil War. In order to earn some needed extra money, the father, Jim (Fess Parker), leaves to spend the summer on a cattle drive out of state. He leaves in charge his fifteen-year-old son Travis (Tommy Kirk) whose sole task is to make sure their corn crop survives the summer so they will not starve to death during the winter. Sharing the farm is the rest of the family, Travis' younger brother Arliss (Kevin Corcoran) who is more interested in playing than working, and his mother (Dorothy Maguire) who is willing to sit back and let her oldest boy prove he has the stuff to be a man.

When a local stray yellow dog begins robbing their henhouse, Travis sets a trap for him and they catch Old Yeller, a mangy mongrel of a dog with charm to boot. Arliss loves him from the start, but Travis finds the dog a nuisance. Only when Yeller saves Arliss' life from an angry bear does Travis begin to recognize Yeller's smarts and courage. Soon enough, Travis and the dog are inseparable. Their bond is cemented when both get badly injured by a marauding pack of wild hogs. The two recover together over the next couple of weeks and grow to deeply love each other. Life on the farm seems perfect. Travis has risen to the challenges. The crop is in good shape for harvesting.

When their cow comes down with rabies, Travis sees no choice but to shoot her. While burning her carcass that night, a wolf charges them out of the dark. Once again, Yeller dashes in and saves their lives, but Travis' mother realizes that the wolf had rabies. As a precaution, they close Yeller up in the corn crib. When the dog starts to turn mean and display the symptoms of rabies, Travis realizes he has no choice but to put him down.

Old Yeller is not just one of the greatest Disney movies ever made, but one of the greatest movies ever made, period. Tommy Kirk gives an amazing performance as Travis, right down to his thick Texas accent. It is almost as if he is channeling a method actor in this movie so complete and dead on is his performance. Looking back, I find it enlightening that his character's name is Travis, the last name of the martyred commander of the Alamo. And like that historical Travis, young Travis here is put in charge of a remote outpost (his family farm) that he must be the stoic commander of while his father is away.

One of the reasons *Old Yeller* had such an impact on me in this time and place was that I was the same age as Travis when I saw it, and I too was just starting to understand what it meant to be an adult, and that it didn't always involve doing what we wanted to do at a particular time. There were chores that needed to be done to ensure success, or even survival, months down the line. There were times when you had to do something alone, and times when it was a sign of maturity to ask for help. And lastly, being an adult was about making the hard choices that broke your heart but were best for all.

Travis has to put on the role of being an adult before he knows how. It is a role he does not feel comfortable wearing at first. Like someone still growing into the role, he becomes militant and tries bossing everyone around. It is his way or the highway, but he soon finds that way doesn't work, particularly on his free-spirited brother who seems naturally bent on rebelling against any attempt to pull him into line. Once he has a partner in Yeller, Travis relaxes. He allows his brother to have a freer rein and he turns into an able helper. He also discovers that being a man is about taking advice and seeing if it works for you, whether it is the incorrect advice of Bud Searsey (Jeff York) about treeing hogs that almost gets Travis and Yeller killed, or it is Burn

Sanderson's (Chuck Connors) more sensible advice to watch out for the onset of "hydrophobia" (rabies).

There are troubles along the way that only a child would find traumatic, like when Burn Sanderson, Yeller's former owner, turns up wanting his dog back. The idea of losing the dog he has just started to love terrifies Travis (much as my own family nearly lost a pet we had just come to love to another owner), but he knows he is honor bound to return him. Fortunately, Sanderson can see how much the family loves Yeller and decides to let him stay by making a trade with Arliss. And there are future "scares" in the way Searsey's daughter Lizbeth (Beverly Washburn) has set her sights on Travis. She is clearly ready for marriage at this young age when he isn't even sure he wants to start dating and that sets the boy on edge (even though there are hints in the film that he will eventually come around).

But over the course of the movie and the summer Travis becomes an adult and Old Yeller teaches him how, even including making the tough (but humane) decision to put the dog down. He not only taught Travis, but he also taught me.

At the end of the summer, Travis' father returns with the horse he promised to bring if Travis was successful. He arrives just as they are burying Old Yeller and Travis is too grief-stricken to care. From Travis' perspective, life is over as he works his way through the final phase and hardest lesson of being an adult, and a Disney staple: dealing with the loss of a loved one, and how, if we are not careful, those feelings of hurt and loss can make us bitter and resentful.

Jim and Travis sit down to have a talk over Yeller's grave and it is a talk that has stuck with me. Jim tells his son:

> What I am trying to say is that life is like that sometimes...now and then, for no good reason a man can figure out, life will just haul off and knock him flat, slam him against the ground so hard it feels like all his insides are all busted. But it's not all like that. A lot of it is mighty fine. And we can't afford wasting the good part fretting about the bad. That makes it all bad...but I'll tell you a trick that might help. If you start looking around for something good to take the place of the bad, as a general rule you can find it.

Wait a minute! There it was again: Pollyanna's Glad Game. Only this time it was phrased a little differently, maybe a little less sentimentally, but the same message: use your time to find the good in life. I vowed (again) to do that right then and there. And Jim Coates was entirely right. A lot of life is mighty fine (that is a massive understatement) and I could very well have missed out on a lot of it if I had chosen only to focus on the bad.

Old Yeller was the last Disney movie or episode to have a lasting impact on me, maybe because, like Travis, I was on the verge of being an adult myself. Even though I would *not* be in charge of the family farm, I would be starting high school in the fall, which has its own pitfalls and challenges. Looking back, it seemed that I saw it at just the right time and at just the right age, just like all the other Disney moments that formed my childhood, so I could take its lessons to heart and carry them forward.

They did air other movies on *All-Disney Saturday Night*, including grown-up Hayley Mills fare like *That Darn Cat!* (1965) and *The Moon-Spinners* (1964). They aired pets-in-peril movies like *The Three Lives of Thomasina* (1963) and *The Incredible Journey* (1963), and wacky comedies like *The Absent-Minded Professor* (1961) and *Lt. Robin Crusoe U.S.N.* (1967). The last *All-Disney Saturday Night* aired on January 29, 1977, and featured *Tonka* (1958). I find it significant that I chose not to watch it.

Disney had taught me enough of what it meant to appreciate life and to appreciate nature, what it meant to be an adult and how to make my way forward as an individual in society. I could sense my childhood was coming to an end and I was okay with that.

It was time to close the door on the past and start embracing the future.

Rich's Top Ten

Here are my top ten favorite songs from *The Wonderful World of Disney*:

1. "The Scarecrow of Romney Marsh Song"
The Scarecrow of Romney Marsh (1964)
Words and music by Terry Gilkyson

2. "The Wonderful World of Disney (Main Title)"
The Wonderful World of Disney (1968)
Music and arrangement by George Bruns

3. "Bella Notte"
From All of Us to All of You (1958)
Originally from *Lady and the Tramp* (1955)
Words by Peggy Lee; music by Sonny Burke

4. "On the Front Porch"
Summer Magic (1963)
Words and music by the Sherman Brothers

5. "You Can Fly! You Can Fly! You Can Fly!"
From All of Us to All of You (1958)
Originally from *Peter Pan* (1953)
Words by Sammy Cahn; music by Sammy Fain

6. "The Spectrum Song"
An Adventure In Color (1961)
Words and music by the Sherman Brothers

7. "The Ballad of Davy Crockett"
Davy Crockett (1955)
Words by Tom Blackburn; music by George Bruns

8. "The Liberty Tree"
Johnny Tremain (1957)
Words by Tom Blackburn; music by George Bruns

9. "The Monkey's Uncle"
The Monkey's Uncle (1965)
Words and music by the Sherman Brothers

10. "The Strummin' Song"
The Horsemasters (1961)
Words and music by the Sherman Brothers

Learning the Ropes of Romance

The Disney Girls

It is difficult to tell at what age a boy's mind turns to thoughts of romance. I suppose it depends on when our hormones start to kick in. Inevitably, our first crushes are safe crushes focused on people who cannot say no. And that means movie stars on the big screen or people on TV. My sisters had their infatuations with Bobby Sherman and David Cassidy and the other teen idols of their day. Since I was a Disney boy, it was inevitable that my first crushes would be on Disney girls. And while they were "romances" that never crossed over into the material world, they still managed to teach me much I needed to know when the fantasies became actualities.

As I grew into my teens, there were girls who captured my fancy with the way they smiled, the way they walked, the knowing twinkle in their eyes hinting that they understood something more than I knew up to that time. While they were attractive, it did seem like some of these women were out of my league, like Susan Hampshire in *The Three Lives of Thomasina* (1963) and Deborah Walley in *Bon Voyage* (1962) and *Summer Magic* (1963). But when it came time there were three Disney girls who stood out in my mind and, in their own way, held my hand and led me into a better understanding of the world of romance.

Hayley Mills

To my mind there were two Hayley Mills. There was the "glad girl" in *Pollyanna* who turned into the exuberant young teen in *The Parent Trap* and *In Search of the Castaways*. But then there was the adult Hayley in *The Moon-Spinners* and *Summer Magic*, with the half-teen, half-grown girl in *That Darn Cat!* bridging the gap.

In Search of the Castaways (1962)

TV Premiere: October 1, 8, 1978

An attempt to recapture the adventure of *20,000 Leagues* by adapting another Jules Verne story, *Castaways* is a fun but odd kind of adventure. Hayley Mills and Keith Hamshere play Mary and Robert Grant, the children of Captain Grant (Jack Gwillim) who was lost at sea. They have teamed up with a French professor (Maurice Chevalier) who has found a message in a bottle from their supposedly lost father. The trio convince Lord Glenarvan (Wilfrid Hyde-White), the owner of the shipping line their father worked for, to set out in search of the title castaways. And it doesn't hurt that they are accompanied on the trip by Lord Glenarvan's cute son, John (Michael Anderson Jr.).

The movie has some of the wildest fantasy sequences Disney ever put on film. Our intrepid party of adventurers find themselves caught over the course of the movie in an earthquake, a crazy slide down the side of a mountain on a chunk of rock that rides like a bobsled, a desert flood that leaves them stranded in a tree, and a fire in said tree. Toss in a hungry jaguar, mutinous sailors, and an oily villain (George Sanders), and you have one rip-roaring adventure tale. The only thing missing this time around is the full Disney touch that would bring the whole thing to life. Perhaps this just wasn't Verne's best story. Perhaps Hyde-White and Chevalier are a bit too old for their roles; there are scenes that make it feel like we are on vacation with our grandparents rather than on a globe-trotting adventure. They make a poor substitute for the dashing Captain Nemo. For whatever reason, the movie plays like a series of action sequences rather than as a unified tale.

However, as a teenage boy watching this in the late 1970s, I found my eyes more focused on sixteen-year-old Hayley than on anything else in the movie. Having already seen her in *Pollyanna* and *The Parent Trap*, I could see this was a girl on the brink of adulthood. Along with all their adventures, there is the budding romance between Mary and John. Played a little too superciliously by Anderson Jr., one minute he is being genuinely sweet and the next moment he is being a bit of an entitled cad.

Still, it is fun to watch how, amid their adventures, the two of them figure navigate their budding romance. This is clearly the first infatuation for both of them and the film nicely captures those moments when your whole body could be thrilled by the touch of a hand, the brush of an arm, or the sweet pleasure of singing a song together (it made me want to learn the guitar).

Hayley Mills had grown from the eager girl in *Pollyanna* to the rebellious twin teens in *The Parent Trap* to the assertive Mary Grant ready to step out with a boy on the deck of a ship and see what the stars may hold under the nighttime sky. And I was wishing to be that boy.

That Darn Cat! (1965)

TV Premiere: May 1, 1976

This movie marked a Disney transition of sorts. It was Hayley Mills' last movie for the studio, but Dean Jones' first. It was also the first of a type of comedy (usually starring Dean Jones) that Disney would specialize in making for the next decade, from *The Ugly Dachshund* (1966) to *Monkeys, Go Home* (1967) to *The $1,000,000 Duck* (1971), with diminishing laughs, involving humans (usually an exasperated Jones) dealing with unusual or exasperating animals. Still, *That Darn Cat!* is one of the best.

The truant title character is D.C., which could be short for District of Columbia since the movie is set in Washington D.C., but is most likely short for Darn Cat. Owned by teenaged Patti Randall (Hayley), D.C. ranges far and wide. Being a Siamese cat, he is a true descendent of the villainous cats in *Lady and the Tramp* (1955), but without their meanness. One night, he returns home wearing a lady's wristwatch in place of his collar. Patti and her older sister Ingrid (Dorothy Provine) contact the police and soon their home is command central for an investigation headed by FBI agent Zeke Kelso (Dean Jones).

They have all reached the conclusion that the wristwatch is owned by a bank teller kidnapped in a recent robbery. If Kelso and his agents tail D.C. on his nightly rounds, he might lead them to the criminals. The humor is inspired and the slapstick comedy moments are among the best in any Disney film. The leads are aided by a strong supporting cast featuring Roddy McDowall, Elsa Lanchester, William Demarest, Frank Gorshin, Richard Deacon, and Ed Wynn.

The only person not given much to do is Hayley Mills. While supposedly the star, the movie revolves around the cat more than her. It doesn't help that she is saddled with a clueless boyfriend named Canoe (Tom Lowell) who is more interested in surfing and surfboards and cars than her. The guy is so clearly beneath her. Even she can see that and there are moments where she treats him more like her kid brother from *In Search of the Castaways* than as her boyfriend. Most of her genuinely loving moments are reserved for her cat.

The Moon-Spinners (1964)

TV Premiere: November 20, 27, & December 4, 1966

The Moon-Spinners is one of the best, and most underrated, action films Walt Disney made. It is one of his few films that seem to have its characters in genuine peril with their lives on the line. There are moments where it feels more like an Alfred Hitchcock film than a Disney production. I discovered this film twice in my life and both times it made a terrifying mark on me.

I first remember seeing it as a five year old when it aired on *World of Disney* in the 1960s. I did not retain the plot beyond the fact that it was set in the Greek isles. What I did remember, what burned its terror on my youthful mind like a brand on a young calf, were two sequences. First, the scene where Hayley Mills was trapped in a windmill and must escape by leaping out a window and riding the blades of the mill down to the ground. Director James Nielsen shot it in such a vertiginous manner that it left me with a dizzying fear of heights that I retain to this day. The second scene happens earlier when Hayley wanders into a local church and finds her date (Peter McEnery) hiding and wounded. His bloody arm shooting up into the frame gave me one of the biggest jolts of my childhood, like the hand shooting out of the water at the end of *Deliverance* (1972).

The second time I discovered *The Moon-Spinners* came a decade later when it aired on *NBC All-Disney Saturday Night at the Movies*. This time around as a teenager I had a much better appreciation for the film and eighteen-year-old Hayley playing her only adult role in a Disney film, as Nikky Ferris, a girl on vacation with her aunt. While staying at a quiet hotel in a coastal town, she finds herself caught up in a jewel heist. For the early part of the film, however, her mind is more focused on meeting cute boys and having a good time. That is how Mark (Peter McEnery) crosses her path and unwittingly gets her involved. There are even hints of romance here and there, but the central mystery soon comes to overwhelm everything else.

Ultimately, Nikky turns into an adult version of the other roles Hayley Mills played at the studio, exhibiting the same traits: a plucky resourcefulness combined with an unerring desire to do what is right.

Summer Magic (1963)

TV Premiere: December 5, 12, 1965

Summer Magic is my favorite of Hayley Mills' Disney films. It is not as wise or profound as *Pollyanna*. It does not have as many laughs as *The Parent Trap* or *That Darn Cat!* And it doesn't have the thrills or high-stakes adventure of *In Search of the Castaways* or *The Moon-Spinners*.

What I like about it is its relaxing charm. It is an escape from everyday reality back into the past, a gently nostalgic tonic that makes us wish for simpler times lived at a more casual pace. I remember watching this movie on *World of Disney* back in 1971 at the age of nine and enjoying it. When I saw it again in 1976 at the age of fourteen, I fell in love with it.

This is the story of the Carey family (based on the classic 1911 novel *Mother Carey's Chickens*) about a widow who discovers after her husband's death that they are now poor. Her daughter Nancy (Hayley Mills) remembers a lovely yellow house in a small Maine town that the family once saw and admired. She writes to the local store and gets the permission of the store's owner (Burl Ives) to move there. The Careys relocate to the yellow house and commence fixing it up. Things change when their cousin Julia (Deborah Walley) comes for an extended stay. The two girls clash over values, but eventually find a common ground: boys. Nancy also lives in constant fear that the house's rich owner, the unseen Mr. Hamilton, will return and demand the house back. In the end, everything turns out right and everyone finds happiness.

Made after *In Search of the Castaways* but before *The Moon-Spinners*, *Summer Magic* finds Hayley on the cusp of adulthood. She has grown into a lovely young woman, but still has tomboy thoughts and ways. Like her other characters, Nancy is a headstrong girl who fixes her mind on something (moving to the yellow house) then uses the same laser-focused determination to not stop until she achieves it. Fortunately, her persistence is now complemented by a generous charm which melts those who choose to stand in her way. Nancy is a prototypical liberated woman of her time. She rejects contemporary women's fashions for a good pair of dungarees. She spouts sufferagette slogans and drops Mrs. Panghurst's name.

Cousin Julia is the polar opposite. The same age as Nancy, she has being a lady down to a tee. She knows just the right way to dress or act to catch a man's eye. When she and Nancy play a lovers' triangle game of croquet with the town's handsome new school teacher (James Stacy), Nancy can't help but get caught up in winning the game. When she does, she raises her hands in triumph, only to discover that Julia and Mr. Brown have abandoned Nancy for a more private pursuit. By winning the game, Nancy has lost the war.

Nancy realizes her approach to life often alienates boys. She convinces Julia to teach her the language of love and how to attract boys. Julia gladly does, instructing her through the song "Talk Feminine" whose lyrics would make feminists' skin crawl today, but still contains some universal truths on how to get a guy's attention.

At the end of the film, Nancy does win her man—and an unexpected one at that—but she does so by combining her newfound feminine ways with the tomboy determination of her true personality. Julia may have being a lady down, but her version of a lady is the 19th century kind that will soon grow out of style. Nancy is a woman who will thrive in the burgeoning 20th century. Hayley plays Nancy well, humanizing her by showing us little moments when we learn that she is not nearly as determined as she appears. She has doubts about everything: whether she can accomplish her plan and keep her family from being homeless, whether she will convince Mr. Hamilton to let them stay, whether she will get someone to share her life with.

It is not a great film, but it is a very good one, and, just like the simpler times it extols, it requires its viewer to sit back and let its rather languid plot unfold at its own pace. The message isn't in the destination but in the journey, and that journey is well supported by a cast which includes veterans like Dorothy Maguire, Una Merkel, Michael J. Pollard, and Peter Brown.

Summer Magic is also graced by one of Richard and Robert Sherman's best song scores. "Flittering" has become a staple played on Main Street, U.S.A. in the Disney parks. Burl Ives' rendition of "The Ugly Bug Ball" became a pop hit, but by far my favorite song is "On the Front Porch"—a lovely ballad about the forgotten glories of just hanging out on the front porch in the evening and enjoying the simple pleasure of being alive. Even Robert Sherman, who penned the lyrics to so many classic Disney songs, selected this one as his personal favorite.

The movie was the perfect vehicle for Hayley Mills as she transitioned from teenager to young woman. It is both a paean to simpler times and an indicator of what it will take to succeed in the new world ahead. But it is also a movie where, as a young boy, I very much wanted to step onto that relaxing front porch in the evening and take the hand of the jilted Nancy and steal a kiss or two.

Janet Munro

Among the Disney girls, few burned as bright or faded so quickly as Janet Munro. She starred in only four films for Disney and only two of them ever appeared on *World of Disney*. When she did appear on the show, it was usually in behind-the-scenes specials publicizing upcoming movies like *Darby O'Gill & the Little People* (1959), *Third Man on the Mountain* (1959), or *Swiss Family Robinson* (1960). *The Horsemasters* was an original two-part episode released theatrically overseas. And then she was gone.

Janet Munro is a bit of a scarlet woman in the Disney lexicon. She had a sexuality to her before I really understood what that word meant. Her characters were free, bent on running headlong into enjoying life without necessarily being tied down by it. In *Darby O'Gill* she plays Katie O'Gill, a lass any man in her small Irish village would gladly marry, but who is just a little past the marrying age (you know, seventeen or eighteen) because she isn't quite ready to settle down into the role of wife and mother. This could be because she has, like Belle in

Beauty and the Beast (1991), surveyed the men in her town and found them wanting. There is even a Gaston-type in the village named Pony Sugrue (Kieron Moore) who is trying to bully her to the altar.

Janet's characters want to be viewed as equals to men even as she understands that men need to feel they are the ones in the lead. Unlike Hayley's characters, Janet's were content to let the boys lead, even while the twinkle in her eye and the giggle in her voice let us know she could take the lead if she wanted to.

Perhaps she hangs back because, when she does barge past the guys, her headstrong nature often finds her in over her head. In *Darby O'Gill*, her refusal to let Michael McBride (Sean Connery) help her retrieve the family horse from the haunted mountain causes her to fall victim to the banshee, the Irish death spirit. In *Third Man on the Mountain*, it results in her getting stuck, hanging off the side of the mountain and getting rescued by Rudy Matt (James MacArthur). In *Swiss Family Robinson,* she gets captured by cannibals and is again rescued by James MacArthur and his brother Fritz (Tommy Kirk).

"I warned you I have a temper," she tells Michael in *Darby O'Gill*.

"Well, I like a lively girl," he smiles back.

Unlike the other Disney girls, Janet also had an androgynous quality as in *Swiss Family Robinson* when she posed as a boy rather successfully. Her characters appear to be in a never-ending competition to prove themselves to the world. She is little interested in conforming to the rules of the societies she inhabited. Her twinkling eyes, her bright big smile, and her pixie nose indicate a mischievous side. This is a game girl willing to try anything once and probably quick to master it as well.

When she is put in charge as Janet Hale in *The Horsemasters*, Munro comes across as a stern martinet, a stickler for drumming in the principles of horse riding and competition with little interest in being loved or admired, even though in private she shows her warm, tender side to the horses. Ultimately, she ends up dating the equally headstrong (but rich) David Lawford (John Fraser).

Like the headstrong colts she tries to tame or the ambitious students she tries to make walk before they run, the real Janet bristled at the Disney roles she was given. She felt they were holding her back as an actress so she plotted her own way out of her contract. While on loan to appear in a British movie, *The Day the Earth Caught Fire* (1961), she posed for a series of risqué publicity photos (topless but covered in all the strategic places by a towel) that earned Walt's wrath and her release from Disney.

The ultimate Janet Munro Disney role is Katie O'Gill in *Darby O'Gill & the Little People*. Lively, vivacious, and flirtatious, Katie enjoys life and even relishes her slightly oddball father who entertains the town with tales of his running encounters with the local leprechauns. She is a girl who wants to be won. "I will have my courtship," she tells the king of the Leprechauns when he asks why she will not settle down and become a wife. She wants the hearts and flowers and the thrills of love. She even becomes the subject of a song "Pretty Irish Girl," the only time Sean Connery ever sang on screen. Perhaps only a virile guy like Connery could contain the fiery Janet.

Annette Funicello

Annette Funicello was the one Disney girl whose reputation preceded me actually seeing her on screen. I was too young to have experienced *The Mickey Mouse Club* the first time around (1955–1959). I only know that when my sisters and cousins got together to play in the mid-1960s, one of our games was "Spin and Marty," the most popular MMC serial about two boys spending the summer on a ranch. Apparently, Annette was a character in the serial because the girls in our group always fought to play Annette (the loser got to be Darlene). So even before I saw her, I learned that Annette (she never seemed to have a last name back then even in the movie credits) was someone girls aspired to be.

Annette Funicello was the pin up, the Betty Grable of the Baby Boomer generation. What was it about her that made her so desired? Maybe it was because Baby Boomers grew up with her. She made her debut on *The Mickey Mouse Club* in 1955 at age 13 and from the get-go she was the most popular Mouseketeer. Annette got more fan letters, the most jewelry, class rings, and engagement rings through the mail than any of her co-stars.

The accepted explanation is that boys followed in her wake because she was the first female Mouseketeer to develop a figure. And while it is true that she did grow to have a most pleasing figure—almost a Rubens or a Renoir figure come to life—I don't think that is the entire answer.

In truth, Annette seemed bemused by the great affection she engendered in men. Like Dinah in *The Horsemasters*, Annette probably felt the burden of high expectations (Dinah's mother was a champion horse jumper until a bad fall ended her career) and doubts whether she can live up to them. In reality, she oozed a sexuality that she felt uncomfortable embracing, perhaps due to a fear or a wariness of the feelings she generated in others.

Annette seemed reluctant to take center stage, but when she did, she shined like a star when she sang "The Strummin' Song" in *The Horsemasters* or "Dream Boy" in *Escapade in Florence* or "Mr. Piano Man" on stage in the Golden Horseshoe Revue at Disneyland.

Annette was a genuine pop star with hits like "Tall Paul," "Pineapple Princess," and others. While singing in *Disneyland after Dark* at the Tomorrowland Terrace, she holds her own with major pop stars of the day, whether singing "I Like to Dance" or sharing the stage with Bobby Rydell. For a time, she dated teen idol Paul Anka and served as his inspiration for the classic song "Puppy Love."

Backstage Party (1961)

TV Premiere: December 17, 1961

Perhaps our most generous glance of the real Annette is in this promo episode highlighting the *Babes in Toyland* wrap party (while also promoting the upcoming movie). Still dressed in her Mary Contrary costume, Annette shows us around the soundstage and introduces us to her fellow cast members, including Ray Bolger, Tommy Sands, Ed Wynn, Mary McCarty, and Tommy Kirk. Each is then given a chance to shine for a few moments and show the person behind the character.

An especially touching moment is when Tommy Kirk presents Ed Wynn with a "Mousekar" award honoring Wynn's fifty years in show business. That is pretty impressive when you do the numbers and realize that Wynn started his career in 1911 when movies were just getting started. Another warm moment is seeing young Ann Jillian singing about her lost sheep and Henry Calvin stepping in to duet with her.

From a Disney fan perspective, the best part of the episode is the beginning when we guests arrive at the gates of the Disney studio for a mini-tour of the place and to see how it was in its heyday.

Overseeing the whole thing is Annette who is warm and welcoming and quick to put us at ease, skills that come naturally to her and contribute greatly to her charm. She was a lovely person with whom it was quiet easy to fall in love, as millions of American boys like me did. She was the ideal embodiment of the perfect girl in that time and place. And nowhere were those qualities on better display than my choice for best Annette vehicle, *Babes in Toyland*.

Babes In Toyland (1961)

TV Premiere: December 21, 28, 1969

Babes In Toyland opens in Mother Goose Village where all the famous fairy-tale characters reside. Mary Contrary (Annette Funicello) is engaged to marry Tom Piper (Tommy Sands), but the evil Barnaby (Ray Bolger) wants her for his own so he can get his hands on the fortune she will inherit. He has Tom kidnapped and Mary's sheep stolen so that the now destitute Mary will be forced to marry him. His plans are thwarted when Tom returns as part of a gypsy troupe and the lovers are reunited.

They flee into the Forest of No Return and discover at its center the fabled Toyland where the Toymaker makes all the toys for Christmas. But Barnaby hasn't given up and follows them there. Will Mary become Barnaby's bride? Will Christmas be saved? What do you think?

Babes was Walt's first attempt at a full-on musical. Looking at it today, the faults in the film are apparent. It consists of a number of interesting elements that never come together as a dramatic whole. The movie never finds its pace and tends to lurch from set piece to set piece. Perhaps Walt should have allowed Ward Kimball to direct instead of Jack Donohue, a dancer and choreographer who seemed more at home as a director on TV than on the big screen. (Kimball temporarily left the studio when he did not get the assignment.) It also doesn't help that the whole film is played in an operetta fashion that probably felt out of date even in 1961.

And yet when I look at the film through the eyes of my childhood, I can see why my sisters and I were so gaga for it. The story itself is a fun blend of Mother Goose fairy tales combined with a different take on the Christmas legend: the Toymaker makes the toys rather than Santa Claus. From Mother Goose Village to Toyland, the production design and costumes are colorful and gorgeous to look at. The trees in the Forest of No Return were scary enough to haunt my childhood dreams, but not too scary to turn those dreams into nightmares.

The movie bursts with inventive special effects, from Little Jack Horner jumping over his candlestick to Grumio's (Tommy Kirk) inventions of the automated toy-making machine and shrinking gun, to the properly famous march of the wooden soldiers, as well as clever throw-away moments like when Roderigo (Gene Shelton) hits Tom over the head with a hammer or when Roderigo slowly sinks into the sidewalk while Gonzorgo (Henry Calvin) relates the tale of Tom's supposed demise in "Slowly He Sank into the Sea." Why the film did not get a special effects Oscar nomination escapes me.

The cast is terrific. Tommy Sands gives his all as Tom with his turn as a gypsy fortune teller and as the commander of the wooden soldiers being his standout moments. Ray Bolger is pitch-black perfect as the evil Barnaby—just like the trees, he is scary without being threatening. Ed Wynn is, well, Ed Wynn, but at this stage of his career no one wanted him to be anything else. Tommy Kirk fills the screen in his moments as Grumio, another inventive genius who doesn't quite think his ground-breaking inventions through before he invents them. Henry Calvin and Gene Shelton are hysterical as Gonzorgo and Roderigo, even if their routine seems a little Laurel and Hardy lite.

And at the center of it all is Annette as Mary. It feels terribly appropriate that "our" Annette is getting married (she was 19 at the time).

Didn't most boys in America want to be marrying her then? It also feels appropriate for Barnaby to be disputing Tom's claim. After all, didn't most boys in America think *they* were the perfect mate for Annette? When Tom romances her with the song "Just a Whisper Away" he was merely voicing the quiet fantasies that most boys harbored at the time.

The only song that rankles our modern sensibilities a bit is "Just a Toy." Mary begins the song by gushing about this beautiful toy doll that some girl will love to receive for Christmas. Tom then turns the song into being about how Mary is also a perfect doll that he is hoping to receive. While singing, he poses her arms and legs like a doll and Mary pliantly goes along with it. You can practically hear feminists grinding their teeth off-screen. However, the sentiments expressed were in keeping with the times before the liberated 60s made those values seem quaint and unwelcome.

In the end, Tom gets his girl. They marry and head out through the snow to start their adult life. In many ways, the movie is about saying goodbye to the teenaged Annette. She was ready to put all that behind her and embrace the joys of marriage and adulthood. In 1965, when the real-life Annette married agent Jack Gilardi, she wore a copy of her *Babes in Toyland* wedding dress at the ceremony.

Annette left Disney in 1963 to star alongside Frankie Avalon in the American International Pictures series of beach movies. Sun, sand, and surf. Annette opted to wear a less-revealing two piece swimsuit, even though she clearly is wearing a bikini in *Bikini Beach* (1964). She is happy to let herself be upstaged by the more flirtatious (and more scantily dressed) sirens of the decade like Linda Evans and Marta Kristen.

Her last moment in the spotlight was *The Monkey's Uncle* when she sings the title song alongside the Beach Boys. At that point, the Beach Boys were the most popular rock band in the U.S.; only the Beatles eclipsed them worldwide. As they sing the title song on stage together, however, it is the Beach Boys who seem to be in awe of Annette, not the other way around. Like the rest of us, they just can't take their eyes off her. And yet the Beach Boys will point the way toward the psychedelic 1960s—a liberated time of sex and drugs and pushing the limits.

Annette wanted no part of that. She opted to retire rather than embrace the more liberated mores of the 1960s. Her personal goals were modest and traditional—a husband, a home, and a family—and out of step with the emerging times. Unlike Hayley or Janet, Annette hesitated to take on more sexual or adult roles post-Disney. That act alone removed her from the scene and ensured that her wholesome image would not be replaced by one that would undermine our memories of her. She remained the girl next door in our hearts and minds: friendly enough to be approachable, but sexy enough to color our dreams.

My Disney Girls

All three of my Disney girls struggled to make the transition from child star to adult actress. Hayley Mills and Janet Munro both did nude scenes for their post-Disney roles, a move they saw as a way to shed their juvenile images, but in doing so they alienated much of their core audience.

Hayley Mills ran headlong into adulthood and hoped us boys would keep up. Fortunately, she managed to realize we couldn't and paused to look back and wait for us. She taught me how to find the beauty in life even in the most trying and depressing situations; to not give up hope and to not stop trying no matter how impossible the task or how many people tell you to quit. She taught me how to embrace your dearest dream and to not give up until you achieved it.

Janet Munro also ran headlong to embrace all of life with a fierce abandon that was both titillating and frightening. In the end, she ran so far ahead that she ended up alone with her demons and her doubts. She taught me that some girls don't always know what is best for them, despite their assured demeanor; that some girls need to shine to fill up the empty space life has placed inside of them; that some need to be held tight and supported to quell the dark thoughts inside, and yet they also require the freedom to explore and find their own way, hopefully back to you.

Annette Funicello strolled alongside us through the course of our childhoods and adolescence until we were fully grown and ready to enter adulthood. She showed us the ropes of gentlemanly romance and then knew when it was time to exit the stage, leaving us with just the right parting image. Although she would probably reject the analogy, she was the perfect embodiment of the fantasy girlfriend and the symbol of what we would be looking for as we began dating in real life: not too naughty, not too nice.

When Annette died in 2013, I experienced the same overwhelming emotions I felt when Walt died in 1966. It was like saying goodbye to both a first love and a best friend, and even though she had been out of the public eye for decades, the world was just that much darker and that much sadder without her.

Between the three of them, Hayley, Janet, and Annette taught me what I needed to know to start dating in real life and how to be a good boyfriend. It was time to take my first steps away from my parents and embrace the future. And it would all start with those six simple words:

"Dad, can I borrow the car?"

CHAPTER THIRTEEN

Embracing the Future

Space, Science, Disney World, and Epcot

As a child growing up in the 1960s, I was raised to believe in the future, and to recognize the history behind me as a steady progression forward from the Renaissance to today, with civilization always advancing and improving. As a group of thirteen English colonies, we shook off the yoke of short-sighted British tyranny and established our own country, the United States of America. We chose to bypass the traditional monarch governments of the time and establish our own (very experimental) democracy.

Through the 19th century, we expanded westward until the country ran from sea to shining sea. There were challenges to our democratic government, but somehow we came out of each challenge stronger than before. And in the process, we established a reputation of equality and opportunity that made immigrants from around the world want to come and live here. And come they did.

Our country was not perfect. We started out as a society where slavery was legal, but ultimately fought a civil war to abolish it. Our manifest destiny of westward expansion devastated the Native Americans living there. Thousands died. They lost their land; they lost their culture; it remains a scar on our heritage.

We spent the first half of the 20th century fighting two world wars and pulling ourselves through the Great Depression. As a result, by 1945 we had replaced the British Empire as the leading political and economic force on the planet.

We still weren't perfect, but we had a knack as a society of seeking out and correcting those parts that still weren't as good as the promises in the Declaration of Independence said they should be. That was why in the 1960s some Americans were marching for civil rights so that blacks could have the freedoms and equal rights afforded them in the 13th, 14th, and 15th amendments to the Constitution. Other citizens were marching against the war in Vietnam. Others were starting to march for equal rights regardless of gender or sexual orientation. Still others were marching and working and organizing to help us appreciate and correct the damage we had done to nature and our environment and to make our planet a better place to live. It was all to build a better America and a better future.

Nobody had taught me more at that point in my life about where we had been and where we were going than Walt Disney.

And there in the mid-1960s it definitely felt that the future was right around the corner. Our TVs were broadcasting in color. Science was creating advances across the board in medicine and engineering and computers. Men were blasting into space. Americans had already explored the heavens with the Mercury space program, and now we with the Gemini space program we were learning all the essentials of living and operating in space, from navigating and rendezvousing and docking and space walking to eating and sleeping. The Soviets were doing the same with their Vostok program. In the race to the moon, we had our Apollo program while the Soviets had their Soyuz program. It was going to be a full-on race to see who would be first to land by the end of the decade.

And if we could reach the moon by 1969, who knows how far out in space we could be by the end of the century: a fully operating moon base? Mars? Even farther? Stanley Kubrick's vision of where we would be in *2001: A Space Odyssey* (1968) seemed dead on.

Our future lay up there in the vastness of space and on 42 square miles of newly purchased swampland in central Florida. It truly was shaping up to be a "great big beautiful tomorrow." And few people had played a bigger role in molding that future than Walt Disney.

I was not alive the first time Disney's "Man in Space" series aired on *World of Disney*. Like many of the late Baby Boomers, I got exposed to the episodes in this series when they were shown as 16mm educational films in the science classes of my elementary and junior high school days. The showing of these films was cause for a school assembly. All grades would gather in our multi-purpose room, sit on metal folding chairs, and the film would whir away. By then it was the early 1970s and we had already landed on the moon, but the films were entertaining and educational regardless.

Looking back, it is fascinating to see how Walt Disney had teamed up with Wernher von Braun and his rocketry collaborators Willy Ley and Heinz Haber to create a show deliberately designed to urge the United States government to fund a space program.

This was not the first time Walt had tried to talk our government into doing something under the guise of making an educational film.

Back during World War II, Walt read Alexander de Seversky's book *Victory Through Air Power* (1942) which argued for the use of strategic aerial bombing to defeat Nazi Germany. Walt became so convinced by de Seversky's arguments that he adapted the book into a feature film the following year. It acted as part persuasive argument for de Seversky's plans, part history of flight. And it helped convince the top brass of the Army Air Corps to adopt the policies presented in the film.

I had two unusual run-ins with *Victory Through Air Power* (1943) during my childhood. The first occurred on a rainy day in the mid-1970s when my gym class could not go outside; we all got herded onto bleachers in the gym and were shown *Victory Through Air Power*. Already a Disney fan, I could not believe what we were being shown or how our teacher had even gotten a copy. I think I was the only one who understood what we were watching. The rest of the class just looked bored. The second happened years later when I served as a manager for our high school track team. One day at practice, someone had piled boxes of books in the locker room. We were told these were leftovers from a school book sale and we could take whatever we wanted. I looked through the boxes and was shocked to find a copy of *Victory*. I scooped it up and still own that book today.

Walt hoped to repeat his *Air Power* success with a series of TV episodes designed to urge America into space. Directed by animator Ward Kimball and featuring Wernher von Braun in place of de Seversky, Walt's plan worked. President Dwight Eisenhower ordered a copy of *Man in Space* and screened it for the Defense Department. By 1959, the U.S. had formed the National Aeronautics and Space Administration (NASA) and our country was on its way to space.

Man in Space (1955)

TV Premiere: March 9, 1955

According to film critic Leonard Maltin, Walt liked to call these episodes "science factual" rather than "science fiction." He saw them as factual because the technology involved was on the cusp of being, and that all it would take was a little know-how and financial backing for the ideas to become reality. In the case of this episode, it was man's first flight into space.

The episode begins with an animated segment taking us through the history of mankind's fascination with space and rockets. It chronicles the early failed attempts to get off the ground as well as the more successful efforts accomplished in fiction like Jules Verne's *From the Earth to the Moon* (1865) which later inspired George Melies' early silent movie *A Trip to the Moon* (1902). Eventually, the story focuses on the career of Robert Goddard, the father of modern rocketry. We are introduced to the basic scientific principles of making a rocket fly in simple, easy to understand illustrations of "action and reaction."

A brief overview of Wernher von Braun and the German efforts to make a rocket culminated in the V2, although the episode pointedly leaves out the fact that the V2 was used to bomb London and other cities late in World War II. Soon enough, the war is over and the German rocket scientists are in the United States, testing and designing missiles for the U.S. Army.

Seeing the flurry of rockets lifting off from the White Sands test site in New Mexico reminded me of a model I helped my father build back then of all the missiles in our military arsenal. In fact, it was called Monogram's Missile Arsenal—31 missiles from the tiny V2 to the Titan rocket which powered the Gemini spacecraft into orbit.

In quick succession, von Braun associate Willy Ley, a rocket historian and rocket engine designer, comes on to explain the basic principles of rocketry. He demonstrates (through animation) how a three-stage rocket can achieve earth orbit and the benefit of having satellites and rockets in space. Heinz Haber then walks us through what it takes for humans to survive in space through the use of space suits and the like.

Lastly, Von Braun walks us through how to build a passenger rocket and in an extended animated sequence runs us through an imagined first space flight. It is a far more advanced flight than either the American or Russian first space flights turned out to be.

Von Braun's idealized first space ship resembles NASA's space shuttle. He proposes testing it first in Earth's atmosphere (just like they did with the test shuttle *Enterprise*). The ship carries a crew of around ten just like a space shuttle would. It is blasted into space atop a large rocket, but when it is done, it re-enters the atmosphere and lands on a runway like a plane, ready to be used again.

The animation makes it look not only plausible, but, as Walt hoped, just around the corner. The narration of Dick Tufeld—who would go on to narrate many a science documentary and even end up as the voice of the Robot on the TV series *Lost in Space* (1965–1968)—gives it an extra level of authenticity. The technology was all there, even if most of it was animated; we just had to decide to go. As the optimistic narration says at the end of the episode: "Next stop: the moon and the planets beyond."

Funny how that was such a given back then.

Man and the Moon (1955)

TV Premiere: December 28, 1955

The second episode picks up where the first left off. We are given more historical detail about man's long-time fascination with the moon and the ancient myths about it, how studying its journey across the sky led to the creation of the calendar, and how early scientists like Galileo and Johannes Kepler added to our understanding about the moon.

Then von Braun returns to describe a journey around the moon, aided again by Ward Kimball's animation. Only this time we have real-life actors playing the astronauts in a real-life set of the spaceship. The inclusion of humans this time around helps raise the "science factual" level of the subject matter from the "possible" to the "plausible."

Von Braun tells us that before we can go to the moon, we must build a large space station in earth orbit as a staging area to build our moon rocket. Watching this part of the show, I am reminded how much the space station and the moon rocket resemble the illustrations in the children's book *You Will Go to the Moon* (1959) by Mae and Ira Freeman. It seems everyone was on the same page about getting to the moon back then. It is also interesting that the animated atomic-powered spaceship being built for this moon mission resembles the spaceships now being proposed for possible trips to Mars.

Watching von Braun narrate us through the moon flight sequence again makes me realize how dead on he was. The pretend ship's flight around the moon is very much like that of the Apollo 8 flight in December 1968. Even the continuous TV coverage updating the public is similar. Halfway to the moon, the ship experiences an emergency (a rupture in an oxygen tank) that foreshadows the Apollo 13 accident in 1970—only in this imagined rendering, an astronaut can space walk and repair the damage so the mission continues on.

The only part of the mission that seems a little weird is when they are on the dark side of the moon and using flares for mapping purposes. One flare momentarily illuminates what appear to be signs of past habitations that resemble abandoned Native American ruins found throughout the American southwest like those of the Anasazi people or Chaco Canyon in New Mexico. There is even a figure that resembles those found on the Nazca plains in South America.

What are they trying to say here? That humans have a deeper past? Difficult to say, as the moment quickly passes and the episode moves on, with the moon ship returning triumphantly to the space station.

In two short episodes, man has traveled in space and journeyed from the earth to the moon and back. There are hints that Mars will be next, something that we still haven't done.

Mars and Beyond (1957)

TV Premiere: December 4, 1957

Mars and Beyond is the least "science factual" of the three. It is conspicuous that von Braun and his associates are absent from this episode. Instead, we have legendary voiceover artist and Disney narrator Paul Frees to provide the commentary and character voices.

Once again, we are given a summary of early man's views of Mars, and how the ancient Greeks had fairly enlightened views on the red planet until classical civilization collapsed and "free and logical thought" was replaced by "stupidity, superstition, and sorcery."

I enjoyed the parts where they discussed literature's contribution to our understanding of Mars, from H.G. Wells' *The War of the Worlds* (1897) to Edgar Rice Burroughs' John Carter series of best-selling books about Mars, or as the Martians like to call their home, Barsoom. It made me want to pick up the books and read them. I would eventually read Wells' book, but I never have gotten around to reading Burroughs.

I even enjoyed Ward Kimball's satire of a standard science fiction storyline from the 1950s, particularly because it was a storyline that could be used even today in the second decade of the 21st century.

The trips to the other planets in our solar system proved illuminating and helped me understand how unique our Earth really is (and, by extension, how it needs to be protected). I learned that the laws of creation are universal and not just confined to Earth. And, lastly, the history of the Earth from its gaseous beginnings to the present day showed just how much change our planet has gone through and just how insignificant we humans are, considering we have only shown up in the last couple millennia on a planet that is millions of years old.

This trip to Mars seemed less engaging, the ship more fanciful than real, even though the blueprint of the base required on Mars in order to survive looks similar to what is being proposed now, sixty years later.

Ironically, what I walked away with from this episode was not a desire to go to Mars, but an appreciation of what we have back here on Earth and how a slight shift in the environment could render it as uninhabitable as Mars or Venus or any of the other planets in our solar system. The series made me want to explore the heavens, but it also made me want to preserve what we had back here at home.

Of course, there were some science episodes that have not aged well.

Our Friend the Atom (1957)

TV Premiere: January 23, 1957

Heinz Haber returns to tell us the glories of atomic energy with the same precision and historical detail as all the other episodes, and Ward

Kimball's animations are just as entertaining as in the others. But in this case, we see all the upsides of atomic energy without seeing the downsides, like radioactive waste disposal. The Three Mile Island accident hadn't happened yet nor had Chernobyl or the movie *The China Syndrome* (1979). It totally overlooks the weaponization of atomic energy, and how countries might scramble to build their own bomb. It does not foresee how terrorist groups might strive to acquire such a weapon to spread panic and destruction in the name of their ideology.

I found the words of Captain Nemo in *20,000 Leagues* echoing in my mind while I watched this: "But there is hope for the future. When the world is ready for a new and better life, all this will someday come to pass, in God's good time."

Early in the episode, Kimball compares atomic energy to being like a genie in a bottle. Many of us wish the genie could be put back in.

Eye in Outer Space (1959)

TV Premiere: April 1, 1962

Even more curious than *Our Friend the Atom*, this episode crosses over from "science factual" to science fiction as it speculated about a day when humans could control the weather. This would be done by a network of satellites circling the Earth and operated by the U.S. Department of Defense. You can see the beginnings of Ronald Reagan's "Star Wars" missile defense system here.

As I watched this episode, I wondered if it was a good thing to do. Perhaps this was the point when we would be passing over into the realm of "playing God" like those mythical Atlantians were accused of doing, and which merely hastened their downfall. Maybe there are some things humans should not have the ability to control; maybe it is better having us be the stewards of the Earth rather than its masters.

The science episodes of *World of Disney* offered us glimpses into the vast possibilities of the future. The use of animation made these theories and possibilities appear on the verge of being when they were, in fact, many decades away from happening.

The "Man in Space" episodes and the other science shows were all "giant wienies" (to use Walt's term) luring us down the road toward the future so we could see the possibilities of "the great big beautiful tomorrow" that lay ahead. Walt had incorporated the concept of the "giant wienie" into Disneyland: the notion that the public needed a lure to get them to move in a new direction. If we were standing on Main Street, U.S.A., then the "giant wienie" was Sleeping Beauty Castle at the end of the street, to lure visitors to the central plaza and get them to experience the other lands of the park. I believe he was trying to do the same with these shows.

I find it interesting that once Walt died, the science shows disappeared from the *World of Disney* schedule. No new ones were made. And, in an ironic kind of way, we as a society decided to ignore the "wienies" of the future, whether it be space travel or atomic energy or improving our way of life for everyone's benefit, to remain where we are and not walk down that street into the future.

"Welcome to a Little Piece of Florida in California"

In the last year of his life, Walt Disney was consumed with planning out his latest and greatest undertaking: the new Disney World project in Florida. He was not so much interested in the theme park section of the vacation resort, though he knew that the Magic Kingdom needed to be built in order to lure visitors to his huge enterprise.

His real interest lay in Phase Two of the Florida Project, namely EPCOT (the Experimental Prototype Community of Tomorrow), the model city he planned to build alongside the park. He called it "the heart of everything we are doing in Florida." In Walt's original layout of Disney World, famously laid out on a cocktail napkin and then later on the ceiling tiles of his hospital room as he lay dying of cancer, visitors would arrive either via an airport (never built, but still included on the Phase One maps as the Lake Buena Vista STOLport when the park first opened) or by car to the vast but welcoming transportation center. There, they would leave their vehicles behind and board a monorail to take them to the theme park. Along the way they would pass the "wienies" of the industrial park and then EPCOT itself before arriving at the theme park area around Bay Lake and the Seven Seas Lagoon.

Visitors would get a tease by passing through EPCOT, hopefully whetting their appetites. Later, after they had had their fill of the Magic Kingdom and the hotels, they might venture back down the monorail line to EPCOT, shop and dine in its pedestrian friendly downtown, and check out what life was like here in a place where, in Walt's words, "people actually live a life they can't find anywhere else in the world today," and maybe even consider moving there.

Unfortunately, at the time of his death, that is all that Disney World and EPCOT were: concept drawings and extensive blueprints ready to be brought into creation. Walt had planned to spend 1967 turning those drawings into an overall master plan while simultaneously raising the vast capital from American industry and corporations necessary to make this a reality. He planned to call in all the goodwill markers he had carefully cultivated with American big business over the previous two decades. So committed was he that Walt planned to delegate the running of the company to his heir apparent, Card Walker, and the running of the movie studio to his son-in-law, Ron Miller, so he could devote all of his energy and time to making Disney World a reality. While not set in stone, he had hopes of opening the Magic Kingdom Phase One theme park area in 1969 and EPCOT Phase Two around 1971.

His death left all of that up in the air.

Project Florida (1971)

TV Premiere: January 31, 1971

Project Florida aired as a half-hour special occupying the second half of the third *World of Disney* episode showing *The Adventures of Bullwhip Griffin*. It was meant to be an update on Disney World's progress. Following Walt's death there had been a great deal of retrenchment and regrouping at the studio. Roy Disney opted to put off his retirement so he could take the company reins and guide at least Phase One of Disney World (now named Walt Disney World at Roy's command) to its completion.

Watching the report, I remember being wowed by all the things they were building and by Walt's last dream actually becoming a reality. The episode featured clips of Walt from the EPCOT promotional film made right before his death (although going back and looking at it now I realize that the company edited out any mentions of EPCOT in the clips shown).

Cameras took us inside the Information and Reception Center Disney opened in February 1969. We saw the large Phase One models and dioramas. I remember the model of the Contemporary Hotel ("as contemporary as tomorrow," the narrator declares) blowing me away. I *had* to stay there some day. Jumping out at me now are the models of the hotels planned, but never built: the Asian Hotel intended for the present site of the Grand Floridian, the Venetian Hotel intended for where the Wilderness Lodge now stands (and looking very much like the Venice Hotel in Las Vegas), and the Persian Hotel planned for north of the Contemporary. In retrospect, it is probably good that none of these were built given the changing times in the decades since. A quick tour of the almost-finished Fort Wilderness campground showed that westerns were still an important feature of the park.

Much of the episode concentrated on progress in the Magic Kingdom. We saw the nearly finished Main Street, U.S.A. and the new

Liberty Square land "dedicated to the American spirit." Updates on the rides whet our appetites. We saw previews of It's a Small World, the Hall of Presidents in Liberty Square, and the Country Bear Jamboree in Frontierland.

And everywhere were signs reminding workers and the public that the park was set to open in October 1971, just nine months away.

I remember watching this episode unfold on TV and being gob-smacked that all of this was starting to come true—Walt's last dream. Even as a child, I knew that our country had suffered a lot of setbacks and events between 1966 and 1971. The Apollo 1 fire, the Summer of Love, Vietnam War protests, the Tet Offensive, the assassinations of Robert Kennedy and Martin Luther King, Jr., a divisive 1968 presi-dential election that saw riots at the Democratic convention, the rise of George Wallace, the election of Richard Nixon, Chappaquiddick, Woodstock, Apollo 13, Kent State.

About the only event that seemed to bring us together during that time was the Apollo 11 moon landing in July 1969, an event Walt Disney had helped put in motion and John F. Kennedy had promised would happen. Much of the drive to make the moon landing happen by the end of the decade had been driven by a desire to fulfill JFK's pledge made even more urgent by his assassination. Many of the workers at Disney and millions of Disney fans felt the same way about the completion of Walt Disney World. The country had suffered its share of recent setbacks, but here was the future now rising up in central Florida. Walt's grandest dream was going to become a reality after all. For a brief shining moment, the future appeared to be bright once again. And it was all beginning in October 1971.

The Grand Opening of Walt Disney World (1971)

TV Premiere: October 29, 1971

Walt Disney Productions made the deadline and Walt Disney World opened in a special two-hour episode hosted by Glen Campbell and Julie Andrews. Jonathan Winters and Bob Hope provided comedy bits. The episode played out like an old-fashioned variety show (Disney rival Ed Sullivan had just recently gone off the air) with lots of singing and dancing in different sections of the Magic Kingdom. We were once again shown the wonder of the Contemporary Hotel. Julie Andrews stopped in the Main Street Cinema to smile at clips from past Disney films like *Steamboat Willie*, *Snow White and the Seven Dwarfs*, *Pinocchio*, *Fantasia*, *Bambi*, *Peter Pan*, *Lady and the Tramp*, *Cinderella*, *101 Dalmatians*, *The Jungle Book*, and even *Song of the South* while she sings "When You Wish Upon a Star."

Being an auto racing fan, I found the segment at the Grand Prix Raceway particularly funny as it featured some of my favorite racers, Indycar stars Mark Donohue and Bobby Unser, and current F1 World Champion Jackie Stewart, going up against Disney stars Buddy Hackett and Herbie the Volkswagon from *The Love Bug* (1969). Guess who won?

The biggest thing I remember from the original broadcast is the 1,076 member marching band under the direction of Meredith Wilson parading down Main Street and the gathering of everyone in the central plaza before Cinderella Castle to sing "When You Wish Upon a Star."

Watching the special now as an adult, other moments jump out at me:

- The low-key opening with Glen Campbell strolling through the Florida wilderness while singing the song "Today Is Mine."

- Julie Andrews riding the monorail and explaining, "Just a few miles from Cape Kennedy where men point their space vehicles to the stars, Walt Disney decided to launch his final dream. A commitment to the future for your children and mine. ... Best of all it is a place to stir the imagination and give us a sense of hope for tomorrow."

- Glen Campbell introducing Liberty Square as "the heart of Disney World" and conjuring up memories of *Johnny Tremain* as he opined, "You know, every now and then I think we get the idea that freedom is our right so we can shape it to our own personal convenience. But I don't think it is meant to be that way at all. You see, freedom isn't a divisible thing that you can cut up and keep the lion's share for yourself with others getting what is left over."

- Bob Hope's tribute to Walt the man: "Walt Disney World is the culmination of a lifetime. ... There's a spirit here, everywhere. It's in the air and everywhere you look. All this is Walt, what Walt wanted for all of us. It is a signal to the minds of children of all ages: cheer up! All is not lost. ... The entire world owes Walt Disney a great debt. He achieved much, but perhaps his greatest accomplishment is that he made children of us all."

Finally, Roy Disney cut the ribbon. The gates were flung open. The future was here.

In retrospect, perhaps it was simply the last gasp of a possible future that no longer had a place in reality.

The Magic of Walt Disney World (1972)

TV Premiere: March 31, 1974

This half-hour promotional film was originally a featurette shown theatrically before the Disney film *Snowball Express* (1972). I remember seeing it with my cousin at the Lans Theater outside Chicago. By the time I saw it, I had actually been to Disney World. My family vacationed there in the summer of 1972. When it aired on *World of Disney* two years later, we had been there twice and even stayed at the Contemporary Hotel. Watching it on TV was like watching a family home movie of a favorite vacation.

Narrated by actor Steve Forrest, the short emphasizes how the park and its facilities "clearly reflect the man Walt Disney and the things he held to be of value: the wonders of nature, the fantasies of childhood, the spirit of America with nostalgia for the past and faith in the future, and, above all, a sense of humor and fun."

It mostly takes us on a whirlwind tour of the Magic Kingdom. Looking back on the film as an adult, I am struck by the large number of multi-ethnic faces shown: white, black, Latino. Happy faces on happy families of all races enjoying the park. I am struck by how new it all looks.

Outside of the park, we catch glimpses of the water ski show by the Polynesian Village Resort—not to mention its magnificent swimming pool with its slide built around a South Pacific grotto.

For its TV premiere, a new section was added to the film promoting the new Tomorrowland about to be opened. The Carousel of Progress was being relocated to Florida from Disneyland. The WEDway People Mover was being added. The biggest addition was Space Mountain, the outer-space roller coaster first conceived by Walt for Disneyland but shelved for lack of space.

Even in the mid-1970s, Walt's influence was still being felt. Could Phase Two of Walt Disney World, EPCOT, be far behind?

The EPCOT Film (1967)

Filmed: October 27, 1966; Privately Premiered: February 2, 1967

There is an urban legend among Disney fans that we all first heard about Walt's city of tomorrow because the EPCOT film was shown on *Wonderful World of Disney*. If you had asked me prior to writing this book, I would have told you the same thing. I have a vivid memory of seeing the film on the show. Yet a detailed look at the show schedule reveals that the EPCOT film never did air in its entirety on *World of Disney*. I believe we were led to think so through a confluence of three events.

First, when Walt Disney Productions announced their plans for Disney World in the spring of 1967, the concept art for EPCOT was front and center in the announcement and provided the illustrations for most of the newspaper articles. I remember looking at the articles and thinking that, to quote lyrics from *Meet the Robinsons* (2007), "the future had arrived."

Second, when Disneyland's new Tomorrowland was featured in the 1968 *World of Disney* episode "Disneyland: From the Pirates of the Caribbean to the World of Tomorrow," a segment chronicled the relocation of the Carousel of Progress from the New York World's Fair. Front and center was the EPCOT model city that greeted the public as they departed the ride. As the narrator says

> And in the Carousel of Progress you can get a view of tomorrow: a model city of the future. It's based on a concept developed by Walt Disney for a community he called EPCOT. ... Realistic to the smallest detail, this animated model is a living blueprint of systems for future cities. The concept for EPCOT is one part of Walt Disney's master plan for the future Disney World in Florida. A city of tomorrow possible today with the technology and imagination of American industry.

Third, the 1971 episode *Project Florida* featured extensive clips of Walt from the EPCOT film rhapsodizing about the Disney World project while removing all references to the actual Experimental Prototype Community of Tomorrow.

Passing decades allowed the three examples to blend together in our minds to give the impression that we had seen the EPCOT film on *The Wonderful World of Disney*. Even film critic Leonard Maltin thought so when he wrote in his book *The Disney Films* (1973), "Ironically, the show that was broadcast the Sunday after his death in December 1966 featured Walt showing plans for his Walt Disney World in Florida. It was a most appropriate tribute to the man."

The big question that hung in Disney fans' minds in the 1970s was, "When would Disney build EPCOT?"

For the first part of the decade, Walt Disney Productions encouraged the expectation that it was going to happen. When my family first vacationed at Disney World in the summer of 1972, we bought a commemorative booklet called *The Story of Walt Disney World* (1971). EPCOT was prominently listed as Phase Two on the checklist of things to build along with an "airport of the future," an industrial park for American industry, the town of Lake Buena Vista, Florida, and lastly, EPCOT. The back page of the booklet titled "The Future World" pictured that now iconic EPCOT concept drawing and the promise "Walt Disney

World is dedicated to how people play, but also to how they live and work. As part of the second phase of its development, Walt Disney envisioned a city...a world of the future planned as an example for today's world."

When my family returned to WDW in 1973, the *Pictorial Souvenir of Walt Disney World* selling at all the Magic Kingdom shops that summer still listed on its Coming Attractions page Space Mountain, Pirates of the Caribbean, the Fort Wilderness Railroad, Tom Sawyer Island, "and one day, the city Walt Disney called EPCOT."

The first edition of Christopher Finch's *The Art of Walt Disney* featured a closing chapter called "The Lessons of the Parks" by Peter Blake that speculated about the building of EPCOT and featured concept art illustrations of its futuristic housing. The book ended with the sentence: "What a wonderfully ironic notion it is that, in this turbulent century, urban man might, just possibly, be saved by a mouse."

Unfortunately, if we looked closer, we could already see that the company was backing away from building EPCOT.

The preliminary Phase One Master Plan for Walt Disney World (dated January 10, 1968) features an area located where EPCOT had been on previous maps but now labeled as "Proposed Residential Community." The concept art in the Finch chapter said the housing could appear either in EPCOT or in the town of Lake Buena Vista that they planned to build to house WDW employees.

In 1975, when the Carousel of Progress ride relocated from Disneyland to the Magic Kingdom, the EPCOT model, which had been the climax of the ride, was removed and relocated as an unlabeled exhibit on the PeopleMover ride.

By the late 1970s, EPCOT had been turned into Epcot Center, not the futuristic world of tomorrow but another amusement park. Even as it celebrated the future and international relations, Epcot Center felt more like a world's fair. It allowed Disney to say they had built Walt's last dream without being on the hook for the municipal headaches that would come with running an actual city.

So why does the EPCOT film even exist? And why am I including it in a book about *The Wonderful World of Disney* when it did not appear intact on the show?

What I find amazing about Walt's EPCOT film is that Disney fans like me and regular watchers of the program all believe that we *had* seen it on the show. I am sure if Walt lived that a version of the film would have ended up appearing on the show, perhaps at around the same time that the *Project Florida* episode appeared.

Walt had intended the film for two audiences. The first was the Florida legislators; Walt needed them to pass a law incorporating Disney World as a city so that they would be free to do all the things necessary to build and operate such an enterprise. The second audience was the general public whom Walt needed to come down and visit and get excited about possibly living there.

The film was rather hastily thrown together at the end of October 1966. Walt pushed to do it because he was planning to enter the hospital at the beginning of November. Even as plans for Disney World and EPCOT pressed forward, Walt had spent a lot of the year battling recurring health issues. His smokers' cough grew worse, he lost weight, his stamina began to falter, and he suffered from chronic neck and shoulder pains from an old polo injury. After putting off dealing with these issues for years, he recognized that he would need to be in perfect health as he spent 1967 courting Florida officials and traveling the country convincing American corporations to sign on to the venture.

He wanted the film done in October because he knew the operation for his neck and back would lay him up for the rest of the year. While he recovered in November and December, the film would be edited together. When 1967 started, he would be back at the top of his game and ready to go, and the film would be his primary selling tool. (In fact, Roy Disney did screen the film to the Florida legislature in February 1967. The mere sight of Walt up on the screen was enough to convince them to pass the laws designating Walt Disney World as the Reedy Creek Improvement District.)

Unfortunately, pre-op X-rays revealed a dark spot on his lungs and the procedure changed from a neck and back operation to lung cancer surgery. The rest we are all sadly aware of. Watching the film now is like watching an alternative history of the future.

In 23 minutes, Walt sketches out his vision for Disney World. The achievements at Disneyland are summarized, including a mention that at the time no one had thought Disney could pull that off either. The opening culminates in a quote from architect James Rouse, "The greatest piece of urban design in the United States today is Disneyland."

The scene shifts to the Florida Project room at WED Enterprises. Walt greets us and gives us a tour of what he has planned. He gives a summary overview of the property, from the arrival airport and entrance plaza to the theme park at the northern edge. He gives only token mention to the theme park and hotel area that is to come first. He doesn't even call it the Magic Kingdom. He is supposed to have said, "build another Disneyland," and left the designers to their own devices. All of his focus and energy is on EPCOT.

Smiling broadly at the camera, he proclaims, "We know what our goals are. We know what we hope to accomplish. And believe me, it's the most exciting and challenging assignment we've ever tackled at Walt Disney Productions."

Walt explains the basic layout of his city, from its radial plan to how the transportation systems will work. I remember finding this part intriguing for a couple of reasons. First, I found it fascinating that EPCOT would be a city where you only needed to use your car to leave. Once you parked your car in the driveway of your home, you could walk or use public transportation to get yourself anywhere in EPCOT or even to the Magic Kingdom. Second, it floored me to see the monorail and PeopleMover being used as transportation systems. I had gotten used to seeing them as rides in the park. I had no idea they could have practical applications for our daily lives. Third, the downtown part of EPCOT with its stores and restaurants and international themes seem to foreshadow the World Showcase in today's Epcot.

The drawings and animation made it easy to fantasize about living in EPCOT, and stepping out the front door of my home that faced not the street but the vast parkland behind. The park featured athletic fields and bike and walking paths (pretty forward for 1966). Walking to the neighborhood PeopleMover station and taking a train into downtown, I could shop, eat, catch a movie or a play or a concert, or maybe transfer to a monorail and take it down to the industrial park where I would walk to work at one of the top research labs or office complexes built by one of our top corporations, or even take a ride up to the park for an evening of fun with the family.

While watching the film, I began to wonder what the houses were going to look like. Sure, you could live in some of the apartment complexes adjacent to downtown, but I wanted a house in the neighborhood. I have always thought they looked like the Incredibles family home in Brad Bird's *The Incredibles* (2004), sort of a retro-futuristic home, an architectural descendant of Frank Lloyd Wright's Fallingwater house.

This was a place I wanted to visit, and to live. To experience what Walt promised would be unlike living anywhere else on earth. As Walt said:

> It will be a community of tomorrow that will never be completed, but will always be introducing, testing, and demonstrating new materials and new systems. ... I believe we can build a community that more people will talk about and come to look at than any other area in the world...that the Experimental Prototype Community of Tomorrow can influence the future of city living for generations to come.

Wrapping up, Walt declares:

> It's an exciting challenge, a once-in-a-lifetime opportunity for everyone who participates. Speaking for myself and the entire Disney organization, we're ready to go right now.

Fade out. End of film.

I cannot think of a better set of words for Walt Disney to leave us with. Even today, the feeling the viewer is left with is that of anticipation. We are ready to go. This feels very much like a beginning, a launching pad to the next phase of the future. Only it is not. It is an ending and that final fade is like the slamming of time's door on a future that will never be.

Walt's Experimental Prototype Community of Tomorrow would never get off the drawing boards, never be anything more than concept art and a promotional film. And maybe that is how it was meant to be: a beacon of possibilities for the future unsullied by the reality of today.

The feeling isn't unlike that at the end of *20,000 Leagues under the Sea*, another movie where the possibility of a glorious future is undermined by the shortsightedness of governments, the military, and big business.

Prof. Aronnax could just as easily be talking to Walt Disney rather than Captain Nemo when he proclaims, "But yours was a dream of the future come true." And just like Nemo, Walt Disney unintentionally chose to take his *Nautilus* (EPCOT) down with him while still leaving the possibilities and the promise dangling before us on celluloid. To take to heart the same words that close out *20,000 Leagues*:

> But there is hope for the future. When the world is ready for a new and better life, all this will someday come to pass, in God's good time.

For me, EPCOT remains Walt's final "big wienie" to motivate us forward down our main streets of today toward the promise of the future, and an unspoken charge to make it happen. He says in the EPCOT film, "with your cooperation," meaning not just the Florida lawmakers and not just American corporations, but us, the American people.

By leaving his last and greatest dream unfinished, Walt unknowingly transferred the responsibility to make it happen from his hands to ours. Rather than leading the way, he left us to create that "great big beautiful tomorrow." And maybe that is the way it ought to be.

Afterword

Somewhere around 1978, when I was fifteen going on sixteen, *The Wonderful World of Disney*'s appeal began to fade for me. It stopped becoming a regular thing on Sunday nights. I would still watch the show sometimes, but many of the episodes were reruns that I had already seen several times before. It seemed like they never aired the really great episodes anymore. And it seemed like the new ones lacked the same quality as the classics. Perhaps I was simply growing up.

I had always read newspapers and watched the news trying to keep up on the political and social developments of the day. And so I found myself suggesting to my parents that maybe we could begin watching *60 Minutes* (which had replaced *Ed Sullivan*) instead of *Disney* and they didn't have a problem with that. I realized then that for the last several years we had only been watching *Disney* because I wanted to, and I didn't want to any longer.

I graduated from high school. I went to college. I experienced my first love. I got my heart broken three or four times. My parents divorced. My family fractured and never fully healed. All by the time I turned 25.

When NBC cancelled *Disney's Wonderful World* (as the show was now called) no one complained much, least of all me. After 28 years on the air, it felt like a show whose time had passed. It was time to put away childish things. *The Wonderful World of Disney* became a distant, though lovely, memory.

I grew up. I became a writer. I became an editor. I became a teacher. I married. We had a son. He grew up. We moved on.

In 2015, my family went to see Disney's *Tomorrowland* on opening day on the big IMAX screen. While the movie has its problems, I found it to be a revelation. The prologue set at the 1964 New York World's Fair took me back to my childhood when I was a young Frank Walker bursting with faith and optimism about the future. And what was the city of Tomorrowland but Walt's EPCOT that had never been built.

As the best movies and TV shows do, *Tomorrowland* got me thinking. Why were my college-age students, particularly the younger ones, so cynical about our future? Why do they believe that civilization is on a downward slope, that people are powerless to change society, that love never lasts, that growing up sucks.

How did they get this way?

Or more importantly, why was I so damn optimistic about everything?

And so I began to think back on how I *did* get to be this way, to believe the way I do. And I came to realize that I believed what I did because:

- Whenever I find myself facing down a bully, I think of Bullwhip Griffin taking on Mountain Ox.

- Whenever I find a mystery that needs solving, I wonder how the Whiz Kids or Scott, Annie, and Catfish would figure it out.

- Whenever I'm faced with an impossible task, I think of Rudy Matt climbing the Citadel or Davy Crockett giving it the "old Crockett charge" or Pollyanna looking to find the good in a bad situation.

- Whenever I see nature threatened, I think of the animals in *One Day at Teton Marsh* and the rangers working to save the forest in *Fire on Kelly's Mountain*.

- Whenever I meet foreigners, I think of Hans Brinker or Hamad or Tom Candy.

- Whenever unjust laws or deceitful politics rear their ugly heads, I ask myself what would Captain Nemo or Dr. Syn do?

- Whenever social change seems impossible, I think of Julie in *A Tiger Walks* or Emil rallying an army of Berlin children to defeat the thieves or Dexter Riley and his group of average college friends butting heads with organized crime.

- Whenever I'm confronted by something that seems bizarre or supernatural, I think of Jim Douglas and Herbie.

- Whenever I face a family tragedy or a deep personal loss, I think of Chris and Smoke, or Mary and Thomasina, or Travis and Old Yeller.

- Whenever I find myself falling in love, the women always had a glimmer of the Disney Girls in their personalities: Janet Munro in *Third Man on the Mountain*, *Darby O'Gill*, and *The Horsemasters*; Hayley Mills in *Summer Magic* and *The Moon-Spinners*; and Annette (just Annette) in, well, everything.

- Whenever I contemplate space and the future, I think of Walt and his Magic Kingdoms, especially EPCOT.

In short, I believed what I did and felt the way I had because I had been taught that by Walt Disney. I discovered that *The Wonderful World of Disney* was not gone but very much alive…in my head. My brain had its own private Disney vault that I could draw on in my everyday life.

And so I came to the conclusion that everything I know, I learned from *The Wonderful World of Disney*. Walt Disney's ideals expressed through his show gave me a strong foundation to build my life on. I could meet the adult challenges of today because Walt Disney taught me how to do that when I was a child. And nothing I have experienced as an adult, the setbacks, the jolts, the losses, the health issues, none of that has changed my mind.

You will have the life you dream. I choose to believe in a great, big, beautiful tomorrow, thanks to my Sunday nights spent with Walt.

To this day, when I watch the opening credits of *The Wonderful World of Disney* and hear announcer Dick Wesson say the title words, I once again smell that intoxicating combination of hot pizza fresh from the oven and just-popped buttered popcorn mixed with the sweet aroma and carbonated hiss of soda pop. It takes me home again. It almost makes me cry.

Thanks to my sisters. Thanks, Dad. Thanks, Mom.

Thanks, Walt.

Acknowledgments

Contrary to popular opinion, no person writes a book alone. There are many people who helped along the way and whom I need to thank for the creation of *Sunday Nights with Walt*.

Thank you to Bob McLain and Theme Park Press for making this book happen.

My work was aided by these other books that I referred to constantly throughout the development and writing process:

- *The Disney Films* (1973) by Leonard Maltin, the first hardcover book I ever bought.

- *The Wonderful World of Disney Television: A Complete History* (1997) by Bill Cotter. Thank you to John Wisniewski for lending me his copy. I hope he doesn't want it back.

- *The Art of Walt Disney: From Mickey Mouse to the Magic Kingdoms* (1973) by Christopher Finch.

- *The Story of Walt Disney World: Commemorative Edition* (1971), which helped me better understand the early history of WDW and realize how prominent EPCOT still was at that point in Walt Disney Productions' strategic thinking. Thank you to my parents for buying it on our first vacation to Disney World in 1972.

Thank you to the following for enabling me to research and watch all those episodes of *Disneyland, Walt Disney Presents, The Wonderful World of Color*, and *The Wonderful World of Disney*: The Walt Disney Company, Walt Disney Treasures, D23, The Disney Movie Club, YouTube and its contributors, Flying Dreams' Gallegher website, the Monroe County (Michigan) Library System, and the Internet Archive.

Thank you to all the talented artists, executives, actors, technicians, musicians, writers, producers, and directors who made *The Wonderful World of Disney* the extraordinary show it was.

Thank you to all the members of the MPI Writers Group for their support and critique of these pages: John Wisniewski, David Galler, Lucie Gillespie, Patrick Neff, Jacob Burkhart, Bub Fish, Alexis Irvine, Naeemah Stewart, and Kevin Ma.

Additional thanks to those who looked over pages and offered their opinions, advice, and unwavering enthusiastic encouragement throughout the writing: Lisa Acton, Linda Brownell Merlo, Robert Eberwein, Terry Hagerty, Robert Coury, Lora & Rene Crombez, Eva Doherty, LeeAnn Doherty, Beth Messner, and Tawny Book.

Thank you to my son Ben for watching hours of Disney television with me over the past six months.

Thank you to my extraordinary wife Betsy for copy editing these pages, offering insights that made the manuscript better, and her unfailing love and support over the past 26 years.

And, finally, thank you to my Rothrock family for sharing Pizza Night with me and helping to create the memories that led to this book: my sisters Patricia Rothrock Banina and Pamela Rothrock Magyar, and my late parents, Paul Rothrock and Dorothy Higgins Rothrock. I would love to have one more Sunday night with all of you.

About the Author

Richard Rothrock is a writer, teacher, and freelance editor with an undying love for film, television, literature, the Indianapolis 500, and all things Disney. He is a proud graduate of George Washington High School in Charleston, West Virginia. He holds a Bachelor of Arts in English and Film from Oakland University and a Master of Arts from Bowling Green State University. His work has appeared in magazines, newspapers, and book anthologies. He has authored a number of award-winning screenplays that got trapped in development hell and currently teaches writing at the Motion Picture Institute in Troy, Michigan. He still wishes to fly in outer space some day and would move to Epcot in a second if it were ever built. This is his first book.

About Theme Park Press

Theme Park Press publishes books primarily about the Disney company, its history, culture, films, animation, and theme parks, as well as theme parks in general.

Our authors include noted historians, animators, Imagineers, and experts in the theme park industry.

We also publish many books by first-time authors, with topics ranging from fiction to theme park guides.

And we're always looking for new talent. If you'd like to write for us, or if you're interested in the many other titles in our catalog, please visit:

www.ThemeParkPress.com

. . . .

Theme Park Press Newsletter

Subscribe to our free email newsletter and enjoy:

- ♦ Free book downloads and giveaways
- ♦ Access to excerpts from our many books
- ♦ Announcements of forthcoming releases
- ♦ Exclusive additional content and chapters
- ♦ And more good stuff available nowhere else

To subscribe, visit www.ThemeParkPress.com, or send email to newsletter@themeparkpress.com.

Read more about these books
and our many other titles at:

www.ThemeParkPress.com

Made in the USA
Columbia, SC
30 December 2017